THE ENTERPRISE IN CONTEMPLATION

The Midnight Assault of Stony Point

Don Loprieno

HERITAGE BOOKS
2009

HERITAGE BOOKS

AN IMPRINT OF HERITAGE BOOKS, INC.

Books, CDs, and more—Worldwide

For our listing of thousands of titles see our website
at
www.HeritageBooks.com

Published 2009 by
HERITAGE BOOKS, INC.
Publishing Division
100 Railroad Ave. #104
Westminster, Maryland 21157

International Standard Book Numbers
Paperbound: 978-0-7884-2574-5
Clothbound: 978-0-7884-8134-5

This book is dedicated to the brave officers and men
of the American Corps of Light Infantry,
the intrepid French volunteers who served with them,
and the valiant British and Loyalist defenders
who fought at the Battle of Stony Point, July 15-16, 1779.

Nec Aspera Terrent

*- Adapted from an inscription in the Memorial Garden
at Stony Point Battlefield State Historic Site*

FOREWORD

If the average reader has never heard of the battle of Stony Point, no ignorance or oversight should be inferred. This brief aspect of the American Revolution is overlooked or barely mentioned in accounts of that war, and when the story of General Wayne's daring nighttime attack against formidable British defenses is told, it is often described incompletely or laced with an unhealthy dose of fiction.

One reason why Stony Point is relatively unknown is that historians seem to believe that a short battle can only have short-term consequences. This writer is not among that group. In fact, it can be persuasively argued that once the British departed from the Hudson Highlands in October 1779, after having failed to lure Washington into a battle on their own terms, their military efforts to control the Hudson River and separate New York from New England and states to the south came to an end. No further attempt – with the single exception of Benedict Arnold's treason the following year – was made by the British to dominate that important maritime highway.

At a time of virtual stalemate and the prospect of an ever-expanding conflict, Sir Henry Clinton's futile attempt to provoke an ill-conceived military response to the British occupation of Stony Point and Verplanck's Point proved to be among the last straws, especially when combined with the recent loss of Philadelphia and the continuing lack of progress in restoring the King's rule to his contentious subjects. Though a southern campaign had been considered previously, Crown forces, in late December 1779, now shifted the focus of their efforts to winning support in Virginia, Georgia and the Carolinas. After an earlier attempt in 1776 had failed, the British attacked Charleston again in May 1780, and this time they prevailed.

Their success, however, was followed by setbacks in other parts of South Carolina, namely at Kings Mountain (October 1780) and Cowpens (January 1781). After a costly "victory" over Nathanael Greene at Guilford Courthouse, North Carolina, in March 1781, Lord Cornwallis, the British commander in the south, marched his troops to the sleepy Virginia port of Yorktown to await supplies and reinforcements, but he and his men were surrounded by the Americans and their French allies in what proved to be the last major battle of the Revolution. It is the author's conviction that the bold, surprise assault of Stony Point created an important impetus to travel down that fateful road, one that would eventually lead to the war's end and independent nationhood.

It is easy, as one tells the story of a conflict that happened long ago, to idealize the actions of those involved and inadvertently add another chapter to the annals of military romanticism. It should be remembered, therefore, that war is always brutal regardless of the age in which it occurs, and no less so than in the 18th century, where, with the exception of artillery, most combat was fought at relatively close quarters and often hand-to-hand; and we should also not forget that almost any human endeavor springs from a complexity of reasons, warfare being no exception. The same action that creates hardship, deprivation and cruelty can also produce courage, daring, and a willingness to be motivated by causes and principles outside of one's self. For that reason, the account that follows focuses not only on strategy and the sequence of events, but also on what has been called the human face of battle – ordinary people reacting to extraordinary circumstances, individuals from another time and place sharing the same frailties and attributes, the same qualities and shortcomings that are common to us all.

No book writes itself, and no author labors entirely alone, and it is therefore appropriate to acknowledge publicly those whose work has helped make the present effort possible, notably Henry B. Dawson, <u>The Assault on Stony Point</u>, and Henry P. Johnston, <u>The Storming of Stony Point on the Hudson</u>. Both historians, writing in 1863 and 1900, respectively, provided a wealth of detail and an abundance of documentation, thus laying the groundwork on which any future volume about the subject must necessarily build.

I have also to thank the following institutions for their cooperation: the New-York Historical Society, The Public Records Office in London; the Historical Society of Pennsylvania; the Lancaster County (PA.) Historical Society, the United States Military Academy at West Point, the Library of Congress and its collection of the George Washington Papers, and Stony Point Battlefield State Historic Site, which I had the privilege and often the pleasure of managing for nearly nine years. Colleagues at the battlefield, including Ellen Abrams, Ted Aron, Joe and Nancy Breen, Gillian Courtney, Jeff Dinowitz, Eliot Hermon, Lisa Kimbark, David Johnson, Lynda Johnson, Bill Laufenberg, Tom Mahoney, Bill and Christina Melvin, Chris Morton, Talia Mosconi, Warren Moseman, Chris Murphy, Tom Olivia, Melissa Pagano, Monica Pellegrino, Ray Russell, Moire Stiskin, Brad Titus, and Brian Ziemba, were always a source of enthusiasm and support.

The contributions of the following individuals should also be recognized: Wallace Workmaster, for his belief in history and those who interpret it: Alan Aimone and Judith Sibley at the West Point library for their assistance in general, and for calling attention to *a Sketch of the Works at Stoney Point*, by Lt. William Marshall, Acting Engineer in charge of British defenses, who was captured during the battle; Matthew Di Biase at the National Archives for his willingness in locating pension records and other important data;

Bruce Carrick for sharing information about Captain Allan McLane; Todd Braisted for locating the court-martial of Lieutenant Colonel Henry Johnson, and Adeline Tucker and Alene Smith, whose ancestor, Robin Starr, fought at the battle of Stony Point, but whose presence there had been largely unknown except to his own family; and to Corinne Will, Editorial Director of Heritage Books, for her publishing experience. I also want to thank my niece Lily Lockhart for her knowledge of photo software, and my brother-in-law Samuel Kerr Lockhart for his legal expertise on author's rights and other literary matters. In each instance, a *quid pro* was generously extended without seeking - so far at least! – the requisite *quo*. Their help is much appreciated.

The most important recognition is also the last. It is safe to say that the present volume might never have been written if it had not been for the constant encouragement and patience of my wife Page Lockhart. In addition to a law background, her research abilities and word processing skills, combined with sound editorial advice, made her indispensable to the creation of this book and to telling the story that needed to be told. Having said that, however, let me add the usual caveat that the responsibility for any omissions or factual errors is mine alone.

Finally – and modestly - I recommend this work and others on historical topics to my children, Nora and Dana Loprieno, and to my grandson Devin, newly arrived this year. May they live in the present, help create a peaceful future, and be nourished by the past.

Don Loprieno
Bristol, Maine
Winter, 2004

CONTENTS

I. The Battle of Stony Point

II. The Prisoners: Captivity and Confinement

MAPS AND ILLUSTRATIONS

III. The Court-Martial of Lieutenant Colonel Henry Johnson

I.

The Battle of Stony Point

General Anthony Wayne by Edward Savage, ca. 1795. Born in 1745, the former Pennsylvania tanner was 34 years of age when he commanded the American forces at Stony Point.

GEN. SIR HENRY JOHNSON, BART. G. C. B.

Born 1748 Died 1835.

This sketch depicts Henry Johnson late in life, but he was only 31 when he led the British defenses at Stony Point. Johnson was promoted to full general in 1809, created baronet (Bart.) in 1818, and wears the Star of the Order of the Bath, Grand Cross Bath (G.C.B.).

Collections of the Historical Society of Pennsylvania

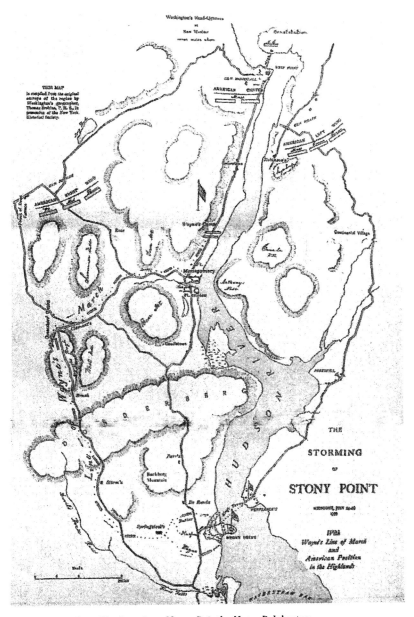

-from *The Storming of Stony Point* by Henry P. Johnston

Schematic Map of British Fortifications and American Attack Routes
(all locations approximate)

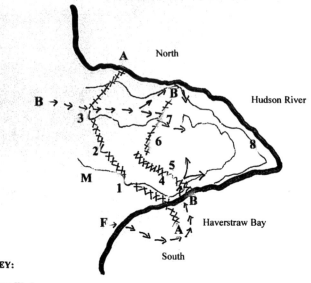

North

Hudson River

A

B → →

B

3

7

6

8

2

5

M

1

4

B

F →

A

Haverstraw Bay

South

KEY:

Outer Works:
1 – Fleche No. 1
2 – Fleche No. 2
3 – Fleche No. 3

Inner Works
4 – Howitzer battery
5 – Left flank battery
6 – Flagstaff battery
7 – Right flank battery

8 – Powder magazine

AxxxxxA   Outer Abatis
BxxxxxB   Inner Abatis

F→-→-→-→   Route of Febiger's column
B→-→-→-→   Route of Butler's column
M   Murfree's detachment

" It is most earnestly wished that you may be able to bring Mr. Washington to a general and decisive action"

On a hot July day in 1779, a small group of men in military uniform ascended on horseback to the top of Buckberg Mountain on the west bank of the lower Hudson Valley of New York, approximately twenty-five miles north of Manhattan and twelve miles south of West Point. The vista was panoramic; as they looked east, they saw the expanse of Haverstraw Bay, the widest part of the Hudson River. The broad scope of the bay narrowed as the river flowed north, passing between two peninsulas less than a mile apart, and entering the tortuous channel of the Hudson Highlands. Approximately a month earlier, British forces had captured these two promontories from American defenders, establishing control over the broad maritime highway that allowed transportation of troops and supplies as well as the advantages of naval support and - if need be - escape.

The observers' attention, however, was drawn to the peninsula closest to them, a rocky eminence of approximately 90 acres that rose 150 feet above the Hudson. In little more than four weeks, the British had constructed imposing defenses, including artillery positions. As the American Colonel Jesse Woodhull reported, "They are at work like a parcel of devils."[1]   The other peninsula, directly across the water, also bristled with enemy troops occupying the American fort they had captured in June, and British ships patrolled the river. As the party watched the ongoing enemy activity, they realized the danger that this new hostile presence created. The imposing figure on horseback -- a tall, dignified Virginian of middle age -- began to confer with a 34-year-old officer from Pennsylvania. General George Washington, commander-in-chief of the Continental Army, and Brigadier General Anthony Wayne, commander of the Corps of Light Infantry, were planning the battle of Stony Point.

But why had Crown forces attacked this area now? By 1779, the American Revolution had raged for four years. The first shots had been fired in 1775, and independence had been declared in 1776, but achieving it would take far longer. Burgoyne had been defeated at Saratoga in 1777, but it would not be until 1783 that peace would actually be concluded. By 1779, England's traditional enemies, France and Spain, had entered the war, and political support for its continuation was waning. The British government was prepared to grant their American colonies almost all the concessions they wanted, short of independence, but independence was now their paramount objective; nevertheless, despite military setbacks, George III still felt compelled to retain the allegiance of his rebellious subjects:

> *I should think it the greatest instance . . . of ingratitude and injustice, if it could be supposed that any man in my dominions more ardently desired the restoration of peace and solid happiness in every part of this empire than I do; there is no personal sacrifice I could not readily yield for so desirable an object; but at the same time no inclination to get out of the present difficulties, which certainly keep my mind very far from a state of ease, can incline me to enter into what I look upon as the destruction of the empire.*[2]

To resolve the conflict that was draining Great Britain's resources, Sir Henry Clinton had received instructions from Lord Germaine, Secretary of State for the American Colonies, to engage the rebels, end the war, and make peace on England's terms:

> *It is most earnestly wished that you may be able to bring Mr. Washington to a general and decisive action at the opening of the Campaign* [of 1779]; *but if that cannot be*

effected it is imagined that . . . you may force him to seek for
safety in the Highlands of New York or the Jerseys, and
leave the inhabitants of the open country at liberty to . . .
return to their allegiance to His Majesty. . . . But besides
these immediate good effects. . . the operations proposed to
be carried on in other parts . . . should be employed upon
the seacoasts of the revolted provinces, the one to act on the
side of New England and New Hampshire, and the other in
the Chesapeake Bay . . .[3]

Sir Henry was an experienced soldier who had been appointed commander-in-chief the previous year. Born in 1738, he was the son of Admiral George Clinton who had served as Governor of New York from 1741 to 1751.

The younger Clinton's military career began in the Seven Years War during which he was promoted to Lieutenant Colonel. In 1775, Clinton became a major general, and two years later was knighted. To comply with Germaine's orders, Sir Henry intended to lure General Washington and the Continental Army away from winter quarters and supply depots in New Jersey. Clinton then planned to capture these storage areas, depriving the Americans of badly needed materiel and hastening the war to a close. However, lack of reinforcements prevented Clinton from seizing these storehouses; instead he hoped that the British occupation of Stony Point and Verplanck's Point would provoke the Continentals into a decisive battle that would return the King's rule to his disaffected countrymen:

An action with Mr. Washington's army was. . . comprised
within the operations I proposed. For, should he be
tempted to hazard one in the defense or recovery of his
Stony Point or Verplanck's forts, I very well knew he must
for that purpose have met me in an angle between the

3

mountains and the river, on terms replete with risk on his
part and little or none on mine."[4]

On May 30, 1779, British forces began to move north up the Hudson from the Yonkers area towards their two objectives: Stony Point, on the west side of the river, and Verplanck's Point, located on the opposite shore and defended by an American defensive work called Fort La Fayette. These two peninsulas guarded not only the southern entrance to the Hudson Highlands, but also the King's Ferry, an important crossing and vital communications link for American troops and supplies traveling between New England and the states to the south. On the morning of May 31, Major General Vaughan landed forces approximately eight miles below Verplanck's Point. At the same time, Sir Henry, with troops of the 17th, 63rd, and 64th Regiments as well as a company of Jaegers, proceeded to within three miles of Stony Point where an American blockhouse was under construction. The arrival of this large enemy force gave the small party of rebels little choice; they burned the blockhouse and fled. To support both landing parties, a British fleet of galleys and gunboats exchanged fire with the small American garrison at Verplanck's Point while Sir Henry's troops occupied the higher ground across the river. By 5:00 AM on June 1, a battery of guns and mortars, which had been offloaded from British vessels during the night, began to fire from Stony Point on the beleaguered American fort less than a mile away. Meanwhile, General Vaughan's troops had approached the rear of Fort La Fayette to prevent an escape by the American defenders. The fort and its garrison of seventy-five men and officers soon surrendered.[5] In little more than a day, both promontories were in British hands. This development had the effect Sir Henry intended: Washington broke camp and headed north from Middle brook, New Jersey, to the West Point area to await further news and consider military options, while the British commander-in-chief withdrew the main body of his troops to an area just above New York City and lamented the lack of reinforcements which prevented him from pursuing

4

a more vigorous campaign. Nonetheless, on July 3, as an added incentive for an American reaction, Clinton directed Commodore Sir George Collier and General William Tryon, royal governor of New York, to conduct a raid against the Connecticut coast, hoping to "force Washington to march to their assistance."[6]   Washington, however, refrained from action, continuing instead to weigh his risks and watch for opportunities, all the while resisting the British provocation.

Meanwhile, the British now occupied both sides of the Hudson, controlling not only the river's narrow passage but also King's Ferry as well. On Stony Point, whose rocky heights rose dominated a marshy area on the mainland, the British began to cut down trees to provide a field of fire, and entangled the sharpened limbs to form two parallel barriers known as *abatis*, spanning the width of the peninsula.[7] Then they constructed two separate sets of fortifications: the Upper (or Inner) Works, built on the highest ground nearest the river, containing the most level terrain -- described by the British as "the table of the hill" -- and protected by an abatis just below it; and the Outer (or lower) Works, situated on lower ground closer to the marsh, with defenses centered on three rocky outcroppings, skirted by another abatis running along their base, and continuing from water to water. The Outer Works was a temporary fortification that was supposed to be abandoned once the Upper Works were enclosed. Stony Point had another defensive advantage; at high tide, the estuarial waters of the Hudson flooded a creek that spanned the peninsula, and much of the rocky point of land became impassable.

On each of the three outcroppings of the Outer Works, engineers placed a v-shaped defensive position open at the rear called a *fleche* from the French word for "arrow." According to Lieutenant William Marshall, Acting Engineer in charge of British defenses, these fortifications were made of earth coated with fascines, and their profiles were twelve feet at the base

5

declining to eight feet at the top.[8] These fleches were designated 1, 2, and 3 – possibly for the number of artillery in each – and oriented westward toward the marsh separating Stony Point from the mainland. The Upper Works, closer to the river, also faced west and mounted two large ship guns in each of the left and right flank batteries, with another cannon near the center.

The British defenders had fifteen pieces of artillery, including nine guns (mostly on truck carriages), five mortars, and an eight-inch Howitzer. [9] From south to north the Outer Works mounted a brass 12 pounder gun (fleche #1), two Coehorn mortars (fleche #2), and two Royal mortars and another brass 12 pounder (fleche #3). In the Upper Works, also south to north, were deployed an iron 18 and 24 pounder (left flank battery), an iron 12 pounder (flagstaff battery), and another iron 18 and 24 pounder (right flank battery).

In addition, a long brass 12 pounder in an unfinished battery oriented toward the river and a ten-inch mortar were located inside the Upper Works. There was also a light 3 pounder positioned in between the Works, and the Howitzer, located below the left flank battery of the Upper Works. The British defense also included at least two fighting ships of the Royal Navy: the *Vulture* to guard the north flank and a small gunboat -- unidentified in records, but possibly the *Cornwallis* -- to guard the south flank by Haverstraw Bay. [10]

The British garrison at Stony Point consisted of eight companies of the 17th Regiment of Foot, two Grenadier companies of the 71st Regiment, a detachment of Loyal Americans, a contingent of 48 men and officers of the Royal Artillery, and 27 artificers and servants, (including at least two African-American boys[11]) for a total of 564, besides a number of women and children. The 17th Regiment, originally formed in Leicester, England, in 1688, was known by the names of its various colonels until receiving a numerical designation in 1751. They arrived in Boston in December, 1775, and fought at the battles of Long Island in 1776, Princeton, Brandywine and Germantown in 1777, and at Monmouth and Newport in 1778. The two Grenadier companies of the 71st Regiment of Foot (Fraser's Highlanders) were commanded by Captain Lawrence Robert Campbell. The regiment's two battalions were raised in Inverness, Stirling and Glasgow in 1775, and had served throughout the war in virtually all the colonies. In 1782, the regiment was sent to Halifax, and the following year returned to Scotland and disbanded.

Loyalists were represented by 69 members of the Loyal American Regiment, under the command of Captain William Robinson,[12] son of the regiment's colonel, Beverly Robinson, whose home, located just twelve miles north of Stony Point on the east bank opposite West Point, had been commandeered by the Americans. Created in the fall of 1776, the regiment had participated in the British assault on Forts Montgomery and Clinton in 1777.

The garrison was led by the 31-year-old Lieutenant Colonel of the 17th, Henry Johnson, who was in fact subordinate to Lieutenant Colonel Webster[13] at Verplanck's Point, the commander of both posts. Commissioned an ensign in 1761 at the age of 13, Johnson advanced to the rank of captain two years later. He was a major in the 28th regiment when it was sent to America in 1775, and three years later, in October, 1778, he was promoted to his present rank. Though a relatively young man, Johnson was held in high regard by Sir Henry Clinton who considered him "a vigilant, active and spirited officer."[14]

Thus, the fortification of Stony Point ultimately brought Generals Washington and Wayne to the top of Buckberg Mountain, a mile and a half from Stony Point. Nearly five weeks earlier when the enemy invasion occurred, Washington, fearing an attack against West Point and hoping to recapture King's Ferry and the two peninsulas now in British hands, expressed concern about the hazards this new enemy threat posed. Writing to President [of the Supreme Executive Council of Pennsylvania] Joseph Reed, he stated:

> *You will no doubt have been informed of the operations of the enemy on the North [Hudson] River. They have taken posts in two divisions on the opposite sides of the River at Verplanck's and stoney [sic] points where the nature of the ground renders them inaccessible. This puts a stop to our lower communication and will greatly add to the difficulty of transportation between the States; while it will enable them to draw additional supplies from the country and to increase the distress and disaffection of the inhabitants residing along the River.*[15]

Washington had already begun the process of gathering intelligence to counteract the British military presence by writing to Major Henry Lee, Jr. on June 6, informing him that "the enemy have now a body at Kings ferry and appear to be establishing a post at Stoney point to which quarter your attention is principally to be directed."[16] The 23-year-old Virginian, having already displayed the dash and daring that would earn him the nickname "Light-Horse Harry," would perhaps be better known to a later generation as the father of Robert E. Lee. Now, the day after he wrote to President Reed, Washington corresponded with Lee again, urging him to use his "best endeavours to obtain satisfactory accounts from time to time of the situation, movements and designs of the Enemy; and in a particular manner, to ascertain what Corps they have at Stoney point, and their strength, the number of Cannon and Mortars the Size, and What Ships . . ."[17]

8

Though Washington's battle plan was still being formulated, it was clear that the nature of the enemy's defenses and their imposing location on the Hudson River would require an attacking force of well-trained, disciplined troops. The elite Corps of Light Infantry, attired in distinctive regimental uniforms and plumed leather caps, and based on the British model of Grenadier and light infantry flank companies, was the obvious choice. Comprised of men chosen from each Continental Army regiment for their endurance and their ability to be deployed quickly in battle, they often served away from their home regiments, gathering intelligence, defending the main army from surprise attack, and raiding enemy outposts. The general chosen to lead them in battle was their new commander who would arrive at his post on July 1.

Anthony Wayne was born January 1, 1745, in Chester County, Pennsylvania; son of a prosperous tanner and veteran of the French and Indian War, Wayne had become a tanner himself, as well as a surveyor whose circle of acquaintances included Benjamin Franklin. On the eve of the Revolution, he was elected to the Pennsylvania legislature and the Committee of Safety. In early 1776, Wayne, whose interest in military affairs had always been keen, was appointed Colonel of the 4th Pennsylvania Battalion. The young officer served in Canada, commanded at Fort Ticonderoga, and fought at Brandywine, Germantown, and Paoli, Pennsylvania, where in September, 1777, he was surprised by a midnight bayonet attack by British troops under General Charles Grey. After wintering at Valley Forge, Wayne earned high praise at Monmouth, in June, 1778, where Washington noted that his "good conduct and bravery through the whole action deserves particular commendations."[18] By 1779, Anthony Wayne had achieved a reputation as a courageous, aggressive soldier whose firm belief in military pride and martial appearance might have struck some as a bit excessive:

9

I must acknowledge that I have an insuperable prejudice in favor of an Elegant uniform & Soldierly appearance, so much so that I would rather risk my life and reputation at the head of the same men in an attack, clothed and appointed as I could wish, merely with bayonets and a single charge of ammunition, than to take them as they appear in common with sixty rounds of cartridges, for good uniforms promoted among the troops a Laudable pride . . . which in a soldier is a Substitute for almost every other Virtue.[19]

Washington was apparently not one to be concerned with such florid sentiments. Later, as President, he would privately express the view that Wayne was "more active and enterprising than judicious and cautious,"[20] but it was the first two qualities that Washington had in mind now, especially for the mission that was being considered. Washington's first communication to his new Corps commander -- one of two written to Wayne on the same day -- left no doubt about impending priorities and the continuing quest for intelligence:

Herewith you will be pleased to receive general instructions for your conduct. This you will consider as private and confidential. The importance of the two posts of Verplanck's and Stoney Points to the enemy is too obvious to need explanation. We ought if possible dispossess them. I recommend it to your particular attention, without delay, to gain as exact a knowledge as you can of the number of the garrison, the state of the creeks that surround the former, the nature of the grounds in the vicinity of both, the position and strength of the fortifications, the situation of the guards,

> *the number and stations of the vessels in the river, and the precautions in general which the enemy employ for their security. It is a matter I have much at heart to make some attempt upon these posts (in the present weak state of the garrisons and before the enemy commence any other operation) if warranted by a probability of success. I must entreat your best endeavors to acquire the necessary information, after having obtained which, I shall thank you for your opinion of the practicability of a surprise of one or both those places, especially that on the west side of the river [Stony Point].[21]*

A few days before Wayne arrived at his new post, Washington had written yet again to Major Lee for more assistance:

> *. . .I have now to request that you will endeavor to employ some person, in whom you can confide, and at the same time is intelligent, to go into the works at Stony-point, or if admittance is not be gained, otherwise to obtain the best knowledge of them he can, so as to describe the particular kinds of works, the precise spots on which they stand and the strength of the garrison. If you should succeed at this point, I must beg you will transmit me without delay a sketch of the work that I may be able to form an accurate idea of them . . .[22]*

Washington added a further request and a word of warning in a postscript: " Describe the number of armed vessels and their situation – and keep the contents of this letter to yourself."

11

On July 2, Captain Allan McLane, an American officer under Lee's command, was designated to carry out the clandestine mission and used a pretext to accomplish it. He had apparently learned that the son of a Mrs. Thomas Smith had recently deserted to the enemy and, using that opportunity, accompanied her under a flag of truce inside the British fortifications to see him. McLane reported to Washington that the Upper Works were incomplete and therefore not enclosed.[23] As an experienced and vigilant officer, he must also have noticed that while both abatis extended across the peninsula, the southern end of the outer one extended into the water and the northern end of the inner abatis stopped on high ground before the river's edge. He also could not have failed to see that most of the enemy artillery were ship guns situated on firing platforms, that these heavy cannon could not easily be moved about, and that they had been deployed on the high points of the peninsula: a ridge and several small, steep hills. They were for the most part confined by embrasures and thus could not turn very far to left or right. In fact, of the fifteen artillery pieces deployed by the British, only four were mounted *en barbette* (unrestricted by embrasures) or in no work at all. This last was a telling observation that may well have shaped the nature of the attack to follow.

The next day, July 3, at Washington's request, Wayne, accompanied by Major John Stewart of Maryland and Colonel Richard Butler, a fellow Pennsylvanian who had drawn an earlier sketch of the British works, reconnoitered Stony Point and reported that the enemy's defenses were formidable, but that a surprise of some sort might be achieved.[24] Three days later on Buckberg Mountain, Washington, accompanied by Wayne, observed the British fortifications for the first time, and confirmed what he must have suspected all the while: that control of Stony Point and Verplanck's Point was vital, but surprising both posts simultaneously would be too difficult.

That fact, combined with McLane's reconnaissance and Washington's own observation that Stony Point occupied higher ground, must have drawn the General to attack that newly-fortified position because of the important military and geographical advantage that a successful assault offered: captured enemy guns could be turned around and fired against the enemy shipping and the lower, opposite promontory of Verplanck's Point occupied by Crown forces. A rain of shot and shell -- British shot and shell -- accompanied by a land attack launched by American troops on that side of the river would complete the victory. If Stony Point fell, so could Verplanck's, and both forts would again be in American hands. In attacking Stony Point first, Washington would take a leaf, so to speak, from recent British annals, since the enemy capture of Stony Point a little more than a month earlier had succeeded using a similar, highly effective strategy: capturing the higher post first, and directing artillery across the river to Verplanck's Point below. Stony Point was also on the same side of the Hudson as the American stronghold at West Point; therefore, the Light Infantry need not attempt a river crossing and could march undetected through the sheltering mountain passes on the west bank.

But how could an attack that had a reasonable chance of success be mounted? The British controlled the Hudson, ruling out a naval assault. A siege was also out of the question since the British could be resupplied, reinforced or even evacuated by means of the same body of water. A frontal landward attack launched against fortifications and artillery would result not only in defeat but also in unacceptable casualties, if it occurred during the day when the enemy could see their attackers, and especially so if the British had advance knowledge of the American plan. Amidst all these factors, the fragments of isolated information, of painstakingly gathered intelligence, were nonetheless beginning to coalesce into a coherent image of the enemy's defenses -- cannon located on the highest points but restricted by embrasures, fortifications incomplete and unenclosed, two abatis, one of which stopped well short of the water line, enemy vessels patrolling both flanks— that might be used to form a viable battle plan, but more details and reconnaissance were still needed to form the one that would soon take shape in Washington's mind.

"...I am called to sup but where to breakfast – either within the enemys lines in triumph or in another world."

On July 9, Washington sent Colonel Rufus Putnam, a skilled engineer and surveyor who had constructed defensive works at West Point, to reconnoiter the works at Verplanck's and Stony Point; he returned to headquarters a few days later with additional information. On the same day, July 9, a vital piece of intelligence also arrived at the General's headquarters in New Windsor, some miles above West Point. A deserter reported a sandy beach on Stony Point's southern flank that was "only obstructed by a slight abatis."[25] The General's thought processes are unknown, but a barrier such as a protruding abatis implies shallow water, deep water being its own defense in an age of non-swimmers. Troops could wade through or around this vulnerable defense, but how could they be protected, and what could be done to increase their chance of success? The daring strategy that was beginning to take shape could not be predicated on chance; therefore, Washington directed General Wayne to "ascertain" the deserter's information. By the next day, July 10, it was apparently confirmed, and Washington communicated his plan to General Wayne:

> *My ideas for the Enterprise in contemplation are these: that it should be attempted by the Light Infantry only, which should march under cover of night and with the utmost secrecy. . . .the approach should be along the water on the south side, crossing the beach and entering the abatis.* [The main body] *is to be preceded by a vanguard of prudent and determined men, well commanded, who are to remove obstructions, secure the sentries, and drive in the guards. They are to advance the whole of them with fixed bayonets and muskets unloaded.*

Washington demonstrated his awareness that a field commander might have a different perspective, and included in his plan several important cautionary notes as well:

> *These are my general ideas of the plan for a surprise; but you are at liberty to depart from them in every instance, where you think they may be improved, or changed for the better. As it is in the power of a single deserter to betray the design, defeat the project, and involve the party in difficulties and danger, too much caution cannot be used to conceal the intended enterprise till the latest hour from all but the principal officers of your corps, and from the men till the moment of execution. A knowledge of your intention, ten minutes previously obtained, will blast all your hopes . . . . A dark night, or even a rainy one (if you can find the way) will contribute to your success. . . .*[26]

Thus, American forces would wade through the water from the sandy beach on the south flank of Stony Point while other troops advanced on the center and north of the peninsula for the purpose of distracting the enemy and cutting off their retreat. Aware that an attack in daylight and the firing of weapons would eliminate the crucial element of surprise, Washington suggested that the troops attack at midnight, armed only with unloaded muskets and fixed bayonets so that an accidental shot would not reveal their presence, and wearing a "visible badge of distinction" to avoid confusion in the darkness. In an era when the limited accuracy of smoothbore firearms was based on the ability to see a fairly close target, a nighttime assault, although unorthodox by 18th century standards, was the most effective way to neutralize British defenses. A corollary benefit would also fall to the attackers: not only would British fire be ineffective in the darkness, it would also identify the defenders and pinpoint their locations.

Any good military plan includes an element of deception. Therefore, to make the British think that a daytime artillery attack was intended, Washington ordered two cannon for the attack force, weapons which could be left behind when the Americans marched.[27] In addition, twenty-four Continental gunners were detached to accompany the attacking force and fire the captured British artillery against the enemy at Verplanck's Point. To confuse the British garrison there and reduce the possibility of enemy reinforcements being sent across the Hudson, Colonel Rufus Putnam, the engineer on whom Washington had relied for an earlier reconnaissance, was ordered to make a feint, or fake attack, against those fortifications at the same time that the real assault was launched against Stony Point.

On July 14, as the Corps of Light Infantry prepared to march, Washington responded to a letter from General Wayne suggesting, for unspecified reasons, a possible postponement of the attack:

> *I have reflected on the advantages and disadvantages of delaying the proposed attempt, and I do not know but the latter preponderate. You will therefore carry it into execution tomorrow night as you desire, unless some new motive or better information should induce you to think it best to defer it. . . .But as it is important to have every information we can procure, if you could manage in the mean time to see Major Lee, it might be useful. He has been so long near the spot and has taken so much pains to inform himself critically concerning the post. . .[28]*

On July 15, 1779, General Wayne inspected his Light Infantry which had been directed by him -- with his usual concern for military appearance -- to be "fresh shaved and well powdered." The Corps was comprised of four regiments, each regiment consisting of two battalions, each battalion having four companies. Their commanding officers were experienced, reliable soldiers. The First Light Infantry Regiment was led by Colonel Christian Febiger, a Dane who had fought at Bunker Hill and Quebec and then settled in Virginia; the commander of Febiger's first battalion, comprised of two companies of Virginians and two of Pennsylvanians, was Lt. Col Francois Teissedre de Fleury. Born in Languedoc in 1749, he had served in the French Army since the age of nineteen. A trained engineer, he had joined the American cause in 1776, and had been wounded at the battle of Germantown and the siege of Fort Mifflin in Pennsylvania. The officer in charge of the second battalion's four Virginia companies was Major Thomas Posey, who, after the war, would settle in the mid-West, become a Major General and the second Governor of Indiana.[29]

Colonel Richard Butler, who had been the temporary commander of the Light Infantry Corps before Wayne's arrival, and who was a skilled, veteran officer with a reputation, led the Second Light Infantry Regiment. The Irish-born Colonel was one of five brothers who served in the Continental Army. A soldier who had served under him described him as brave but fiery. "Whenever he had a dispute with a brother officer . . . he would never resort to pistols and swords, but always to his fists. I have more than once seen him with a black eye, and have seen other officers that he had honored with the same badge."[30] Butler's first battalion of four Pennsylvania companies was under the command of Lieutenant Colonel Samuel Hay of the same state. Major John Stewart had been captured on Staten Island in August, 1777, and now took charge of the second battalion and the four companies from his native state of Maryland.

18

The Third and Fourth Light Infantry Regiments, with one exception, were comprised of New England companies. Colonel Return Jonathan Meigs of Middletown, Connecticut, commanded the Third Regiment The 39-year-old officer had fought at Lexington and Concord and took part in Arnold's march to Quebec; he was voted an "elegant sword" by Congress for his daring raid at Sag Harbor, New York in 1777.[31] Lieutenant Colonel Isaac Sherman, from New Haven, led the first battalion's four Connecticut companies. He was the son of Roger Sherman, one of the Signers of the Declaration of Independence, and had served at the battles of Trenton and Princeton. Captain Henry Champion of Colchester, acting as Major, commanded the four Connecticut companies of the second battalion.

The Fourth Regiment was under the nominal command by Colonel Rufus Putnam, but, as previously noted, he had been ordered to divert the enemy garrison at Verplanck's Point when the Light Infantry began its attack on Stony Point. In his place was Major William Hull, who also commanded the first battalion of four Massachusetts companies. Finally, the Fourth Regiment's second battalion was led by Major Hardy Murfree and consisted of two Massachusetts companies and two companies from his home state, North Carolina. Murfree had already fought at Brandywine and Monmouth and would add further distinction to his name in the action to come.

The inspection completed, General Wayne ordered the troops to march south from their camp at Sandy Beach, near Fort Montgomery just below West Point and approximately eleven miles north of Stony Point. Civilians encountered along the way were arrested to prevent their bringing word to the British. The Light Infantry, whose final objective had yet to be revealed except to a few principal officers, marched single file fourteen miles along the steep narrow trails leading around Bear Mountain and over Donderberg Mountain to the fate that awaited them.

Shortly before sunset on July 15, they arrived at Springsteel's farm, approximately a mile and a half west of Stony Point. General Wayne, accompanied by several chosen officers, then conducted a final reconnaissance of the enemy fortifications.[32] The Light Infantry now paused to regroup — an opportunity not only for rest and refreshment, but also for sober consideration of the risks they would soon face. Colonel Febiger, referred to affectionately as "Old Denmark", composed a brief note disposing of his effects if he joined "the deceas'd heroes of America." Wayne wrote a letter asking a friend to take care of his family and dated it "Springsteel's . . . near the hour & scene of carnage." The first sentence sounded a dramatic note "This will not reach your eye until the Writer is no more," that was repeated at the end, " . .I am called to sup but where to breakfast – either within the enemys lines in triumph or in an other world"[33] Similar thoughts, perhaps more mundanely expressed, must have occurred to other men. Private Eli Mix and Corporals Jacob Bailey and John Rundle of the Second Connecticut Battalion may have had well-placed forebodings. All three would be killed in battle. Robin Starr, a 28-year-old black slave from Connecticut, would survive. Born in Africa in 1751, by war's end he would have served seven years as a soldier, have been wounded twice, and finally be able to buy his freedom.[34]

Tensions were also high behind the British lines at Stony Point on the evening of July 15, and extra precautions were in effect. Chevaux de Frise had been brought over from Verplanck's Point to create temporary barriers on the right flank of the Upper Works.[35] To reduce access to the fortifications by unauthorized persons at night, passwords — paroles and countersigns — were not allowed, and a total of 88 sentries — nearly 20% of the garrison's infantry force — had been posted outside the British defenses. Four days earlier, on July 11, Lieutenant Colonel Johnson had been informed by scouts that an attack would soon occur, and had established alarm posts for his men, making a decision that might well have haunted him in later years. This change in deployment, based on available information and probable assumptions about the enemy and the kind of attack they would launch, would have fatal consequences for the ability of the garrison to defend itself: four companies of the 17th Regiment were to join the two Grenadier companies of the 71st Regiment along the outer abatis,[36] thereby leaving less than half the men under Johnson's command to guard the unfinished (and unenclosed) Upper Works, the main fortification and the obvious target of any assault. As events would later confirm, too many of the Colonel's men would soon prove to be in the wrong place. Now, after dark on the 15th, as the Americans were arriving at Springsteel's farm, two more scouts repeated the warning of an attack.[37] The anxiety that all inside the fort must have felt was probably heightened by the moonless night and the unseasonably frigid weather. One American soldier, encamped on the other side of the Hudson, remembered the "brisk wind at northwest and cold. I never came nearer perishing with cold in the middle of summer in all my life."[38] It was a bitter wind that could numb the British sentries and muffle the sound of approaching troops. The defenders lay on their packs, weapons at the ready, and waited for first light.

General Wayne now informed his troops that they would attack Stony Point that very night with unloaded muskets, and protected by the advantage of surprise. To help achieve this goal, Wayne had the approaches to the British fort secured prior to the battle by a small detachment of troops to prevent discovery of the advancing Americans. In addition, he ordered other military units in the area to be of assistance.[39] These were added to a reserve force of 300 under General Peter Muhlenberg that had been ordered by Washington.[40] Major Lee and his men would also be close by. Amending the General's plan as he had permitted him to do, Wayne had also increased the attacking force; instead of the 100–200 men recommended by Washington, approximately 1,150 troops would launch the attack. Wayne also added a second column and expanded the concept of distraction proposed by the commander-in-chief.[41]   Thus, one column of Light Infantry - 700 Connecticut, Massachusetts, Virginia, and Pennsylvania soldiers under the command of Colonel Febiger and with General Wayne at its head - would wade through the shallow water on the south flank of Stony Point, climb the hill, and overwhelm the summit fortifications. A second column - 300 Maryland and Pennsylvania troops led by Colonel Butler - would approach around the north side of Stony Point. Officers would be armed with espontoons, which had been requested a few days earlier by General Wayne in order to practice with them.[42] As the columns swept around the flanks and through the defenses, Major Hardy Murfree's two companies of North Carolinians, the only American troops with loaded muskets,[43] would mount a "perpetual and galling" fire in the center of the peninsula to "amuse" the British defenders and make them think that the Americans were attacking in front.   Murfree's men would march with Butler's column, break off when they approached a causeway constructed by the British to span the creek in front of the Outer Works, and start firing when the attack began. General Wayne's order of battle explained the mission that the two vanguards would perform, the number of men in each, and how they would be armed:

> *Col. Fleury will take charge of One Hundred and fifty determined and picked men, properly Officered, with their Arms unloaded, placing their whole Dependence on the Bayonet . . . . He is to detach an officer and twenty men a little in front whose business will be to secure the sentries and Remove the Abbatis and obstructions for the Column to pass through. The Column will follow close in the Rear with shouldered muskets led by Col. Febiger and General Wayne in person. . . . Col. Butler will move . . .preceded by One Hundred chosen men with fixed Bayonets, properly officered and Unloaded muskets. . . these hundred will also*

22

detach a proper Officer and twenty men a little in front to Remove the obstructions... [44]

Each vanguard's detachment of twenty men was called, in military parlance, a "forlorn hope," since they had a small chance of returning alive or unwounded. Lt. John Gibbon of Pennsylvania led the forlorn hope of Butler's column; Lt. George Knox, also of Pennsylvania, led the forlorn hope from Febiger's column. But as Wayne's order makes clear, each group of twenty would be selected from the vanguard of their respective columns. The vanguards, in turn, armed only with unloaded muskets and "placing their whole dependence on the bayonet" would follow closely behind and meet the brunt of enemy resistance, while the rest of the troops in each column followed with muskets shouldered. The one hundred men of the vanguard from Butler's column would serve under Major John Stewart of Maryland, and the one hundred fifty men of the vanguard from Febiger's column would be commanded by Lt. Colonel Fleury of the Virginia Line. Fleury was one of two French volunteers that night in the Light Infantry, the other being Major Rene-Hippolyte Penot Lombart de Noirmont (misnamed in official records as Noirmont de la Neuville or Noirmont de Laneuville) who served in the forlorn hope of Colonel Butler's column and was later praised by Washington for the military service he had rendered during the war, particularly at Stony Point. [45]

Once the Americans were inside the Upper Works, they would shout the watchword, "The fort's our own!" To identify the Americans to each other in the impending combat, the soldiers would wear a piece of white paper -- the "visible badge of distinction" directed by Washington -- in their hats. As an incentive, troops would receive not only a share of the value of any captured ordnance and supplies, but also monetary rewards as explained by Wayne in final instructions to his men:

The General cannot have the least doubt of a glorious victory, and he hereby most solemnly engages to reward the first man who enters the works with five hundred dollars and immediate promotion; to the second four hundred, to the third three hundred, to the fourth two hundred, and to the fifth one hundred dollars. But should there be any soldier so lost to every feeling of honor, as to attempt to retreat one single foot or skulk in the face of danger, the officer next to him is immediately to put him to death, that he may no longer disgrace the name of a soldier, or the corps or state he belongs to.[46]

3

"for God's sake, why are not the Artillery here made use of, as the Enemy are in the hollow, and crossing the Water.."

Though it had been planned to begin at midnight on July 16, the attack was delayed until twenty minutes past twelve because the marsh below the approach of the fort was "overflowed by the tide."[47] Lt. John Ross[48] of the 71st Regiment commanded a picket of 30 men deployed in front of the Outer Works to the right of fleche #2, and was among the first defenders to realize — though not immediately -- that an attack had begun:

> . . .one of the Centries [sic] that I had Posted fired a Shot, upon which I sent a Corporal & some Men down, to know what was the cause of it, and they brought up the Man that had fired, who seemed to be of opinion that there was a body of the Enemy in front, the Corporal and the rest of the Men were of the same Opinion; another Sentry posted at the same place then fired a Shot, and I then got the Picquet collected together, and order'd the Drummer to beat to Arms, that a little after, the visiting Officer, Lt. Cumming came up to me and advised me to retire with my Picquet, for that the Enemy were assuredly in motion back and forward, in different places; I told him that I saw No Enemy; the Night being extremely dark and very Windy, made me suppose that what the Men reported to me to have heard, was occasioned by the Wind rustling amongst the Bushes, and that the Orders I had received from the Picquet was to retire only in case of danger; that I had hardly said this, when I heard a Volley of Small Arms from the part of our own Works, where Capt.Tew commanded, and where I was

to retire through; upon this I got all the Sentries collected, and retired by the 3 Pdr. and Capt. Tew desired me to fall in with his Company and to line the [outer] Abbatis; that I had just got within the Works when I receiv'd the Push of a Bayonet from a Man who knocked me down the Hill with the Butt end of his firelock, imagining that this was one of our own Men, who had done it thro' a mistake I damn'd him for a Scoundrel, whereupon several Shots were immediately fired from behind us and Capt. Tew immediately ordered Lt. Cumming to go up and see, who those were that were firing, as we did not know whether they were Rebels or our own Men. . .[49]

Simon Davies of the 17th Regiment of Foot was also among the British sentries to respond to the American attack as the Light Infantry approached the outer abatis. Davies was posted near fleche #1 and heard the shots fired to his right in the darkness from the picket commanded by Lt. Ross, and shortly thereafter also heard ". . . a Noise in the Water on my left [by the sandy beach on the south flank] which appeared...to have been Occasioned by a large body of Men wading through it. . . .I retired into the Work, where Lt. Horndon of the Artillery was, with a Short 12 Pdr. . . "[50]

At fleche #1, on the south flank of the Outer Works, Lieutenant Horndon's gunners ". . .heard a great firing of Musquetry from right to left, & Consequently began firing the 12 Pdr to a particular Object, to which they were Order'd to point that Gun, in case of an Alarm.. ."[51] The volleys may have been the "perpetual and galling" fire of Major Murfree's diversion. As the cannon boomed, its muzzle flashes revealed the south column of Light Infantry wading through Haverstraw Bay, but the embrasure prevented the gun from being turned toward the water. Horndon's men fired their muskets at the silently advancing figures in the intense darkness, but the Americans passed the British position and pressed on towards the Upper Works.

At almost the same time, the north column of Light Infantry under Colonel Butler began to enter the outer abatis, despite a fusillade from the fort's defenders as well as sixty-nine artillery rounds from a 3-pounder cannon, which killed or wounded a number of the first twenty Americans in the forlorn hope. Most of the resistance the Americans encountered was from the two Grenadier companies of the 71st Highland Regiment, whose alarm post was close by. Their commanding officer, Captain Lawrence Robert Campbell, was wounded in both legs with musket balls almost as soon as the fighting began, but managed to escape to a British transport in the river after it was apparent that the battle would be lost. He was one of only two British officers to avoid capture.[52]

Lieutenant John Roberts of the Royal Artillery was the other, and recounted his experience:

> . . about 12 o'Clock on the Night of the Attack, there was an
> Alarm given, by the Sentries firing, [and] . . imagining this
> might arise from the Sentries who might have fired
> inconsiderately (there having been several false Alarms
> before) I waited about a Minute & a half at my Tent when I
> heard several more Shots fired . . . I went to Capt. Tiffin,
> whom I found getting out of his Tent; I being the Officer of
> the inner Work that Night, then repaired to the Battery on
> the left flank, where there were an 18 and 24 Poundr. &
> where I found Capt. Clayton of the 17th Regiment; and a
> party of Men lining the Parapet; that Capt. Clayton seeing
> that I belonged to the Artillery (tho' I believe he did not
> know [me] to be an Officer, from the Manner in which he

spoke to me), said, for God's sake, why are not the Artillery
here made use of, as the Enemy are in the hollow, and
crossing the Water.. . [53]

Roberts knew full well the reasons and explained them to Clayton: these guns were kept unloaded at night, and ammunition was not kept in the batteries. In addition, because of their design and location, these large ship guns, which were intended for long-range daytime targets, could not be depressed to fire on the attackers below. Roberts now headed for the Howitzer, which *did* have ammunition but wasn't firing as it should have been because it guarded the south flank that was now under heavy enemy assault. This weapon, capable of lobbing a 46 pound exploding shell 1200 yards, would have made short work of the Americans wading around the abatis, but the Light Infantry overran the battery before the British gunners could open fire. In addition, a gunboat which had been assigned to guard the shallow waters on the south flank was absent from its post, as was the *Vulture*, normally deployed on the opposite flank, possibly because of high winds. Lieutenant Roberts was nearly captured, and reached the same conclusion as Captain Campbell: the fort was, or was about to be, in American hands:

. . I went towards the Howitzer Battery, knowing that the
Howitzer could be of considerable Service against the
Enemy, as they were coming up the Side of the Hill; that
when I had got within 10 or 20 Yards of the Howitzer
Battery, I found the Enemy were in Possession of it, at least
I had great reason to imagine so, from the Noise I heard
within the Work; . . .I then waited some little time there, not
being positive that the Enemy were in Possession of the
Work, and during this time several people were passing and
repassing, and after being there about a Minute and a half I

heard a Body of them Approaching, and I then concluded that the Enemy were in Possession of the Howitzer Battery, and were pushing for the Upper Work, upon which I also bent my Steps that way, but fell over a Log of Wood, and several People fell over me before I recovered myself, and I have great reason to believe that the Enemy entered the upper Work at the Barrier [the inner abatis just below the Upper Works] *at the same time that I did; I was then going down the hill in the rear of the Work, where the Encampment of the Artillery was, near where a Block house had stood, when I found the Enemy had not only turned the flank, but had got into the rear; that finding I could not return to the Work again without being in danger of being taken Prisoner, I immediately made for a Spring, which I myself had made, and the passage to which was thro' a very intricate Path, and before I got to the Water side I heard a Huzza on the top of the hill, which convinced me that the Enemy had got Possession, that I then thought of making my Escape by wading thro' Haverstraw Bay & crossing the Country, imagining it a more certain Way, than going to the other side; & I accordingly took the Water and forded a considerable Way, I suppose near a half a Mile, with all my Cloaths on, but hearing the Vulture Sloop of War, which I could not see, from the darkness of the Night, fire a Gun, I undressed myself & Swam to her, reaching her, whilst she was under way. . .*[54]

Thus, amid the sounds of gunfire and the wind howling down river through the cold darkness, Roberts swam to safety on board the *Vulture*, which, like the gunboat, had weighed anchor, apparently to avoid being blown ashore because of the high winds previously mentioned. With the gunboat missing and the Howitzer captured, opposition to the 700 men of the main attack column was proving futile - the battle was nearly lost, the post about to be taken.

The element of surprise, so important to American success, was also combined with the equally vital element of speed. So rapidly did the Light Infantry advance that only two of the fifteen artillery pieces were fired during the battle, and none from the Upper Works, the main objective.[55] Captain William Tiffen, the British artillery commander at Stony Point (and possibly the unluckiest man on either side that night because he had arrived at his post less than twenty-two hours before) was in the Upper Works and stated after his capture that only the 12-pounder at fleche #1 and the 3-pounder between the Works went into action.[56] Neither affected the outcome of the battle.

Colonel Butler's column, preceded by its forlorn hope and vanguard, was delayed by the resistance it encountered, but nonetheless swept around the north end of the Upper Works' abatis, in the area known as "the precipice," and through the embrasures of the right flank battery.[57] Meanwhile, the main column, under Colonel Febiger, having waded through the water by the sandy beach, came through the Upper Works abatis, approximately ten yards from the left (south) of the Howitzer battery.[58] Within minutes of each other, both attacking Light Infantry columns converged on the summit. Lieutenant Colonel Fleury entered the main fortifications first and struck the British flag.[59] He would later divide his five hundred dollars reward among his men, as Lieutenant George Knox of the 9th Pennsylvania regiment, the second man inside the Upper Works, would also do with the four hundred dollars he received. Fleury also declined the immediate promotion that accompanied his reward if it meant leaving his command in the Light Infantry.[60] The French volunteer and the Pennsylvania Lieutenant were almost immediately followed inside the fortifications by three other soldiers in advance of the main column: Sergeants Baker and Spencer of Virginia, and Sergeant Dunlop, also of Pennsylvania, most of them wounded and all from the forlorn hope of the south column. Lieutenant Colonel Johnson, the British commander, while attempting to direct the defense of his troops near the Outer Works, returned to the summit fortifications only to be taken prisoner by Colonel Febiger, signaling the end of major resistance.

Failure to tell friend apart from foe also played a role in the British defeat. Lieutenant William Armstrong, part of a small defensive force in the Upper Works, "received a Contusion in the head, from a [musket] Ball, which render'd him insensible, and in that situation he was taken Prisoner."[61] He was probably fired upon by British troops, since the only Americans with loaded weapons that night -- Major Murfree's two companies -- remained outside the fortifications to continue drawing attention away from the advancing columns.

The only officer killed on either side during the battle was Captain Francis Tew of the 17th Regiment, and he, too, was the victim of friendly fire. Tew was a celebrated soldier with a distinguished career. He was a veteran who had been wounded in Canada and the West Indies during the Seven Years' War, and his long and faithful service had been personally recognized by George III. Lieutenant John Ross of the 71st Highlanders, who had accompanied Tew as they ran from the outer abatis to help defend the main works, recorded his fate: ".. .a body of the Rebels presented themselves. . . and desired us to surrender on which Capt. Tew made use of some hasty expression, which I do not remember but Capt. Tew was immediately fired on and killed.'[62] The "rebels" were undoubtedly redcoats who mistook the Captain for the enemy and were apparently responding to his intemperate language, the general nature of which can easily be imagined.

The heaviest fighting lasted approximately half an hour. 144 men on both sides had been wounded, and 15 Americans and 20 British lay dead, buried to this day where they fell in battle. Lt. Col. Hay of the Pennsylvania Light Infantry was wounded, though not fatally. Major William Hull, whose military career would come to an ignominious end many years later when he surrendered Detroit to the British in 1812, lost two men killed, but was, in the present conflict, unscathed and with reputation intact, suffering only "one ball. . . through my hat, another struck my boot."[63] Seven Virginians in Col. Febiger's regiment were killed, as were three men each from Col. Butler's and Col. Meigs's regiments. Captain Ezra Selden of Connecticut was seriously wounded in the hip, but eventually recovered sufficiently to command a small American force at Stony Point later in the war. Colonel Febiger, the Danish-born commander of the Virginia Light Infantry, wrote to his wife to tell her that, other than a musket ball scraping his nose, no other damage had been done to "Old Denmark."[64] At 2:00 AM on July 16th, despite a head wound,[65] Wayne wrote this brief report to General Washington: "The fort and garrison with Colonel Johnston [sic] are ours. Our officers and men behaved like men who are determined to be free."[66]

Despite the blustery weather, the sounds of battle could be heard across the river by the British at Verplanck's Point who had listened intently to the conflict and who were at first mistaken about the outcome. Major William Hull was a witness to the result:

> *Three long and loud cheers were now given* [by the Americans] [67], *and reverberating in the stillness of night amidst rocks and mountains sent back an echo in glad response to the hearts of the victors. They were quickly answered by the enemy's ships of war in the river, and by the garrison at Verplanck's Point, under the belief that the Americans were repulsed.*[68]

At least one British officer at Stony Point was also confused about the American victory and subsequent change in command. Major Hull continues:

> The officer of the British artillery was requested to furnish the key of the powder magazine; he hesitated, and said that he only received his orders from Colonel Johnson. He was informed that Colonel Johnson was superseded in command, and there must be no delay, or the consequences might be unpleasant. The key was produced, the pieces of ordnance loaded, and the news of what had happened sent to the shipping from the mouths of the cannon.[69]

Twenty-four American artillerymen, under the command of Captains Pendleton and Barr, had swung into action and turned the British cannon against Verplanck's Point and the British ships, which slipped their cables to escape downriver out of range. The gunners had accompanied the Light Infantry in battle and demonstrated their bravery and dedication to duty:

> The officers and men of the artillery are highly commendable; they marched to the charge without a single weapon offensive or defensive, and on their entering the work their officers seemed unhappy until they were employed against the enemy.[70]

The valor and initiative of the artillerymen, as well as that of the Light Infantry, helped overcome a brave though futile defense - but Stony Point was only one half of the American goal.

4

"When I came to examine the post at Stony Point,
I found it would require more men to maintain than we could
afford. ."

Controlling the Hudson meant seizing both sides of the river; however, Washington's plan to capture Verplanck's Point as well as Stony Point failed because of a miscommunication that even the most carefully planned attack could not predict or control. General Washington explained the situation to Congress:

> *The evening appointed for the attack, I directed Major-General* [Alexander] *McDougall* [at West Point] *to put two brigades under marching orders to be moved down toward Verplanck's as soon as he should receive intelligence of the success of the attempt on this side, and requested General Wayne to let his dispatches to me pass through General McDougall, that he might have the earliest advice of the event. But through some misconception, they came directly on to Head Quarters* [at New Windsor] *which occasioned a loss of several hours. The next morning, Major General* [Robert] *Howe, was sent to take command of those troops, with orders to advance to the vicinity of the enemy's works and open batteries against them. It was hoped that this might either awe them into a surrender under the impression of what had happened on the other side, or prepare the way for an assault. But some accidental delay, in bringing on the heavy cannon and trenching tools necessary for an operation of this kind, unavoidably retarded its execution, till the approach of the enemy's main body made it too late.[71]*

His plan having miscarried, General Washington inspected the captured British fortifications to determine if they could be defended. Washington reluctantly decided to abandon the captured post and so informed Congress:

> *When I came to examine the post at Stony Point, I found it would require more men to maintain than we could afford, without incapacitating the army for other operations. In the opinion of the engineer, corresponding with my own and that of all the general officers present, not less than 1300 men would be requisite for its complete defence; and, from the nature of the works, which were opened towards the River, a great deal of labor and expense must have been incurred and much time employed, to make them defensible by us. The enemy depending on their shipping to protect the rear, had constructed their works solely against an attack by land. We should have had to apprehend equally an attack by water, and must have enclosed the post.*[72]

According to Major Hull, the day after the battle was spent burying the dead.[73] The prisoners, 543 in all,[74] had to be marched away from the captured post.[75] Meanwhile the wind -- having blustered down river since the night of the battle -- continued to prevent a British naval counter-attack. The time gained by the Americans was used to dismantle both abatis, destroy the fortifications, and remove large quantities of tents and other military supplies, including 334 muskets and 28,752 cartridges.[76] On July 18, much effort was expended removing the fifteen pieces of artillery that had fallen into American hands. Washington provided the details:

For want of proper tackling . . . we were obliged to send them to the fort [West Point] *by water. The movements of the enemy's vessels created some uneasiness on their account, and induced me to keep one of the pieces for their protection, which finally could not be brought off without risking more for its preservation than it was worth. We also lost a galley* [possibly the Lady Washington] *which was ordered down* [the Hudson] *to cover the boats. She got under way on her return the afternoon of the 18ᵗʰ. The enemy began a severe and continued cannonade upon it, from which, having received some injury which disabled her for proceeding, she was run ashore. Not being able to get her afloat till late in the flood tide, and one or two of the enemy's vessels under favor of the night* [having] *passed above her, she was set on fire and blown up.*[77]

Writing on July 26 to Lord Townsend in London, Major General James Pattison of the Royal Artillery described the same scene from a different viewpoint:

The Enemy. . . [was intent on] *carrying off all the brass cannon and stores in a large armed galley. . .which they sent down the river for that purpose. But luckily on her return up again and ill befriended by the wind* [still blowing from the northwest] *Lieutenant Douglas, who commanded the artillery at Verplanck's, played upon her so successfully with an 18 pounder that having hulled her several times, they ran on shore to prevent her sinking, then set her on fire and she burned to the water's edge. . . . Endeavors were afterwards used* [by the British] *to recover the cannon, but as they have not succeeded, it is presumed that the rebels*

with their usual industry found some means under favor of
the night to carry them up the river.[78]

By the night of July 18, the Americans had departed from Stony Point with fourteen cannons, having left the one behind that "could not be brought off without risking more for its preservation than it was worth," though that weapon was apparently retrieved later by the British.[79] But that same day, there was other military business to be conducted. Among the captured defenders of the British fort were six American deserters who had apparently joined the 71st Grenadiers.[80]   On July 18, at a General Court Martial, five of the six - William Fitzgerald of the 9th Pennsylvania Regiment, Isaac Wilson of Colonel Bradford's Regiment, John Blackman of Col. Bradley's Regiment, John Williams of the 4th Maryland Regiment, and Joseph Case of the 1st Connecticut - were found guilty and hanged at the Flagstaff Battery.[81] The one deserter who was not tried and executed might well have been the son of Mrs. Thomas Smith, the woman whom Captain Allan McLane accompanied into the British fort to gather intelligence prior to the attack.

Before the Americans left, there were also the enemy wounded to care for, and this was the special concern of Richard Auchmuty, the captured surgeon of the 17th Regiment who wrote to General Wayne that "The situation of the wounded belonging to His Majesty's service is such that I must request your interposition in ordering them to be forwarded to our lines.*"[82]*

The same day General Wayne tried to resolve the situation by suggesting an accommodation with the commanding officer of the British ships lying down river from Stony Point:

I transmit you the copy of a note received from Doctor Auchmuty. I have no objection to sending the wounded officers and men on board the British ships lying below this post on condition that a like number of officers and men belonging to our army now, on the honor of Sir Henry Clinton, be released on demand in exchange for these persons. I have no boats to convey the wounded and therefore am under the necessity of requesting that you will send a proper number to receive them. They amount to about forty.[83]

This arrangement was apparently agreed to, since Abraham Skinner, the American Deputy Commissary General of Prisoners, listed 39 men and 4 officers sent to New York, presumably by the ships mentioned in Wayne's letter.[84]   These men had already been left behind, however, since prisoners were marched away from the captured post on the 16th, the day of the battle. That night, at Kakiate, located south of Stony Point and midway between Haverstraw, New York and Suffern, New Jersey, an escape attempt resulted in the wounding of nine men from the 17th Regiment. They were left there by Deputy Skinner with two fellow soldiers to care for them.[85]

The prisoners' lot was not an easy one, and difficulties were encountered on the march to captivity. On July 20, 1779, the captured British commander, Lieutenant Colonel Johnson wrote to General Wayne from Goshen, New York:

The distressed situation of not only the officers but also the privates made prisoners at Stony Point from not having necessaries or even money to purchase them induces me to request you will be so good as to grant a permission for an officer of each corps to go to New York in order to execute the several commissions given them on that head. You may depend on the strictest attention being paid to the time limited for their return. [I] Should be glad if permission could be given to two women likewise to go to New York – one whose husband was killed at Stony Point, the other whose husband is at New York.[86]

General Wayne forwarded the letter to Washington who responded two days later, agreeing to Lieutenant Colonel Johnson's request and directing Deputy Commissary General of Prisoners Skinner to carry it out, with the stipulation that the women who desired to go to New York — and any other women on the march who wanted to go there as well -- simply not return.[87] Skinner had his own troubles with the prisoners in his charge and on the same day (July 20) that Johnson had written to General Wayne, Skinner also corresponded from Goshen describing his situation:

. . We arrived at this place last Evening, and the Prisoners behave much better than I expected. The greatest difficulty is occasioned by the Women and Children, who amount to near Seventy, and who must Starve unless furnished with Provisions. I have hitherto drawn for them but would wish to have your particular directions whither I shall continue to supply them, as I know of no Resolution of Congress empowering the Commissary of Prisoners to do this, tho their particular situation requires it. We shall proceed as soon as a Waggon or two can be got to carry Some of the Party who are unable to keep up and who are fallen Lame in crossing the Mountains to this place. ..[88]

The letter bears poignant witness to the harsh effects of captivity on civilians as well as soldiers, particularly at a time when women and children were often a part of garrison life.   The prisoners continued to march away inland away from the Hudson and possible rescue from British raiding parties. Their precise route has not been fully determined, but it is known that after Goshen, they arrived in Hardystown, Pennsylvania, on July 24. On that day, Lieutenant Colonel Johnson took the opportunity to write Sir Henry Clinton about the loss of Stony Point:

> *The bearer, Lieutenant Armstrong, of the 17th Infantry, will give a full and perfect account of the unfortunate event of the morning of the 16th instant, whereon the post of Stony Point fell into the hands of the enemy. I am inclined to think that upon a just representation you will be fully convinced that it was not any neglect on my part, nor of the troops under my command, but the very superior force of the enemy that caused the capture of the place. . .The very distressed situation of our people, for want of necessaries of every kind, occasioned my application for a flag, in order to have them provided. General Washington's permission to send a subaltern officer of each corps I received but this instant. The Commissary of prisoners being under the necessity of returning immediately, obliges me to draw a conclusion, referring your Excellency to Lieutenant Armstrong for any further particulars.[89]*

Lieutenant Colonel Johnson would benefit from a standard military practice of the time, that of paroling officers. He and 22 others were being sent to Easton, Pennsylvania,[90] and thence to Lancaster to be billeted in private houses, having given their parole –- from the French for "word' –- that they would refrain from escape, avoid political and military discussions with local civilians, pay their own expenses, and be subject to a kind of house arrest until they were exchanged for enemy officers of equal rank. Until they arrived at their final destination, however, the captured officers would continue to march along with their men.

Their passage was noticed by Ensign Thomas Hughes, who was also a British prisoner in Lancaster. Hughes had been captured at Ticonderoga in 1777 and kept a journal. On August 3, he entered the following information:

> *Col. Johnson and most of the officers taken at Stony Point*
> *came here on parole. The wounded were permitted to go to*
> *[New] York and their men are sent to Philadelphia gaol –*
> *they were all plundered.*[91]

As previously noted, wounded officers and men had already been sent to New York on British ships as a consequence of Surgeon Auchmuty's request to General Wayne. On December 29, a further entry appears in Hughes' journal:

> *The [men of the] 17th Regiment were brought here under*
> *guard and are to be sent to Virginia – the poor fellows are*
> *ragged and the weather piercing cold.*[92]

The prisoners languished in their respective locations, but finally, by October 25, 1780, after more than a year in captivity, an exchange was agreed to, and Lieutenant Colonel Henry Johnson and his fellow officers were released. Among the exchanged prisoners was Lt. William Marshall of the 63rd Regiment of Foot, who, on June 26, 1779, had been appointed Acting Engineer in charge of the British defenses at Stony Point. Marshall was captured inside the Upper Works near the ruins of an American blockhouse when the post was attacked.[93] Marshall stayed in Lancaster from early August of 1779 to at least March 13, 1780, the date of his last letter from that location.[94] During that time, he may have drawn his highly detailed *Sketch of the Works at Stoney Point*, the only extant map of the battleground by a participant. In September of that year, prior to his exchange, Marshall acquired a new rank, having been promoted to Captain. Returning to his own lines, the relatively unknown officer would soon play an unexpected role in a later event that would help determine the responsibility and possible   negligence for the loss of Stony Point.

5

***"You have nobly reaped Laurels in the Cause of your Country and in the
Fields of Danger and Death."***

Meanwhile, there was widespread praise for the victorious Light Infantry
and their successful assault against Stony Point.   In his report to
Washington, written on July 17 when the captured British fort was still
occupied by the Americans, General Wayne was among the first to voice
approval for the brave men who had carried out the brilliant *coup de main*:

> *Too much praise cannot be given to Lt. Col Fleury (who
> struck the enemy's standard with his own hand), and to
> Major Steward* [sic], *who commanded the advanced parties,
> for their brave and prudent conduct.   Colonels Butler,
> Meigs, and Febiger conducted themselves with that
> coolness, bravery and perseverance, that will ever ensure
> success. Lt. Col. Hay was wounded in the thigh, bravely
> fighting at the head of his battalion.   I should take up too
> much of Your Excellency's time, was I to particularize every
> individual who deserves it, for his bravery on this occasion.
> I cannot, however, omit Major Lee, to whom I am indebted
> for frequent and very useful intelligence, which contributed
> much to the success of the enterprise, and it is with the
> greatest pleasure I acknowledge to you, I was supported in
> the attack by all the officers and soldiers under my
> command, to the utmost of my wishes.[95]*

In his letter to Congress of July 20, 1779, in which Wayne's report was
enclosed, General Washington added his own accolade:

> *To the encomiums he* [General Wayne] *has deservedly bestowed on the officers and men under his command, it gives me pleasure to add, that his own conduct throughout the whole of this arduous enterprise merits the warmest approbation of Congress. He improved upon the plan recommended by me, and executed it in a manner that does signal honor to his judgment and to his bravery. In a critical moment of the assault, he received a flesh wound in the head with a musket ball, but continued leading on his men with unshaken firmness.* [96]

Newspapers printed accounts, not always accurate, of the battle, while military colleagues and civilian officials — including President Reed of Pennsylvania, Dr. Benjamin Rush and even General Charles Lee, on whose court-martial Wayne had recently sat -- continued to compliment the Corps of Light Infantry and their commanding officer. A word of praise, one that General Wayne would never see, also came from an unlikely source, none other than Sir Henry Clinton, the British commander-in-chief who stated that the "bold and well-combined attempt" on Stony Point "procured very deservedly no small share of reputation and applause to the spirited officer who conducted it." [97]

Congress, too, acknowledged the daring nighttime attack mounted against formidable enemy defenses and conducted by troops armed only with fixed bayonets. An Act of Congress was passed on July 26 and John Jay sent a personal letter and a copy of the resolutions to General Wayne:

> *Your late glorious Achievements have merited, and now receive the Approbation and Thanks of your country; They are contained in the enclosed act of Congress which I have the Honor to transmit. This brilliant action adds fresh*

44

Lustre to our arms and will teach the Enemy to respect our Power if not to imitate our Humanity. You have nobly reaped Laurels in the Cause of your Country and in the Fields of Danger and Death. May these prove the earnest of more and may victory ever bear your Standard, and Providence be your Shield.

The Resolutions raised the level of praise to a virtual crescendo and must have been the high point of all the communications received by General Wayne for the action at Stony Point.

Resolved, unanimously, That the thanks of Congress be presented to Brigadier General Wayne, for his brave, prudent and soldierly conduct in the spirited and well conducted attack of Stoney Point.

Resolved, unanimously, That Congress entertain a proper sense of the good conduct of the officers and soldiers under the command of Brigadier General Wayne, in the assault of the enemy's works at Stoney Point, and highly commend the coolness, discipline and firm intrepidity exhibited on the occasion.

Resolved, unanimously, That Lieutenant Colonel Fleury, and Major Stewart, who, by their situation in leading the two attacks, had a more immediate opportunity of distinguishing themselves, have, by their personal achievements, exhibited a bright example to their brother soldiers, and merit in a particular manner the approbation and acknowledgement of the United States.

> Resolved, *unanimously, That Congress warmly approve and applaud the cool, determined spirit with which Lieutenant Gibbon and Lieutenant Knox led on the forlorn hope, braving danger and death in the cause of their country.* Resolved, *unanimously, That a medal, emblematical of this action, be struck: That one of gold be presented to Brigadier General Wayne, and a silver one to Lieutenant Colonel Fleury and Major Stewart respectively..*[98]

The medals were a unique badge of honor since each one was individually designed and cast; not many were awarded, and only one was given to a foreign officer serving as a volunteer: Lt. Colonel Fleury, who had also earned the admiration of George Washington. Describing Fleury's service in America to his fellow countryman the Marquis de La Fayette, the General stated that the French nobleman had always "behaved with that intrepidity and intelligence which marks his conduct on all occasions."[99]

Prior to 1779, only two medals had been conferred by Congress: one to General Washington for the evacuation of Boston by the British in 1776; and one to General Horatio Gates for the defeat of Burgoyne at Saratoga in 1777. By the end of the Revolution – the second longest war in American history -- only eleven medals would be issued for the eight long years of conflict and sacrifice.[100]   The midnight assault of Stony Point, involving less than a half hour of combat, was the first of only two battles for which three medals were given.[101] The medals represented not only the bravery of the recipients themselves; but also the country's increased pride in a military force that could launch a daring, well-planned assault that equaled the highest standards of trained professional soldiers.

Congress had also approved the monetary rewards that General Wayne had offered in his order of battle to the first five men who entered the main British defenses, and had confirmed as well the appraised value of the ordnance and stores captured at Stony Point, which was calculated to total $160,141.82/90.[102] This amount was then distributed among the troops, based on rank. A private's share, for example, was $78.92, whereas General Wayne received $1420.51.[103]

Some officers, however, were disgruntled by another concern, namely that they had been omitted from the congratulations that continued to be offered to General Wayne from all quarters. Perceiving a Pennsylvania bias, they expressed their complaints. On August 10, 1779, Major Thomas Posey of Virginia wrote directly to General Washington and sent a copy to General Wayne on the 12th, two days later:

> . ..I feel a most Sensible Mortification . . . by finding myself totally Neglected. It is not even mentioned that such a field Officer was at the Attack. It is perfectly well known to General Wayne that I led the Battalion which Composed the front of the Right Column, where he himself marched until we Came to the Beach, Where General Wayne left the head of the Column, After which I had the sole Guidance and direction of it. . . .As I have had an equal share in the danger and fatigue attending the reduction of Stony Point I expected an equal share of the honor resulting from the Success of that enterprise. I expected to have been mentioned to my Countrymen; this is all I ask, all I want, and all I wish to receive. . .[104]

Twelve days later, on August 22, Colonel Return Jonathan Meigs of Connecticut voiced a similar opinion, this time only to Wayne himself:

47

*I think it my duty to inform your honor that the account
contained in your honor's letter to his Excellency of the
Reduction of Stony Point is exceptionable to many Officers
in the Brigade* [the Third and Fourth Light Infantry
Regiments, consisting primarily of troops from Connecticut
and Massachusetts]. *. as the Account now Stands, the
Public must be induced to believe that Lt. Col. Fleury,
Major Stewart, Lieutenants Gibbon and Knox, forced their
way in the Works, which made the advancing of the
Columns comparatively easy – while the fact is that the
volunteers of the Right Column did not suffer more in
proportion than the Columns in General - the Gentlemen*
[officers of the Brigade] *don't object to the encomiums
given in your honors letter of any of one of the Officers
there mentioned, who upon every principle ought to be
distinguishingly noticed But think that there is the
appearance of partiality in not mentioning any wounded
Officer except Lt. Col. Hay* [of Pennsylvania] *whose
wounds are equally honorable, & no more so than the
Others . . The honorable mention made of my name with
the Other Colonels is to the utmost of my wishes – As Major
Hull Commanded a Regiment in the Attack, I could have
wished that his name had been mentioned with the
Colonels. . .* [105]

Meigs, however, was certain that whatever omissions had occurred in
Wayne's Report to Washington stemmed from the best motives:

*. . I would not think that your honor would deliberately
shew a partiality to any particular Corps or State, On the*

48

contrary, I am convinced that you are actuated by
Sentiments as great as the magnitude of the cause in which
we are mutually combined. . [106]

These two letters – one passionate and accusatory, the other balanced and diplomatic – were the first salvos in a battle of words that would threaten not only the esprit de corps of the Light Infantry, but also undermine the unity exemplified by their recent triumph.

On the same day of Colonel Meigs's letter, August 22, Lieutenant Colonel Isaac Sherman, also of Connecticut, wrote to General Wayne. His initial remarks set a considerably less temperate tone that, with few exceptions, was maintained throughout his communication:

Can it be supposed that the officers of the New England line
are totally void of sentiment, that those fine and delicate
feelings which ever distinguish the generous and manly soul
are incapable of making any impression on them .. .Your
brave and spirited behavior in the action of Monmouth
endeared you to your brethren in the field, and merited the
highest applause; but your letter to General Washington on
the reduction of Stony Point, in the minds of many judicious
persons, has in some measure tarnished the luster of your
character, and rendered your command less agreeable.
However, we wish to believe it was owing to the variety of
business that demanded your attention at that time, rather
than any other cause. . . . [107]

Sherman warmed to his subject and pointed out that he was speaking for others, lest Wayne think he was acting entirely out of self-interest.

Are we not embarked in the same cause, and does not our independence rest on our united efforts? But rather than be injured, rather than be trampled upon and considered as insignificant beings in the scale – <u>my blood boils at the thought. Nature recoils, and points out a mode, the only one of redress</u> . . .[emphasis in original] *I am not writing for myself, but I feel for those officers under my command as well as others who merit as much as those most distinguished by you. . .You have not arrived beyond the regions of censure, and our feelings as well as interest require that there should be a more full and impartial representation of facts than you have made[108]*

General Wayne was either more sensitive than his military critics imagined or he had already heard about the dissatisfaction of some of his fellow officers because on August 10, before any of the letters cited here were written, he had corresponded with John Jay, the President of Congress, to correct omissions in his original report:

I feel much hurt, that I did not in my letter to him [Washington] of the 17th of July Mention (among Other Brave & Worthy officers) the Names of Lt. Col. Sherman, Major Hull, Murphey [sic] & Posey – whose good Conduct & Intrepidity justly entitled them to that attention.[109]

On August 23, in a lengthy and detailed response to Meigs's letter, Wayne noted that the problem had already been addressed in his letter to Jay and pointed out that if he had to name every officer who distinguished himself at Stony Point "I should have to recapitulate the names of every Officer in the Corps, otherwise not have done justice to their merit, and perhaps it would not have rested here, but must have gone down to every Non-commissioned

50

Officer and private – the Absurdity is too Obvious to admit of a serious comment."[110] Wayne requested Meigs "to place this matter in its proper point of view – not only to the Officers of your Regiment – but to others who may have read my letter and returns with a Prejudiced or Inattentive eye – and assure them that I wish for nothing more than an Opportunity of Producing a Conviction to the World that I detest Local Prejudices as much as I pity the man who would unjustly suspect me of them."[111] However, in a postscript to Meigs, Wayne plainly took strong personal exception to some of Sherman's comments:

> I have received a letter dated yesterday from Lt. Col. Sherman, of a very extraordinary Nature – which at a Proper Season will require a very Serious & particular explanation – for although I don't wish to Incur any Gentleman's displeasure, yet, I put up with no man's Insults.[112]

Meigs must have conveyed Wayne's obvious displeasure to Sherman because the Lieutenant Colonel very quickly wrote to Wayne again to clarify his original remarks:

> To insult you, I declare upon my honor, never was my intention; my view was to acquaint you there was an uneasiness among the Officers of your command, and the cause . . . I am sensible that I expressed myself with a good deal of warmth arising from my feelings at the time . . .[but] So far from thinking to make use of compulsive measures to gain redress, that I can assure you, it never entered my mind.[113]

Major William Hull, who had also expressed concern that he was not mentioned in Wayne's original report, learned that he was included in Wayne's letter to Jay. Further, he had been invited to discuss the matter personally with Wayne, had apparently done so, and was mollified, stating ". . . ample justice is done me, and the Cause of the Omission clearly pointed out – I am only unhappy that I imputed the Neglect to the wrong Cause, and am now firmly persuaded that you was actuated by no other Principles, than equal and impartial Justice to your Corps."[114]

But there was still Thomas Posey, the Virginia major who wrote the first letter complaining that, among other things, he felt " a most Sensible Mortification . . . by finding myself totally Neglected. " Wayne's initial response set the stage:

> *Your very Laconic note of the 12th Instant enclosing a Copy of a long letter to His Excellency General Washington – I purposely delayed Answering until you had an Opportunity of being convinced that I had made use of the first Opening of doing justice to your merit.*

Next, he addressed some of the statements in Posey's letter. He observed, for example, that Colonels Fleury, Meigs, Febiger, and Sherman were all in Posey's column, and when Wayne left it and pushed ahead, had a better right to claim command than the lowly Major. Wayne affirmed that Major Posey was included in the many individuals who did their duty the night of the attack, and had been identified by name in the letter to Jay, a copy of which he enclosed. Wayne now sought clarification for some of the language Posey had used in his letter to Washington:

. . .perhaps on cool reflection you may find that there are some expressions made use of tending to hold up an Idea of want of Prowess in me – which was Supplied by you. Was that really your Intention, and you still Continue in the same Opinion – I know that you will have Candor enough to acknowledge it (not to me as your Superior Officer) but to me as a Private Gentleman very tenacious of my Honor – which honor is now plighted to meet you on that ground only. But should you have no Intention to cast a Shade on my Military Character (as a Gentleman of those nice feelings which I believe you to possess)- I now call on you to place that matter in a proper point of View.[115]

Major Posey got the letter –- and the message -- and responded the same day:

.. I had no intention . . to cast any reflection upon your military Character, or your character in any manner whatsoever. . . your letter to Congress [in which Posey was named] *is a sufficient one, & I hope this will be a satisfactory one to you.[116]*

Wayne was not about to have his comments to Jay interpreted by Posey as an apology and fired off a final shot in the seemingly endless war of letters:

As you seem to attribute my Letter to the president of Congress (of the 10th ultimo) to the effects of yours to me on the 12th, I must beg leave to put you right by a perusal of the enclosed, as published by order of Congress – & in which you'll find the real & only cause that could possibly produce it.[117]

53

By enclosing yet another copy of his letter to President Jay, Wayne intended Posey to observe something he had obviously overlooked -- that Wayne's reason for writing to Jay was that Wayne himself felt "much hurt" that he had neglected to mention more officers in his original report of the assault, and that the letter to Jay, written on August 10th, could hardly be viewed as a response to a letter written by Posey on August 12, two days later. The correspondence had lasted far longer than the battle of Stony Point itself, but it was now at an end.

6

"Good God, Col. Webster, did I not always say that these points ought not to be defended?"

The British had not remained idle during the aftermath of battle, and had in fact returned to the abandoned post of Stony Point. Brigadier General Sterling, with the 42nd, 63rd, and 64th regiments, approached the area on July 19, the day after the Americans left, though the British return may have been as late as July 21 or 22.[118] The reason for the possible delay may have been the inclement weather, namely "the northerly winds, rather uncommon at this season" that had favored the Americans throughout the battle and were continuing to impede British reaction.[119]   When Crown forces landed unopposed, their work was cut out for them:

> . . [We] *found the Works dismantled & the Abatis torn up, & the Platforms destroyed. We began immediately upon the defense of the Post, first by carrying* [constructing] *an Abatis round the Table of the Hill* [inside the remains of the Upper Works] *& then erecting the enclosed Work, with Six Block Houses as delineated on the Plan,. . .   The Work on the Table of the Hill being enclosed, a Block house was erected in front upon a Knoll where there had latterly been a fleche* [fleche #1 in the ruined fort].[120]

This new defensive system, with its enclosed works and a circular abatis, took six or seven weeks to complete, and was, of course, very different from the fortifications recently captured by the American Light Infantry, a fact that did not escape Lieutenant Colonel Johnson:

> . . *respecting the Necessity of having an enclosed Work on the Table of the Hill. . I am fully persuaded that had that*

Plan [for the second fort] *been originally adopted, the Enemy never could have taken it by Assault, & from the Opinions given me by several of the Rebel Officers, have reason to think that they never would have attempted it.*[121]

Captain Patrick Ferguson of the 71st Regiment would play a key role in the new fort and had observed the American assault on July 16 from his post at Verplanck's Point.[122] He agreed with Lieutenant Colonel Johnson and had had several discussions prior to the attack with him and Lieutenant Colonel Webster, the commander of both British forts at the time, and under whom Johnson served. Captain Robert Douglass of the Royal Artillery recalled the conversation:

Captain Ferguson from the first moment disapproved of the mode in which Stony Point was fortified. It was his almost constant conversation in my hearing, and I have every reason to believe he held up the same idea to Lt. Col. Webster that if ever Stony Point was attacked during the night that it would be carried. And that he himself with 600 or 700 men would undertake to effect it . . .Captain Ferguson meant that the post in general as his common objection was that there was no enclosed work.[123]

By late August, the second British post at Stony Point was nearing completion, having been garrisoned with between 500 and 600 troops, about the same number as the earlier fort. Once again, Washington was concerned about the continuing presence of the enemy in a vital military area, and made several requests for information from General Wayne, including one on October 3. He was to arrange for General Du Portail[124] to reconnoiter for a second time "the post of Stony Point and to ascertain the distances from the Enemys works to the places proper for establishing batteries . .

.P.S. . . . I am to request you will take pains to ascertain whether the enemy have bomb proofs in Stony point, what number, extent and thickness. This is an essential point to know towards any operations against that post."[125]

However, an attempt to re-take Stony Point would soon prove unnecessary because by 1779 the war had expanded: the British were now fighting France and Spain, America's new allies, and consequently experiencing shortages of men and supplies. On September 9, 1779, Sir Henry Clinton lamented his situation to General Sir Frederick Haldimand:

> . . .The Reinforcements which I have been so long expecting from Europe arrived here on the 25th of last month . . . and consists only of two raised Regiments and the British recruits for the Army. . . .The unfortunate affair at Stony Point . . retarded me much, and I was obliged to leave a strong garrison there to repair the work which two days' foul wind had given the enemy time to demolish. . . . I am [also] disappointed in my expectation of a Reinforcement from the West Indies, and, weak and miserable as I am, I am obliged to comply with your requisition, and therefore, Sir, I send you three Regiments, one of which is British, and considering the large detachments that have already been made from this army, is a great proportion.[126]

On October 21, Washington informed Wayne that deserters had told him a speedy evacuation of Stony Point and Verplanck's Point appeared likely, and that Verplanck's Point may have been abandoned the previous evening.[127] The next morning, Washington ordered Wayne to provide a covering party of "about 100 men" as the commander-in-chief intended to ride the following day to Verplanck's Point and see the situation for himself.[128] Apparently, the departure of the British from both posts, and their destruction of the fortifications on each, must have been evident because on October 26, Washington advised Wayne that "there will be a necessity of throwing up a small work upon Stony Point to protect the communication by King's Ferry."[129] The Americans could not be absolutely certain at the time, but the British departure was permanent - they would not be back.

A small American garrison would remain at Stony Point throughout the war, but the short battle had long consequences. There may well have been less talk from London about luring "Mr. Washington" into a military situation from which he could not withdraw, and there was a new respect accorded to the professional ability of the American army. It was becoming abundantly clear that the rebellion was out of hand, and that a military resolution against a more experienced enemy was becoming considerably less likely. In fact, the war would last another four years, but Crown forces would not make another military effort to control the Hudson and achieve their goal of separating New England from New York and other colonies, and they would never again threaten the Hudson Highlands. Instead, attention would focus on the American south which held much promise for British arms but whose efforts would nonetheless culminate with Cornwallis's defeat at Yorktown in the fall of 1781.

That a British fort on a high, rocky peninsula, with two sets of defenses, two abatis, fifteen pieces of artillery, a garrison of more than 500 professionally trained troops, supported by a second garrison of about the same size in another fort less than a mile away and protected by ships of the Royal Navy, could be captured in less than a half hour raises several important issues. A close look at those defenses may shed light on the British response to the American attack on the night of July 15-16, 1779.

The most serious shortcoming of the British defensive situation was that there was no enclosed work and no physical connection between the two existing sets of fortifications. In a reference already cited, both Lieutenant Colonel Johnson and Captain Patrick Ferguson mention the former defect before the battle, yet no permanent measures were taken to remedy the situation prior to the American attack. Part of the reason for this might have been a lack of communication between different branches of the service, a problem not confined to the eighteenth century. The comments of Captain Alexander Mercer, Commanding Engineer, are instructive:

Q. As you have said that you had several Conversations with Lt. Col Webster relative to the defense of Verplanck's and Stony Point, do you recollect whether you gave your Opinion relative to the Number of Men necessary for the defense of that Stony Point or of the disposition of the Troops?

A. I cannot recollect that I did. . .

Q. Had you any conversation with Lt. Col. Johnson relative to the defense of Stony Point?

A. I do not recollect that I had.

Q. Had you Offered any lights or Instructions to the Commanding Officer of the defense of Stony Point?

A. I do not recollect that I did.

Q. Did you Consult with Anybody with regard to the disposition of those Works in the defense of Stony Point?

A. I cannot recollect that I particularly Consulted with any Person on these Works, as they were carried on in some Measure under the immediate Eye of the Commander in Chief [Sir Henry Clinton]. . .

Q. Is it not usual and proper in the Service for a Commanding Engineer, being ordered to fortify a Post, to give his Ideas of the Defense to the Officer who is left to defend it?

A. Yes, and as Lt. Col Webster was left in Command of both Posts . . . I did, in general Conversation, and I think on delivering him a Copy of my Letter of Instruction to Lt. Stratten, give him my Ideas on this subject. . .

Q. You have said that in your idea the defense should have been confined to the Table of the Hill. Were you ever consulted or did you ever give it as your Opinion Officially to Lt. Col. Johnson or Lt. Col. Webster that the several Pieces of Artillery in the fleches along the outward Abatis should remain in their fleches after the Works were reported to be in a state of Defense?

A. I do not recollect that I ever had any Conversation with Lt. Col Johnson relative to the defense of Stony Point, but I very well remember in general Conversation with Lt. Col. Webster on this Subject telling him that these fleches were never intended as Objects of Defense, and I further recollect on returning to Verplanck's Point [after the battle] *with the Commander in Chief* [Sir Henry Clinton], *I used this*

Exclamation to Lt. Col. Webster: "Good God, Col. Webster, did I not always say that these points ought not to be defended?"[130]

This apparent missing link in the chain of command made a unified defense all the more difficult. The contact between Captain Mercer and Lieutenant Colonel Johnson was indirect at best, and it appears that Johnson was never told to abandon the Outer Works and bring in its guns in the event of an attack. Had he done so, rather than deploying more than half the garrison along the outer abatis instead concentrating all his troops in the Upper Works, the garrison might have resisted further, possibly long enough for the tide of battle to turn, even though the primary fortification was not enclosed. The defenders would also have been more able to tell friend apart from foe in the confusing darkness if all the Colonel's forces had been deployed inside a single set of defenses.

The two abatis – normally effective obstacles in themselves - formed lines across the peninsula but did not enclose anything, a mistake the British corrected in their second fort. Both barriers could be (and were) flanked for different reasons: the southern end of the outer abatis extended into shallow water; the northern end of the inner abatis stopped short on a high place the British called "the precipice," above the shoreline. Neither water nor precipice stopped them: in the darkness, without firing a shot, the Americans swept around them both.

The artillery would have been highly effective in a daytime battle, when the 18 and 24 pounders on the flanks of the Upper Works could have provided a devastating, long-range initial fire. At night, however, line-of-sight guns were extremely limited. British eye-witnesses also tell us that only two cannons fired: the light brass 12-pounder, commanded by Lt. William Horndon at fleche #1, which ran out of ammunition as it tried to hit targets the gunners could not see, and the 3-pounder cannon which was on a field carriage. This gun, the only one at Stony Point that was not in a work, was, as previously noted, located in the middle of the two sets of fortifications; it fired 69 rounds, probably case shot, directed toward the advancing Americans as they entered the outer abatis by fleche #3. The other artillery pieces played no role in the fort's defense, nor could they have done so: as we have seen, the heavy ship guns in the Upper Works were kept unloaded at night and were placed on the ends of a high ridge, allowing an enemy to pass below unscathed. Lieutenant John Roberts states:

> *Q. What were your reasons for Asserting that the 18 and 24 Prs . . . could be of no Service on the Night of the Attack?*

> *A. Because they could not be depressed to the Object, on Account of the projection of the brow of the Hill; they were intended for distant Objects, & laid accordingly for a Hill in front; and as it was naturally supposed that they would not be wanted on a Night Attack, the Ammunition for them was not deposited on the Batteries . . .[131]*

These guns, as well as the other 12 pounders, were also confined in embrasures, thus restricting their side-to-side movement. The 12-pounder located at the Flagstaff Battery on the right flank was *en barbette*, but, like the heavy ship guns, was mounted on a hill and could not fire at an enemy rushing forward in the darkness below. The two Royal mortars and the 12-pounder at fleche #3 were overrun by the advancing Americans,[132] and the 10 inch land mortar in the Upper Works –- like the Coehorns in fleche #2 -- would have killed defenders and attackers alike had it lobbed shells blindly into the all encompassing night. Most of these weapons would have made little if any difference to the results of the battle, but there was one important exception: the Howitzer battery which alone could have repulsed the

American advance and altered the outcome of the battle. Its location was the key to defense because it overlooked the sandy beach on Stony Point's southern flank that was "only obstructed by a slight abatis": the very area where the 700 men of the Light Infantry's right column were wading through the shallow water, going around the abatis, and ascending to high ground   The importance of this weapon was obvious, as Lt. Roberts confirmed:

> *Q.   To what Object was the 8 inch Howitzer pointed in General?*
>
> *A.   At Night it was always depressed so as to point to. . Haverstraw Bay.. .*
>
> *Q.   Had those shots been fired from the Howitzer. . .would it not have had a very seasonable effect and galled the Enemy in their Approach that way?*
>
> *A.   I conceive that it would. . .*
>
> *Q.   Was there Ammunition deposited in the Howitzer Battery during the Night?*
>
> *A.   There was.*
>
> *Q.   Do you imagine the Howitzer not being fired was Occasioned by the Rapid Success of the Enemy in taking Possession of the Howitzer Battery or from what other cause did it proceed?*

A. I believe it was from the Rapid Movement of the Enemy, & the Men of Artillery who were Attached to that Battery laying so far from it, as they lay the furthest off of any of the Troops in Garrison. . .

Q. What length of time intervened between your hearing the first Shots fired. . . from which you drew your conclusion that the Enemy were in Possession of that Battery?

A. Twelve or thirteen Minutes. . .

Q. What did the Ammunition consist of, fixed Shells or Case Shot?

A. Both.

Q. Were any Precautions taken by fixing Stakes, etc., as is usual, in order to bring the Howitzer to point at the same Object again, after the Natural & Common Alteration that might have been occasioned by every Recoil?

A. No, had it been necessary to fire Shells to 150, 200 or 250 Yards, that Precaution, I suppose, would have been taken, but as the distance was so short, at which they were to fire Case Shot,. . .it consequently could not have missed its Object, particularly as the Battery was <u>en Barbette</u> & the Howitzer might have been traversed, without the danger of injuring an Embrazure.[133]

The weapon was aimed toward Haverstraw Bay, had ammunition close by, and could have had a "very seasonable effect and galled the enemy" if the artillerymen ("they lay the furthest off of any of the troops in the garrison") had gotten there before the Americans. But the Light Infantry got there first and quickly, advancing through the marsh at the front of the fortifications, passing below fleche #1 in the Outer Works and through the shallow waters of the bay, going around the first abatis and climbing the slope to the Howitzer battery — all in twelve or thirteen minutes, as Lt. Roberts tells us. How did they know where it was and that it was vital to capture it before it fired? The answer may well lie in the careful and detailed reconnaissance conducted by observant, experienced officers directed by Washington himself.

7

"Had the Gun Boat been at her station and the People in her Vigilant I do not think it possible for a Column of Men to have waded thro' the water without being heard"

Though the historical record is not clear, it seems likely that the Howitzer's strategic location must have been obvious to Captain McLane on July 2 when he gained entry to the British fortifications, and he or the others who gathered information on Stony Point's defenses must have conveyed that fact to General Washington. The potential danger to the American plan would have then been apparent: if shells were lobbed or case shot fired at virtually pointblank range toward the troops wading in the shallow water below Stony Point, the Light Infantry assault would probably have gotten no further and sustained numerous casualties as well. The Howitzer, however, remained silent, leaving only a gunboat to protect the crucial south flank.

But the gunboat wasn't there. As noted earlier, The *Vulture*, which, although it was intended the protect the north side of Stony Point, was anchored on the night of the battle in the middle of the Hudson, most likely to avoid being blown aground by blasts of the northwesterly wind which had begun on the night of July 15 and continued for several days; the gunboat which was supposed to guard the south flank was probably tethered to her for the same reason. The unreliable defense of ships guarding the watery flanks proved so erratic that it was, in fact, dispensed with altogether by the second British fort, with its enclosed works and circular abatis. On the night it could have made a difference, however, the gunboat was manifestly not where it should have been, and its whereabouts is one of the most frequently asked questions in Lieutenant Colonel Johnson's trial. It was not unusual for it to be missing, as Ensign Henry Hamilton indicates:

Q. Was the Gun Boat which was usually on the left Flank at her Station on the Night of the Attack?

A. It was not.

Q. Under whose Orders was this Gun Boat supposed to be?

A. As it was so frequently taken away, I cannot say under whose Orders she was.

Q. Had not the Gun Boat been taken away several Nights previous to the Attack?

A. Yes, very often..

Q. Did you not often hear Lt. Col Johnson express his dissatisfaction at the Gun Boat being taken away?

A. I have often seen him displeas'd at it.

Q. Do you know whether the Gun Boat was at its station the Night before the Attack?

A. I believe that it was not.

Q. Supposing [the enemy] *to have enter'd between the first and second Abatis, had the Gun Boat been at her station do you think it possible for a Column of Men to have waded thro' the Water without being heard by those in the Gun Boat?*

A. Had the Gun Boat been at her station and the People in her Vigilant I do not think it possible for a Column of Men to have waded thro' the water without being heard, notwithstanding the Darkness of the Night.[134]

The apparently unpredictable deployment of the gunboat, regardless of the weather, made the Howitzer all the more critical, but if the gunboat had been at its station, it alone, like the Howitzer, could have very likely stopped the main American column in the water. Of course, the Howitzer and gunboat combined would have had even more devastating consequences for the Light Infantry assault, but when both failed to defend the vital south flank, the battle was lost in the murky waters below the heights, the same place where, with a successful defense, it might well have been won.

There were also other means available that might have helped the defenders during a nighttime attack. The Coehorn mortars at fleche #2 in the Outer Works were capable of firing lightballs[135], which could have been lobbed toward the marsh in front to illuminate the attackers, and in fact, a composition for them had been prepared. As a signal to the *Vulture,* there were also rockets[136] located at the opposite end of the peninsula, attached to the frame of a hut.[137] Lieutenant William Marshall was asked about both of these devices:

Q. Were any light Balls fired on the Night of the Attack, or do you know of any Signal to the Vulture being framed & prepared?

A. I think that no light Balls were made use of on the Night of the Attack, nor do I know of any Signals being prepared in Order to be made to the Vulture.[138]

It is unlikely that signals could have brought any assistance, since the high winds would have made navigation across the river very difficult, and, as previously noted, the British garrison at Verplanck's Point was the object of a feint led by Colonel Rufus Putnam, which must have seemed real at the time. Beacons of some sort, possibly brush piles ready to be ignited, might have helped the garrison identify the attackers and reduce the confusion that ultimately aided the Americans, but none had been prepared. Captain Mercer, the commanding engineer, was asked his opinion:

> *Q. Do you mean . . . that the Table of the Hill only was to be defended; that this should have been the Case in the Night only, or both by day & Night?*

> *A. I will abide by the same disposition, by day and Night, only with this difference, that by Night I would have Beacons on the flanks to have lighted; and had I been informed of the Approach of an Enemy I would have the beacons constantly lighted.*

> *Q. Did you signify the foregoing Ideas to Lt. Colo. Johnson, or Lieut. Colo. Webster, or to whom?*

> *A. I do not remember to have mentioned the Idea to anybody; it appeared to me too Obvious to render this Necessary.* [139]

Deception also played a role in determining the kind of attack the British might anticipate. As stated earlier, the orientation of their artillery — mostly toward the landward side of peninsula — suggested the expectation of a daytime frontal assault. General Washington promoted that view in order to conceal the nature of the impending attack, and, as cited previously, wrote to

General Wayne that he had "ordered down a couple of light fieldpieces. When you march, you can leave the pieces behind."[140]   The probable consequence of that ruse aided the American effort to cover their true intentions, as confirmed by Lieutenant Colonel. Johnson:

> *The intelligence I received between eight and nine o'clock on the night of the 15th [of July] from the scouts I had sent out the preceding evening. . . gave me reason to expect an attack, . . from the enemy's moving with heavy cannon.*[141]

Another factor in the British defeat was an unforeseen development that has affected many battles throughout the ages: the weather - in particular, the high winds and the intense darkness of the night.   As has been shown, a cold, brisk wind blew out of the northwest and lasted three days, from July 15 to July 18, when Washington decided to abandon Stony Point.   Among several officers who commented on the weather during the attack, Captain Robert Clayton refers to "the high Wind and darkness of the Night."[142]   As cited earlier, Lieutenant John Ross of the 71st Regiment related that he could not at first detect the enemy because the "Night being extremely dark and very Windy, made me suppose that what the Men reported to me to have heard was occasioned by the Wind rustling amongst the bushes."[143] Corporal Simon Davies, one of the sentries posted near the south flank, observed that sentries were relieved by ship's bells but the wind "blew so hard that Night, that I could not hear them."[144]

Several important advantages now fell to the Americans because of the wind: the British vessels guarding the north and south flanks of the peninsula were anchored in the middle of the Hudson away from their posts; and the attacking columns were far more difficult to hear and locate.   The darkness, of course, made the Americans more difficult to see, combined with the fact that the attacking columns had unloaded muskets, and therefore did not reveal their presence in the dark by firing. That also meant fewer Americans would accidentally be wounded by their own men or lose precious time during the assault to aim or load. Finally, the blackness of the night also protected them from whatever enemy artillery and musketry could be brought to bear, and rendered most of the British defensive measures ineffective.

One can only speculate as to why the British failed to take the precautions and preventive measures that might have changed the course of the battle. It may have been a matter of perception, a feeling that their military opponents — "Mr. Washington" and his "rebels" — were simply not as well trained or experienced. That may have been true in the early years of the war, but, by 1779. that had all changed, never to be altered again. Had the Americans at Stony Point been considered professional soldiers, and the British taken the same precautionary measures they would have thought necessary to guard against their European counterparts, defeat might well have become victory.

8

***"a tale hardly worth considering, a poor tradition . . .the exploit would
have been mentioned at the time. . ."***

The battle of Stony Point not only had military repercussions and increased
American morale; occurring as it did during a period of relative stalemate in
the war, it also seized the public imagination, sometimes leading to
misconceptions and legends. Because of General Wayne's unfortunate and
misleading sobriquet, the battle has occasionally been oversimplified from a
well-planned and coordinated assault into a headlong, suicidal charge led by
"Mad Anthony."

The facts, of course, do not substantiate this view of the American strategy,
though a brief look at the origin of the General's nickname may help explain
how it came about. One author tells how the appellation of "mad",
meaning an aggressive and perhaps foolhardy approach to battle, became
attached to the intrepid Pennsylvanian in 1781:

> *It seems that he [Wayne] had an eccentric private in his
> army called 'Commodore' or 'Jimmy the Drover,' who was
> arrested by the civil authorities and who demanded that
> Wayne intervene in his behalf. When told that the general
> refused to do so, or had sentenced him to the lash should he
> be derelict in duty in the future, Jimmy exclaimed, 'Anthony
> is mad! Farewell to you; clear the coast for the
> Commodore, 'Mad Anthony's friend.' This story, like so
> many anecdotes about men in high places during the
> Revolutionary War, spread like wildfire through the ranks
> of America's armies, and thereafter for the troops General
> Wayne was 'Mad Anthony.'*[145]

A more plausible explanation is offered by the same source and derives from Wayne's encounter with the British at the battle of Green Spring Farm on the Virginia peninsula in July, 1781. Unexpectedly confronted with a large enemy force and outnumbered five to one, he charged the startled redcoats with bayonets and ordered his three cannon to commence firing. General La Fayette, under whom Wayne was serving, was aghast at what seemed an imprudent strategy at best, but Wayne's men were able to withdraw, though with some losses. Word of this episode soon appeared in local newspapers, including the New Jersey Gazette which declared, "Madness – Mad Anthony, by God, I never knew such a piece of work heard of – about eight hundred troops opposed to five or six thousand veterans upon their own ground."[146] Wayne's calculated but unexpected attack had caught the British off guard, lending support to an assessment of his career and abilities by a later historian. Writing in 1863, Henry B. Dawson wrote that the fact that General Wayne was authorized by General Washington to alter the plan of attack on Stony Point if he saw fit is evidence "of the great confidence General Washington reposed in the good judgment and military abilities of the commander of the Light troops, and an unanswerable argument in opposition to that indefinite and very questionable credit which has popularly been awarded to him, as 'Mad Anthony.'"[147] General Wayne was certainly bold and aggressive in battle, bluff in manner, and had more than a touch of the martinet – but he was not inattentive to military concerns, and he was neither careless nor mad.

Another misconception is that General Wayne was assigned to conduct the assault on Stony Point because he had been the victim of a similar bayonet attack at Paoli, Pennsylvania, in September, 1777, and that the American Light Infantry shouted "Remember Paoli!" as they stormed the British fort on the Hudson. No witnesses to the battle on either side report hearing that phrase, though an echo of what has been described as "the Paoli Massacre" in which as many as 150 Americans fell to British steel can be detected in

Wayne's report to Washington on July 17, 1779, in which he comments on "the humanity of our brave soldiery, who scorned to take the lives of a vanquished foe calling for mercy, reflects the highest honor on them, and accounts for the few of the enemy killed on the occasion."[148]   In any case, Stony Point should not be confused with Paoli. There is no record, for instance, that Wayne's troops were ordered to remove the flints from their muskets at Stony Point, as the British were at Paoli -- in fact, the Americans might have had to load and fire if circumstances changed -- and the geography, the defenses, and the strategies in each battle were very different.   Washington's choice of Wayne to lead the assault was simply a straightforward military decision. He was selected because of his experience and qualifications, revenge or retaliation playing no role at all.   Similarly, two years later, in October, 1781, when Washington directed General Benjamin Lincoln to receive the surrender at Yorktown of Lord Cornwallis's army by his deputy, General Charles O'Hara of the Coldstream Guards, it was not retribution for Lincoln's disastrous loss of Charleston the year before.   It was, instead, a simple case of one second-in-command submitting to another.

A third misconception that has appeared frequently in print, often taken from one author and repeated by another, is the assertion that the Light Infantry killed all the dogs near the British fort to prevent the enemy from learning that the Americans were close by.   Not a single first-hand account – letters, battle orders or official reports – mentions this alleged part of the attack plan.   The one reference is second hand at best, and therefore less than reliable.   In his journal, Commodore Sir George Collier, who was not directly involved in the battle of Stony Point, makes the following entry:

> . . *The rebel troops, under a General Wayne, formed two*
> *attacks with fixed bayonets and unloaded arms during the*
> *darkness and silence of the night; it was said that they had*

taken the precaution to kill every dog two days before that was within some miles round the post, to prevent their approach being discovered by their barking. .[149]

Though the claim is improbable since the total absence of barking dogs for two days might also arouse suspicion, the Commodore's remark, couched in the language of hearsay ("it was said") and uncorroborated by primary sources, has taken on a life of its own and appears as unquestioned fact in many accounts of the battle.

Misconceptions sometimes become exaggerated through embellishment, with the result that individuals become larger than life and are transformed into legend or myth. One of the best examples is the story of Peter Francisco, a Virginia soldier born around 1760 who served in numerous battles throughout the war. The following claim for Francisco's exploits is typical:

He [was] a 6-foot 6 –inch giant weighing 260 pounds. . .[and] was one of the 20-man forlorn hope led by Lt. James Gibbon at Stony Point (July 16, 1779) and one of the four who reached the final objective. In this action he first used the huge, 5-foot broadsword Washington had ordered made for him . .[150]

In other versions, he strikes the British flag or is the first man to enter the main fortifications, or is a "one-man army." Francisco may have been at Stony Point -- lists of the American participants are incomplete -- and the description of his size may well be accurate, but there are important historical discrepancies that undermine the credibility of his exploits. Even though it would seem likely that someone of his stature wielding such a formidable weapon would have been noticed, his name and the role he is supposed to have played in the battle are not mentioned by any eyewitness, British or American. [151] Further, General Wayne's report to General Washington on the day after the battle not only fails to identify Francisco or describe his alleged actions, but instead specifically commends Lieutenant Colonel Fleury and states that he ".. struck the enemy's standard with his own hand."[152] In addition, Fleury, writing from Fort Montgomery, New York, July 21, 1779, confirms what no one at the time doubted: he had entered the fort first and struck the flag, followed by the next four soldiers whom he lists in order: Lieutenant Knox of Pennsylvania, Sergeants Baker and Spencer of Virginia, and Sergeant Donlop also of Pennsylvania.[153]

These men were members of the right column's forlorn hope and entered the main British works first. The forlorn hope of Lieutenant Gibbon, of which Francisco allegedly was a part, was comprised of men from the vanguard of Butler's left column, which approached around the north side of Stony Point. Gibbon and his men entered the main fortifications after Lieutenant Colonel Fleury and his volunteers, having been delayed by unexpected enemy resistance, most likely the intense fire from the enemy's 3-pounder cannon referred to earlier. Thus, the historical record runs counter to the claims, and accounts purporting to describe other aspects of Francisco's role (if any) during the battle of Stony Point remain unsupported until any new primary source materials are discovered.

Perhaps a more elaborate example of an individual embellished into legend associated with the battle of Stony Point is the account of Pompey Lamb, an early version of which appeared in print in *The Pictorial Field-Book of the Revolution,* written in 1852 by Benson Lossing:

> *Mr. Ten Eyck, the old ferryman at Stony Point, informed me*
> *that he knew this negro* [Pompey] *well. His name was*
> *Pompey, and for his services on that night his master gave*

him a horse to ride, and never exacted any labor from him afterward. Pompey's master was a warm Whig, and himself was a shrewd negro. Soon after the enemy took possession of the Point, Pompey ventured to go to the fort with strawberries to sell. He was kindly received; and as the season advanced, and berries and cherries became plentiful, he carried on an extensive traffic with the garrison, and became a favorite with the officers, who had no suspicion that he was reporting everything to his Whig master. Finally, Pompey informed them that his master would not allow him to come with fruit in the daytime, for it was hoeing-corn season. Unwilling to lose their supply of luxuries, the officers gave Pompey the countersign [password] regularly, so that he could pass the sentinels in the evening. He thus possessed a knowledge of the countersign on the night of the attack, and made good use of it. That countersign was "The fort's our own," and this was the watchword of the Americans as they scaled the ramparts.[154]

Pompey, a one-time member of the Orange County, New York militia and a slave belonging to a Captain Lamb, is also alleged to have served as a guide to the Americans during the attack. A few pages after this account is related, Lossing mentions that the ferryman, David Ten Eyck, "held up a bottle of whiskey and proffered a draught [offered a drink]"[155] and then enjoyed the beverage himself with two of his neighbors. A few sentences later, Lossing identifies Ten Eyck as an octogenarian, and refers to his "adventurous tales." At no time did Ten Eyck claim to have been at the battle, which had occurred 76 years before, nor did he offer documentation of Pompey's role except that "he knew [him] well."[156]

The tale has been repeated many times since in print, though with further embellishments added. Sometimes Pompey overcomes the sentries, one by one, by himself or with the aid of another black slave. In a recent version, he is even credited with thinking of a way "to storm the fort," though Washington's plan, dated July 10, 1779,[157] is a matter of historical record.

Continuing efforts have failed to locate any primary source that would support the version of events related by "the old ferryman," and not a single eyewitness on either the British or American side mentions Pompey or any individual who did what the account claims. The tale refers to the apparent willingness of British officers to compromise the fort's security for occasional fresh fruit — part of their "supply of luxuries" — but that is also highly implausible since to do so would have been a capital offense under the Articles of War in effect at the time.[158] A closer look at Lieutenant Colonel Johnson's court-martial further undermines this crucial element of the Pompey version. Two officers, Ensign Henry Hamilton [159] and Captain William John Darby,[160] both captured during the battle, testify that Lieutenant Colonel Johnson would not allow passwords - paroles and countersigns -- on the night of the battle or any other night, (probably because of security concerns) -- and if there was a countersign, the chance that it would by coincidence also be the American watchword ("The Fort's Our Own!") defies belief.

Finally, as Ensign Hamilton states, there were no fewer than 88 sentries on duty during the night of the battle and other nights as well, deployed into six pickets or groups, with individual sentries between each picket, forming a human chain across the peninsula: far too many soldiers to be overcome by one or two men.[161]

The credibility of the Pompey legend was questioned during the very century in which it first appeared in print. Henry Dawson, writing in 1863, considered it "probably an entire fiction,"[162] and later, in 1900, Henry P., Johnston, author of one of the most comprehensive accounts of the battle of Stony Point, thought the tale "hardly worth considering, a poor tradition," and pointed out that "the exploit would have been mentioned at the time among the numerous other incidents."[163] The eminent African-American historian Benjamin Quarles, in his The Negro in the American Revolution, published for the Institute of Early American History and Culture in Williamsburg, Virginia, conducted extensive research into the military role played by black Americans during the Revolutionary War and concluded that "it is doubtful that a Negro slave, Pompey, guided the assaulting parties commanded by General Wayne at Stony Point"[164].

Pompey Lamb, like Peter Francisco, may have played some unproven minor role in the battle of Stony Point -- in Pompey's case, perhaps by providing some information to the Americans -- but their colorful yet unconvincing stories are at variance with what is known, and will remain so unless new contemporary records are found. Both figures may well have been enlarged beyond their real selves by the common human tendency to expand an account well past what actually happened. Unfortunately, the result is that the legend tends to replace the facts, and those whose deeds have been proven are overlooked and forgotten. The exaggeration of contributions that an individual may have made to a given event therefore becomes a poor substitute for new insights gleaned from documented research, and often creates a whole body of misinformation that impedes the search for historical truth.

Epilogue

When the newly released British officers reached New York in December, 1780, the unexpected loss of Stony Point was still a subject of concern and discussion. Lieutenant Colonel Johnson's reputation as a competent soldier very likely suffered during his captivity, and that may explain why he requested his own court-martial, a not uncommon practice when military judgment was in question, as was Johnson's, at least by Lieutenant Colonel Webster, the former commander of both Verplanck's and Stony Point.[165] Ironically, General Wayne, facing a similar situation in 1777, had also asked for a military trial to resolve any doubts about his judgment during the American defeat at Paoli, Pennsylvania.

The proceedings against Lieutenant Colonel Johnson began in New York on January 2, 1781, and included the testimony of no fewer than 22 officers and men; Lieutenant William Marshall, the Acting Engineer, would be one of the key witnesses. On February 20th, after a lengthy adjournment and time for the accused to prepare his defense, the court-martial announced its decision:

> *The Court having Considered the Evidence for and against Lieut. Colonel Johnson, together with what he had to Offer in his Defence, is of Opinion that he is, in suffering the Post of Stoney Point to fall into the hands of the Enemy, Culpable in the following instances,*

> *viz. 1st. In a mistaken Disposition of the Troops, which for which the Defence of the Post, ought to have been confined to the Table of the Hill* [in the Upper Works or main fortification].

2dly. In not remonstrating against the frequent Absence of the Gun Boat [guarding the shallow water on the south flank] *notwithstanding he knew of it, which the Court is of Opinion, are Errors of Judgment, and consequently think his Conduct <u>reprehensible</u>; . . . At the same time, the Court is of Opinion that . . .Lieut. Colonel Johnson, in common with the officers and soldiers at his Post, behaved with an Alertness, Activity, and Bravery, that do them Honor.*[166]

With this mixed verdict, Johnson continued his military career as best he could, but not without being captured again, along with his regiment, at Yorktown in 1781. Despite the stigma of defeat, he had, by 1799, achieved the rank of Lieutenant General, and would live to the age of 87.[167]

The battle of Stony Point was one of the most daring military exploits of the American Revolution, and though the world has changed in countless ways since 1779, the valor and bravery shown during that brief struggle are timeless attributes, still relevant to our own age. As the two armies clashed by night, there was no lack of daring or risk, and all who were engaged in this brief, momentous action must have remembered it all their lives, as did Captain Henry Champion of Connecticut. The 25-year-old officer, who died in 1836 at the age of 82, was with General Wayne in the south column and never forgot it. Every year, on July 16, he observed what he called "Stony Point Day," and he must have recalled that time of conflict when dangers were faced and overcome. He may also have reflected, not only on tactics and strategies, but also on the turmoil and struggle of battle, on the courage and sacrifice of men whose strengths and weaknesses we all share: human beings very much like ourselves, motivated by the same considerations, tempered by the fears and determinations that shape us all.

---

[1] *Letter from Colonel Woodhull to Colonel Malcolm*, June 7, 1779, Johnston, Henry P., The Storming of Stony Point, James T. White & Company, New York, 1900, p. 154.

[2] *George III to Lord North, June 11, 1779, ibid.,* p. 105.

[3] *Lord Germaine to Sir Henry Clinton, January 23, 1779, ibid.,* p. 28.

[4] *Clinton, Sir Henry, The American Rebellion, Sir Henry Clinton's Narrative of His Campaigns, 1775-1782, with an Appendix of Original Documents....,* Willcox, William B., ed., Yale University Press, New Haven, 1954, pp. 122-23.

[5] *Sir Henry Clinton to Lord Germaine,* June 18, 1779, Johnston, Henry, *op.cit.,* pp. 109-111.

[6] *Sir Henry Clinton to General Sir Frederick Haldimand, ibid.,* p. 56.

[7] An abatis consists of trees that have been cut down and placed side by side, with the sharpened limbs oriented toward the likely direction of enemy attack.

[8] *Testimony of Lieutenant William Marshall,* The Court-Martial of Lieutenant Colonel Henry Johnson, Public Records Office, London, 1781, pp. 99-100. After the battle of Stony Point and his release from captivity, Johnson was court-martialed at his own request. The trial was held in New York City, January 2, 1781.

[9] 18th century artillery had three types of cannon, all smoothbore: guns which used a range of projectiles except shells, and were identified by the weight of the ball they fired; mortars which lobbed exploding shells in a high arc; and Howitzers which could fire solid shot, canister (a kind of scattershot), or shells, all at a lower trajectory. Mortars were mounted on flat beds, whereas guns and Howitzers were mounted on carriages, sometimes using large wheels for field carriages or small wooden or iron wheels called "trucks" for ship or garrison carriages.

[10] The *Vulture* was a sloop - a small warship with two or three masts. The gunboat would have been a shallow draft boat mounting one or two guns at bow and stern, and could be rowed, sailed or both. Ensign Henry Hamilton testified at the court-martial of Lieutenant Colonel Henry Johnson that there was usually a detachment from the British garrison at Stony Point on board the vessel, apparently to man the oars.

[11] *Abraham Skinner to Colonel Richard Butler, July 18, 1779,* Dawson, Henry B., The Assault on Stony Point, Houghton Co., Cambridge, Mass., 1863, p. 111.

[12] Captain Robinson's first name is given as 'William' by the American officer James Chrystie in a prisoner list prepared at Stony Point on July 16, 1779 (Johnston, Henry, op. cit., p 213); however, he is identified as "Morris Robinson" by Deputy

Commissary of Prisoners Abraham Skinner in a list of officers on parole sent to Robert H. Harrison, aide-de-camp to General Washington on July 20, 1779, from Goshen, New York (George Washington Papers at the Library of Congress, 1741-1799: Series 4. General Correspondence. 1697-1799.)

[13] Lieutenant Colonel James Webster of the 33rd Regiment was a capable, resourceful soldier who eventually rose to the rank of Brigadier General. In late December, 1779, he sailed with Sir Henry Clinton's expedition to Charleston, South Carolina, and served under Lord Cornwallis particularly at the battle of Camden, South Carolina, in August, 1780. He was mortally wounded at Guilford Courthouse, North Carolina on March 15, 1781. His fellow officer, Banastre Tarleton, wrote that he "united all the virtues of civil life to the gallantry and professional knowledge of a soldier." Boatner, Mark Mayo III, Encyclopedia of the American Revolution, David McKay Company, New York, 1976, pp. 1178-1179.

[14] Sir Henry Clinton, The American Rebellion, Sir Henry Clinton's Narrative of His Campaigns, 1775-1782, with an Appendix of Original Documents, William B. Willcox, ed. New Haven, Connecticut, 1954, p. 132.

[15] George Washington to Joseph Reed, June 14, 1779, The Writings of George Washington from the Original Manuscript Sources, 1745-1799, John C. Fitzpatrick, Editor.

[16] George Washington to Major Henry Lee Jr., June 6, 1779, ibid.

[17] George Washington to Major Henry Lee Jr., June 15, 1779, ibid.

[18] Letter from General Washington to Congress, July 4, 1778, Nelson, Paul David, Anthony Wayne-Soldier of the Early Republic, Indiana University Press, Bloomington, 1985, p.82.

[19] Letter from Wayne to Washington, July 4, 1779, ibid., p.3

[20] The Writings of George Washington from the Original Manuscript Sources, op. cit., volume 31, p. 510.

[21] Letter from Washington to Wayne, July 1, 1779, The Writings of George Washington from the Original Manuscript Sources, op.cit.

[22] George Washington to Major Henry Lee Jr., June 28, 1779, ibid.

[23] Diary entry of Captain McLane, July 2, 1779, reprinted in Johnston, Henry, op.cit, p. 199

[24] Letter from Wayne to Washington, July 3, 1779, reprinted in Dawson, Henry, op.cit., p. 24.

[25] Letter from Washington to Wayne, July 9, 1779, ibid., p. 27.

[26] *Washington's Instructions to Wayne, July 10, 1779,* Johnston, Henry, *op.cit.*, pp. 156-57.

[27] *Washington's Instructions to Wayne, July 10, 1779, ibid.,* p. 57.

[28] *General Washington to General Wayne, July 14, 1779, reprinted in* Charles J. Stille, <u>Major-General Anthony Wayne and the Pennsylvania Line in the Continental Army</u>, Kennikat Press, Port Washington, New York, first published 1893, reissued 1968, p. 400.

[29] Johnston, Henry, *op.cit.,* p. 69.

[30] *Martin, Joseph Plumb, <u>Private Yankee Doodle</u>* edited by George E. Scheer, Acorn Press, 1979, p. 136.

[31] Boatner, Mark Mayo III, *op. cit.*, p. 699.

[32] Dawson, Henry, *op.cit.,* p. 44.

[33] *Letter from Wayne to Sharp Delany, July 15, 1779, ibid.,* p.46.

[34] *Pension Application of Robin Starr,* 2nd Connecticut Regiment, File S36810, Volume 2, Page 898, National Archives, Washington, 1818.

[35] Chevaux de Frise or "horses of Frisland" are freestanding field fortifications, a number of which can be linked together to form a portable barrier. Viewed from the side, each resembled a series of "x"'s around a central axle, with the sharp points of each "x" tipped with iron. Their name derives from the province in North Holland where they were first designed and used in the 16th century.

[36] *Testimony of Ensign Henry Hamilton,* <u>Court-Martial</u>, *op.cit.*, p.3.

[37] *Ibid.,* p. 6.

[38] Martin, Joseph Plumb, *op.cit.,* p. 163

[39] *General Wayne to General Washington, Fort Montgomery, July 15, 1779.* ". .I have taken the liberty to order Col. Ball's Regiment stationed near Rose's farm to follow in my rear and shall give out that the whole Virginia Line are to support us .", reprinted *in* Stille, Charles J., *op.cit.,* p. 399.

[40] *George Washington to Peter Muhlenberg, July 15, 1779,* The Writings of George Washington from the Original Manuscript Sources, *op.cit.*

[41]*Letter from Wayne to Washington, July 15, 1779,* Dawson, Henry, *op.cit.,* p.35.

[42] *General Wayne to General Washington, July 10, 1779,* The Writings of George Washington from the Original Manuscript Sources, *op.cit.* An espontoon

(or "spontoon") is a spear-shaped half- pike, used as a weapon and an officer's badge of rank.

[43] Colonel Christian Febiger, writing in 1779 shortly after the battle, asserted that the men of Lieutenant John Gibbon's forlorn hope from Colonel Butler's column "instead of advancing with musquettes unloaded, halted outside of the enemy's main Works and kept up a fire." (Johnston, Henry, op.cit., p. 183). Since Febiger was with the other column on the south side of Stony Point, it is not clear how he could have distinguished American gunfire from British, particularly under very dark and windy conditions, nor is it clear what his motivation might have been for making the statement. Febiger added that although Gibbon "was heard to say that he had 17 men killed and wounded out of the 20 [in the forlorn hope], I must likewise contradict that . ." (ibid., p. 183). Here the record tends to bear him out. In a list of American casualties prepared by Captain Benjamin Fishbourn, aide-de-camp to General Wayne, Febiger's column has seven men killed, compared to a loss of three for Butler, with thirty-eight wounded in Febiger's column, and thirty in Butler's. (Anthony Wayne, July 16, 1779, Report on American Casualties at Stony Point, George Washington Papers at the Library of Congress, 1741-1799, op. cit.) Colonel Febiger, in a letter to Governor Thomas Jefferson of Virginia, dated July 21, 1779, writes that "Seven of my men in the forlorn hope who entered first were either killed or wounded." (Johnston, Henry, op. cit., p. 188). Though the exact number of killed and wounded in each forlorn hope is unknown, it would not seem that Lt. Gibbon has the greater claim.

[44] *General Wayne's Order of Battle*, Johnston, Henry, *op.cit.*, pp. 158-59.

[45] *George Washington to Rene H.L. de Noirmont de la Neuville, October 1, 1779*, The Writings of George Washington from the Original Manuscript Sources, *op.cit.*

[46] *General Wayne, Order of Battle, July 15, 1779*, Dawson, Henry, *op.cit.*, p.38. Major William Hull reports an instance where Wayne's threat was carried out by a young Lieutenant who reported after the battle that he had killed one of his men for disobedience to orders and was feeling remorse. Hull responded by saying, "You have performed a painful duty, by which, perhaps, victory has been secured, and the life of many a brave man saved. Be satisfied." (Johnston, Henry, *op.cit.*, pp. 192-93.)

[47] *General Wayne to General Washington on the Success of the Assault, July 16, 1779, ibid, p.162.*

[48] Excerpts from the testimony of Lieutenant Ross and other witnesses are in the question-answer format of Lieutenant Colonel Johnson's court-martial. In order to conform to modern usage, the language has been changed from third person to first person.

[49] *Testimony of Lieutenant John Ross*, Court-Martial, *op.cit.*, pp. 21-22.

[50] *Testimony of Corporal Simon Davies, ibid.*, p. 71.

[51] *Testimony of Lieutenant William Horndon, ibid ,* pp. 32-33.

[52] *Testimony of Captain Lawrence Robert Campbell, ibid. ,*pp. 39,44.

[53] *Testimony of Lieutenant John Roberts, ibid.,* p. 55.

[54] *Testimony of Lieutenant John Roberts, Ibid.,* pp. 56-57.

[55]Despite this fact, several American accounts mention intense exposure to enemy artillery. Major William Hull of Massachusetts, for example, refers to a "heavy fire of artillery and musketry," and Captain Henry Champion of Connecticut writes that "the fire was very brisk from cannon and grapeshot." It certainly must have seemed so to both officers in the reverberating darkness and the ordeal of battle.

[56] *Testimony of Captain William Tiffen,* Court-Martial, *op.cit.,* pp.28-30.

[57] *Testimony of Lieutenant William Armstrong, ibid,* pp.46-47.

[58] *Ibid.,* p. 46.

[59] Writing in 1821, Lieutenant Gibbon, the officer in charge of the forlorn hope from Colonel Butler's column, claimed that one of his men struck the British flag and that it was handed to Colonel Fleury. While it is true that Gibbon's men entered the Upper Works closer to the Flagstaff Battery, it's also plausible that Fleury and the soldiers in the other forlorn hope could have fought their way across the fortifications to that location since Stony Point peninsula is not very wide. However, no one has ever officially disputed that Fleury removed the enemy flag and earned the promised reward for being the first man inside the Upper Works. If that had not been the case, dissension would surely have occurred, as it did later when officers felt that their names and deeds were omitted from Wayne's account of the battle to Washington. Further, two of the first five soldiers inside the Upper Works were Virginians (Sergeants Baker and Spencer), and there were no Virginia troops in Butler's column.

[60] *Francois de Teissedre de Fleury to Anthony Wayne, July 21,1779,* Stille, Charles J., *op.cit.,* p. 403

[61] *Testimony of Lieutenant William Armstrong,* Court-Martial, *op.cit.,* p. 45 (in this instance the transcript is quoted *verbatim* in the original third-person tense).

[62] *Testimony of Lieutenant John Ross, ibid.,* p. 22-23.

[63] *Memoirs of the War* by William Hull, Johnston, Henry, *op.cit.,* p.193.

[64] *Colonel Febiger's Letters to his Wife, Stony Point, July 16, 1779, ibid.,* p.186

[65] In a letter to Congress dated July 20,1779, Washington stated "In a critical moment of the assault, he [Wayne] received a flesh-wound in his head with a musket-ball, but continued leading on his men with unshaken firmness,"(*ibid.*, p.165). However, Major William Hull, who was with Wayne in the main column, indicated that Wayne ". . remained on the spot until the British surrendered, when some other officers and myself bore him into the fort, bleeding, in triumph," (*ibid.*, p. 192.) Colonel Christian Febiger, also in the same column, confirms Hull's recollection (*ibid.*, p. 186).

[66] *General Wayne to General Washington, July 16, 1779, ibid.,* p.85.

[67] These cheers or "huzzas" may well have been the same heard by Lt. John Roberts of the Royal Artillery just before he determined that the battle was lost and decided to swim to the *Vulture.*

[68] *Memoirs of the War* by William Hull, reprinted in Johnston, Henry, *op.cit.,* p.192.

[69] *Memoirs of the War* by William Hull, *ibid.,* p.192.

[70] *Manuscript of Colonel Christian Febiger, ibid.,* p.185.

[71] *Washington to the President of Congress, July 20, 1779, ibid.,* pp. 166-67.

[72] *Ibid.,* p.167

[73] *Memoirs of the War* by William Hull, *ibid.,* p.193.

[74] The prisoners included one soldier from the Volunteers of Ireland, a provincial regiment raised by Lord Francis Rawdon-Hastings in 1778. This lone representative is unidentified except by rank (Sergeant) in Lt. Col. Johnson's return of killed, wounded, missing, and taken prisoner (Johnston, Henry, *op.cit.,* p. 129) but is given the name "John White" and is listed as a private by Deputy Commissary of Prisoners Abraham Skinner (Abraham Skinner to Robert H. Harrison, July 20, 1779, General Report on British Prisoners Taken at Stony Point, New York, George Washington Papers at the Library of Congress, 1741-1799: Series 4. General Correspondence. 1697-1799). The Thomas Bradford Papers in the Historical Society of Pennsylvania has a copy of Skinner's report cited above and White's first name has been changed to "Thomas".   White's presence at Stony Point is unexplained, but his regiment was not part of the garrison.

[75] *Abraham Skinner to Robert H. Harrison, July 20, 1779, General Report on British Prisoners Taken at Stony Point, New York,* George Washington Papers at the Library of Congress, 1741-1799: Series 4. General Correspondence. 1697-1799

[76] *Return of Ordnance and Stores taken at Stony Point, July 15, 1779 at night,* Dawson, Henry, *op.cit.,* p.80-81.

[77] *Letter from Washington to the President of Congress, July 20, 1779,* Johnston, Henry, *op.cit.,* p. 168.

[78] *Major General James Pattison to Lord Townsend, July 26, 1779, ibid.,* p. 132.

[79] *George Washington to Henry Lee Jr., July 22, 1779.*
". . .The 24 pounder said to be taken off by the enemy, if gone is only the loss of an Iron piece" The Writings of George Washington from the Original Manuscript Sources, *op.cit.*

[80] *Anthony Wayne, July 16, 1779, Report on British casualties at Stony Point, New York.* George Washington Papers at the Library of Congress, *op.cit.*

[81] *George Washington, July 18, 1779, General Orders.* The Writings of George Washington from the Original Manuscript Sources, *op.cit.*

[82] *Richard Auchmuty to Anthony Wayne, July 17, 1779,* George Washington Papers at the Library of Congress, *op.cit.*

[83] *Anthony Wayne to the Commanding Officer of the British Ships lying below Stony Point, July 17, 1779, ibid.*

[84] *Abraham Skinner to Robert H. Harrison, July 20, 1779, List of British Privates Sent to New York, ibid., and Abraham Skinner to Robert H. Harrison, July 20, 1779, List of British Officers Sent to New York, ibid.*

[85] *Abraham Skinner to Robert H. Harrison, July 20, 1779, List of British Prisoners Wounded in Escape Attempt, ibid.*

[86] *Lieutenant Colonel Henry Johnson to Anthony Wayne, July 20, 1779, ibid.*

[87] *George Washington to Abraham Skinner, July 22, 1779,* The Writings of George Washington from the Original Manuscript Sources, *op.cit.*

[88] *Abraham Skinner to Robert Harrison, July 20, 1779,* George Washington Papers at the Library of Congress, *op,cit.*

[89] *Lieutenant Colonel Johnson to Sir Henry Clinton, July 24, 1779,* Johnston, Henry, *op.cit.,* p. 127-128.

[90] *Abraham Skinner to Robert H. Harrison, July 20, 1779, List of Officers on Parole Sent from Stony Point, New York, to Easton, Pennsylvania.* George Washington Papers at the Library of Congress, *op.cit.*

[91] *Journal of Ensign Thomas Hughes, Prisoner of War at Lancaster, May, 1779 to November, 1780,* Papers of the Lancaster Historical Society, Vol. LVIII, No.1, 1954, p.5.

[92] *Ibid.,* p.11.

[93] *Testimony of Lieutenant William Marshall,* <u>Court-Martial</u> *op.cit.,* pp. 116.

[94] *Letters of Lieutenant William Marshall,* collections of the Historical Society of Pennsylvania, Philadelphia.

[95] *General Wayne to General Washington, July 17, 1779,* Johnston, Henry, *op.cit.,* p. 163.

[96] *George Washington to Congress, July 20, 1779, ibid.,* p.165.

[97] Nelson, Paul David, *op.cit.,* p.101.

[98] *John Jay to Anthony Wayne, July 27, 1779,* Dawson, Henry, *op.cit.,* p.61.

[99] *George Washington to the Marquis de La Fayette, September 30, 1779,* The Writings of George Washington from the Original Manuscript Sources, *op.cit.*

[100]They were: Washington for Boston; Gates for Saratoga; Wayne, Fleury and Stewart for Stony Point; Henry Lee for Paulus Hook; Daniel Morgan, John Eager Howard, William Washington for Cowpens; Nathanael Greene for Eutaw Springs; and John Paul Jones, for the victory of the *Bonhomme Richard* over HMS *Serapis.* A modern version of Fleury's medal is issued to members of the U.S. Army Corps of Engineers.

[101] The other was the battle of Cowpens, South Carolina, January 17, 1781.

[102] *George Washington to Anthony Wayne, August 15, 1779,* The Writings of George Washington from the Original Manuscript Sources, *op.cit.*

[103] Dawson, Henry, *op.cit.,* p.56. Although usually associated with maritime operations wherein captured enemy ships and their cargo were sold in friendly ports, prize money was also infrequently applied to land battles as well, though the battle of Stony Point appears to be the only instance of this practice in the Continental Army. Because of Congress's limited financial resources, such arrangements may have been restricted to special military situations during which extraordinary motivation would be necessary. The daring nighttime assault at Stony Point – conducted largely through water by troops armed only with fixed bayonets - would certainly have qualified. Of course, the weapons and supplies that fell into American hands were used throughout the war, and the fourteen cannons lost by the British were especially valued. Those that have survived can still be identified today because each has the same inscription – "Taken at the Storm of Stony Point, July 15, 1779" – suggesting that they were engraved at the same time, probably at West Point, and soon after their capture.

[104] *Major Thomas Posey to General Washington, August 10, 1779, ibid.,* pp.128-29.

[105] *Colonel Return Jonathan Meigs to General Wayne, August 22, 1779, ibid.,* p.130-31.

[106] *Colonel Return Jonathan Meigs to General Wayne, August 22, 1779, ibid.,* p.130.

[107] *Lieutenant Colonel Isaac Sherman to General Wayne, August 22, 1779, ibid.,* pp.131-32.

[108] *Lieutenant Colonel Isaac Sherman to General Wayne, August 22, 1779, ibid.,* pp.132-33.

[109] *Anthony Wayne to the President of Congress, August 10, 1779, ibid.,* p.126.

[110] *Anthony Wayne to Colonel Return Jonathan Meigs, August 23, 1779, ibid.,* p.134.

[111] *Anthony Wayne to Colonel Return Jonathan Meigs, August 23, 1779, ibid.,* p.135.

[112] *Anthony Wayne to Colonel Return Jonathan Meigs, August 23, 1779, ibid.,* pp.135-36.

[113] *Lieutenant Colonel Isaac Sherman to General Wayne, August 24, 1779, ibid.,* p.136.

[114] *Major William Hull to General Wayne, August 25, 1779, ibid.,* pp.138–39.

[115] *General Wayne to Major Thomas Posey, August 28, 1779,* Stille, Charles, *op.cit.,* pp. 414-416.

[116] *Major Thomas Posey to General Wayne, August 28, 1779,* Dawson, Henry, *op.cit.,* pp.141-42.

[117] *General Wayne to Major Thomas Posey, September 2, 1779, Ibid.,* p.142.

[118] Testimony of Major Charles Graham, Court-Martial, *op.cit.,* p.124.

[119] *Sir Henry Clinton to Lord Germaine on the Loss of Stony Point, July 25, 1779.* Johnston, Henry, *op.cit.,* p. 124.

[120] Testimony of Major Charles Graham, Court-Martial, *op.cit.,* p.124.

[121] *Testimony of Lieutenant Colonel Henry Johnson, ibid.,* p.125

[122] Patrick Ferguson (1744-1780), inventor of the first breech-loading rifle adopted by the British Army, was an influential officer whose brief military career included having fought at Brandywine, being involved in the capture of Stony Point and Verplanck's Point in late May, 1779, and serving at Charleston later in the war. Ferguson, who was held in high regard by Sir Henry Clinton, played a key role in the direction and planning of the new fortifications at Stony Point. Ferguson was killed at the battle of Kings Mountain, South Carolina, October 7, 1780. Rankin,

Hugh F., *An Officer Out of His Time: Correspondence of Major Patrick Ferguson, 1779-1780, Reprinted in* <u>Sources of American Independence</u>, Volume II, Howard H. Peckham, editor, Chicago and London, 1978, pp. 287-298.

[123] *Testimony of Captain Robert Douglass,* <u>Court-Martial</u>, *op.cit.*, p.120-121. Captain Ferguson voiced a similar, more detailed assessment of Stony Point's vulnerability in a letter written to Sir Henry Clinton on July 6, 1779, ten days before the American attack, stating that " Stony Point with very little labor & no expence may certainly be rendered secure against assault from an Army, & put in Condition to stand a Siege with a Garrison of 300 Men; for which purpose it is only necessary to occupy the Table of the hill with one good capacious closed work, surrounded by a thorough abbati . . ." Ferguson continued his strategic analysis by predicting, seemingly with clairvoyance, almost exactly the kind of attack that occurred, commenting that ". . were a Strong Corps of the Enemy at Dawn of Day, when our little advanced works would have little effect with their fire, to enter any Part of the abbati, the flanks of which may be turn'd almost unseen from the works or were they to steal or force a landing, the Post & Garrison might be lost in a few minutes as the works are all open behind," Rankin, Hugh F., *An Officer Out of His Time: Correspondence of Major Patrick Ferguson, 1779-1780, Reprinted in* <u>Sources of American Independence</u>, Volume II, Howard H. Peckham, editor, Chicago and London, 1978, pp. 325-26.

[124] Louis Le Begue de Presle Duportail, 1743-1802, French engineer and Continental Army general.

[125] *George Washington to Anthony Wayne, October 3, 1779,* The Writings of George Washington from the Original Manuscript Sources, *op.cit.*

[126] *Sir Henry Clinton to Sir Frederick Haldimand, September 9, 1779,* Johnston, Henry, *op.cit.*, pp. 141-144.

[127] *George Washington to Anthony Wayne, October 21, 1779,* George Washington Papers at the Library of Congress, *opus.cit.*

[128] *George Washington to Anthony Wayne, October 22, 1779, ibid.*

[129] *George Washington to Anthony Wayne, October 26, 1779, ibid.*

[130] *Testimony of Captain Alexander Mercer,* <u>Court-Martial</u>, *op.cit.*, pp.86-87

[131] *Testimony of Lieutenant John Roberts, ibid.*, p. 61

[132] *Testimony of Lieutenant William Nairne, ibid.*, pp.68-69.

[133] *Testimony of Lieutenant John Roberts, ibid.*, pp. 57-60.

[134] *Testimony of Ensign Henry Hamilton, ibid.*, pp. 3-5.

[135] Defined by Lieutenant Roberts as a "composition of mealed powder and other materials," *ibid.*, p. 65.

[136] The terms "rocket" and "lightball" are used interchangeably in the court-martial.

[137] *Testimony of Lieutenant William Marshall, ibid.*, pp 110-11.

[138] *Testimony of Lieutenant William Marshall, ibid.*, p. 111.

[139] *Testimony of Captain Alexander Mercer, ibid.*, p. 91.

[140] *George Washington to Anthony Wayne, July 10, 1779,* Johnston, Henry, *op.cit.*, p. 157.

[141] *Testimony of Lieutenant Colonel Henry Johnson,* Court-Martial, *op.cit.*, p.118.

[142] *Testimony of Captain Robert Clayton, ibid.*, p.16.

[143] *Testimony of Lieutenant John Ross, ibid.*, p.22.

[144] *Testimony of Corporal Simon Davies, ibid.*, p.70.

[145] Nelson, Paul David *op.cit.* p. 125.

[146] *Ibid.*, pp. 136-37.

[147] Dawson, Henry, *op.cit.*, pp. 33-34.

[148] *General Wayne to General Washington, July 17, 1779,* Johnston, Henry, *op.cit.*, p. 164.

[149] *Extract from the Journal of Commodore George Collier,* Johnston, Henry, *ibid.*, p. 134.

[150] Boatner, Mark Mayo III, *op.cit.*, pp. 392.

[151] Inquiries made of the Virginia Historical Society in Francisco's home state, and of Guilford Courthouse National Military Park in North Carolina where Francisco apparently served during the battle fought there in 1781, failed to produce any primary source material to support his presence or actions at Stony Point, or any corroboration of the claim that Washington had ordered a five-foot long sword for his use.

[152] *General Wayne to General Washington, July 17, 1779,* Johnston, Henry, *op.cit.* p. 163.

[153] *Extract of Brigade Light Infantry Orders, July 15, 1779, including a letter to General Wayne From Lieutenant Colonel Fleury, July 21, 1779,* Stille, Charles J., *op.cit.*, p. 403.

[154] Lossing, Benson J., <u>The Pictorial Field-Book of the Revolution</u>, Harper & Brothers, New York, 1852, vol. 2, p.176. footnote 3.

[155] *Ibid.*, p.183.

[156] *Ibid,* p. 176, footnote 3.

[157] *General Washington to General Wayne, July 10, 1779,* Johnston, Henry, *op.cit.,* pp. 155-57.

[158] *Section XIV, Article XV, "Any Person Belonging to Our Forces Employed in Foreign Parts, Who Shall Make Known the Watchword to any Person Who is not Entitled to Receive it According to the Rules and Discipline of War, or shall presume to give a Parole or Watchword different from what he received, shall suffer Death, or such other Punishment as shall be ordered by the Sentence of a General Court-martial"*, <u>from Rules and Articles for the better Government of His Majesty's Horse and Foot Guards and all other His Majesty's Forces in Great Britain and Ireland, Dominions beyond the Seas, and Foreign Parts,</u>, Charles Eyre and William Strahan, London, 1778.

[159] *Testimony of Ensign Henry Hamilton,* <u>Court-Martial</u>, *op.cit.,* p.5.

[160] *Testimony of Captain William John Darby, ibid.,* pp.12-13.

[161] *Testimony of Ensign Henry Hamilton, ibid.,* p.9.

[162] Dawson, Henry, *op.cit.,* p. 44.

[163] Johnston, Henry, *op.cit.,* p. 92, footnote 1.

[164] Quarles, Benjamin, <u>The Negro in the American Revolution</u>, University of North Carolina Press, Chapel Hill, 1961, p. xi.

[165] "No apology can be made for the place [Stony Point] being carried at all," Lt. Col. Webster to Sir Henry Clinton, July 29, 1779, quoted in Sir Henry Clinton, <u>The American Rebellion</u> . . ., William B. Willcox, ed. (New Haven, Connecticut, 1954), p. 133, note 23. Sir Henry apparently had a different view of Lieutenant Colonel Johnson's abilities, since, as previously noted, he described him as a "vigilant, active and spirited officer." On the other hand, Clinton also states that Lieutenant Colonel Johnson was "honorably acquitted" by a court-martial despite the fact that Clinton, as Commander in Chief, reviewed the proceedings that, while acquitting Johnson of the main charge, nonetheless found him culpable on two counts. *ibid.,* p. 133.

[166] <u>Court-Martial</u>, *op.cit,* pp. 127-28.

[167] Boatner, Mark Mayo III, *op.cit.,* pp. 560-61.

INDEX

A

B

C

Collier, Sir George (Commodore), *instructed to raid Connecticut coast, p. 5, extract from journal regarding alleged killing of dogs by Wayne's troops, p. 74.*

Cornwallis, Lord Charles, *defeat at Yorktown mentioned, p. 58; sending substitute to surrender ceremony at Yorktown, p. 74.*

Cumming, Patrick (Lieutenant), *mentioned in testimony of Lt. Ross at court martial of Lt. Col. Johnson, p. 25.*

D

Darby, William John (Captain), *testimony at court martial of Lt. Col Johnson quoted, that Johnson would not allow passwords, p. 78.*

Davies, Simon (Corporal), *sentry on duty at Stony Point, testimony quoted, p. 26; further quoted regarding weather during battle, p. 70.*

Dawson, Henry B., *opinion that Washington had great confidence in Wayne quoted, p. 73; opinion that Pompey Lamb legend a fiction quoted, p. 79.*

Donderberg Mountain, *part of Wayne's route of march, p. 19.*

F

Febiger, Christian (Colonel), *commanded First Light Infantry Regiment, brief history, p. 18; referred to as "Old Denmark", p. 20; commander of south column at Stony Point, pp. 22; takes Lt. Col. Johnson prisoner, p. 31; loses seven men during battle, p. 32; writes wife of being scraped by musket ball, p. 32; mentioned by Wayne in report to Washington of July 17, 1779, p. 43.*

Ferguson, Patrick (Captain), *of 71st Regiment, opinion regarding fortifications at Stony Point as quoted by witness at court martial of Lt. Col. Johnson, p. 56.*

Fitzgerald, William, *hanged as deserter after battle, p. 37.*

Fleury, see Teissedre de Fleury

Fort Clinton, *assaulted by Loyal American Regiment, p. 7.*

Fort La Fayette, *British forces take, p. 4.*

Fort Mifflin, *Lt. Col. Fleury wounded at battle of, p. 18.*

Fort Montgomery, *assaulted by Loyal American Regiment, p. 7; Wayne's forces camp at Sandy Beach near, p. 19.*

Fort Ticonderoga, *Wayne commands at, p. 9; Ensign Hughes captured at, p. 41*

Francisco, Peter, *legend discussed, pp. 75-76.*

Franklin, Benjamin, *Wayne acquainted with, p. 9.*

G

Gates, Horatio (General), *awarded medal for defeat of Burgoyne at Saratoga, p. 46.*

George III, *attitude toward American rebellion quoted, p. 2; personally recognized service of Captain Tew, p. 31.*

Germaine, Lord George, *instructions to Clinton, pp. 2-3.*

Germantown, PA, *17th Regiment fights at battle of, p. 7; Wayne fights at battle of, p. 9, Fleury wounded at battle of, p. 18.*

Gibbon, John (Lieutenant), *led forlorn hope of Butler's column, p. 23; mentioned for bravery in Congressional Resolution, p. 46; mentioned in Meigs's letter to Wayne, p. 48; mentioned in discussion of Peter Francisco legend, p. 75.*

H

Haldimand, Sir Frederick (General), *Clinton complains of lack of reinforcements to, p. 57.*

Hamilton, Henry (Ensign), *testimony regarding gun boat at court martial of Lt. Col. Johnson quoted, pp. 66-68; testimony regarding passwords referred to, p. 78; testimony as to number of sentries posted referred to, p. 78.*

Hay, Samuel (Lt. Colonel), *commands Butler's first battalion, p. 18; wounded during battle, p. 32; mentioned in Wayne's report to Washington, July 17, 1779, p. 43; mentioned in Meigs's letter to Wayne, August 22, 1779, p. 48.*

Horndon, William (Lieutenant), *mentioned in testimony of Cpl.Davies at court martial of Lt. Col. Johnson, p. 26; fires 12 pounder during battle, p. 26; runs of out ammunition during battle, p. 61.*

Howe, Robert (Major General), *commander of abortive attempt against Verplanck's Point the day after the battle of Stony Point, p. 34.*

Hughes, Thomas (Ensign), *British prisoner in Lancaster, PA, notices British captured at Stony Point passing through, p. 41.*

Hull, William (Major), *field commander of Fourth Regiment of Light Infantry, commander of first battalion, p. 19, struck by musket balls through hat and boot during battle, surrendered Detroit to British in 1812, p. 32; quoted regarding cheers given by Americans during battle, p. 32; describes how key to powder magazine was obtained from British officer, p. 33; states that dead were buried the day after the battle, p. 35; mentioned in Meigs's letter to Wayne, August 22, 1779, p. 48; mentioned by Wayne in letter to John Jay, August 10, 1779, p. 50; mollified after not being mentioned in Wayne's original report, p. 52.*

J

Lee, Henry Jr. (Major), *Washington writes to watch British at Stony Point, nicknamed "Lighthorse", p. 8; Washington requests further intelligence from, pp. 8, 11; Captain Allan McLane under his command, p. 12; Washington suggests Wayne see regarding Stony Point, p. 17; part of reserve at battle, p. 21; mentioned in Wayne's report to Washington, July 17, 1779, p. 43.*

Lee, Robert E., *son of Major Henry Lee jr., p. 8.*

Lexington, MA, *Lt. Return Jonathan Meigs fought at battle of, p. 19.*

Lincoln, Benjamin (General), *received surrender at Yorktown from counterpart General O'Hara, p. 74.*

Lombart de Noirmont, Rene-Hippolyte Penot (Major), *mentioned as one of two French volunteers at Stony Point, p. 23.*

Long Island, NY, *17th Regiment fought at battle of, p. 7.*

M

Marshall, William (Lieutenant), *description of fortifications at Stony Point, pp. 5-6; described, held prisoner, may have drawn Marshall Map during stay at Lancaster, PA, promoted Captain, pp. 41-42; testimony at court martial of Lt. Col. Johnson quoted, p. 68; one of key witnesses at court martial, p. 80.*

McDougall, Alexander (Major General), *mentioned in Washington's letter to Congress regarding failure to take Verplanck's Point, p. 34.*

McLane, Allan (Captain), *reconnoiters British fort at Stony Point under flag of truce, p. 12.*

Meigs, Return Jonathan (Colonel), *commander of Third Regiment of Light Infantry, background, p. 19; mentioned in Wayne's report to Washington, July 17, 1779, p. 43; letter to Wayne, August 22, 1779, pp. 47-48.*

Mercer, Alexander (Captain), *testimony at court martial of Lt. Col. Johnson quoted, pp. 59-61; further testimony quoted, p. 69.*

Mix, Eli (Private), *killed at Stony Point, p. 20.*

Monmouth, NJ, *17th Regiment fought at battle of, p. 7.*

Muhlenberg, Peter (General), *commander of reserve force at Stony Point, p. 21.*

Murfree, Hardy (Major), *commander of Second Battalion of Fourth Regiment of Light Infantry, fought at Brandywine and Monmouth, p. 19; companies of North Carolinians the only troops with loaded muskets, to create diversion, p. 22; their fire perhaps seen by gunners in Fleche No. 1, p. 26.*

N

Newport, RI, *17th Regiment fought at battle of, p. 7.*
New Windsor, NY, *Washington's headquarters, p. 15.*
Noirmont, *see* **Lombart de Noirmont.**

O

O'Hara, Charles (Brig. General), *deputy for Cornwallis at surrender of British troops at Yorktown, p. 74.*

P

Paoli, PA, *Wayne surprised by midnight bayonet attack at, p. 9; legend that Light Infantry shouted "Remember Paoli", p. 73; "Paoli Massacre" contrasted, p. 74; Wayne requests court martial after loss at, p. 80.*
Pattison, James (Major General), *description of American attempt to remove cannon from Stony Point quoted, pp.36-37.*
Posey, Thomas (Major), *commanded second battalion's (First Light Infantry Regiment) four Virginia companies, later Governor of Indiana, p. 18; letter to Washington, August 10, 1779, quoted, p. 47; mentioned in Wayne's letter of Jay, August 10, 1779, p. 50; Wayne's response to complaints of, pp. 52-53; Posey's response to Wayne, p. 53.*
Princeton, NJ, *17th Regiment fights at battle of, p. 7.*
Putnam, Rufus (Colonel), *reconnoiters Stony Point, p. 15; ordered by Washington to make a feint against Verplanck's Point, p. 17; nominal commander of Fourth Regiment of Light Infantry, p. 19.*

Q

Quarles, Benjamin, *book <u>The Negro in the American Revolution</u> cited, p. 79.*
Quebec, *Col. Febiger fought at battle of, p. 18.*

R

Reed, Joseph, *Washington writes to as President of Pennsylvania, p. 8; compliments Wayne and Corps of Light Infantry, p. 44.*

Roberts, John (Lieutenant), *escape from Stony Point, pp. 27-29; testimony at court martial of Lt. Col. Johnson quoted, pp. 62-64.*

Robinson, Beverly (Colonel), *colonel of Loyal American Regiment, residence opposite West Point, p. 7.*

Robinson, William (Captain), *son of Beverly Robinson, commander of Loyal American forces at Stony Point, p. 7.*

Ross, John (Lieutenant), *commands picket at Stony Point, testimony at court martial of Lt. Col. Johnson quoted, pp. 25-26; with Captain Tew when Tew killed, p. 31; testimony quoted regarding weather, p. 70.*

Rundle, John (Corporal), *killed at Stony Point, p. 20.*

Rush, Benjamin, *compliments Wayne and Corps of Light Infantry, p. 44.*

S

Sag Harbor, NY, *Col. Meigs's raid on, p. 19.*

Sandy Beach, NY, *location of Light Infantry camp, p. 19.*

Saratoga, *battle of mentioned, p. 2; General Gates awarded medal for victory at battle of, p. 46.*

Selden, Ezra (Captain), *wounded at Stony Point, p. 32.*

Sherman, Isaac (Lt. Colonel), *commander of four Connecticut companies of first battalion, Third Light Infantry Regiment, son of Roger Sherman, served at Princeton and Trenton, p. 19; writes to Wayne August, 22, 1779, pp.49-50; writes again, p. 51.*

Skinner, Abraham, *lists British Prisoners, p. 38; leaves wounded British prisoners at Kakiate, p. 38; directed by Washington to effectuate Col. Johnson's requests, writes regarding condition of prisoners, p.39.*

Smith, Mrs. Thomas,, *visit to her son the pretext for Captain McLane to visit Stony Point, p. 12; her son not listed as hanged, p. 37.*

Springsteel's Farm, *stopping point on Wayne's route of march, location of Wayne's eve of battle letter, p. 20.*

Starr, Robin, *soldier in Light Infantry, serves throughout Revolutionary War and buys freedom, p. 20.*

Sterling, (Brig. General), *commander of British forces that retake Stony Point after battle, p. 55.*

Stewart, John (Major), *reconnoiters Stony Point with Colonel Butler, p. 12; commands second battalion of Second Light Infantry Regiment, p. 18; his command includes vanguard, p. 23; mentioned in Congressional Resolutions and awarded medal, pp. 45-46.; mentioned in Meigs's letter to Wayne of August 22, 1779, p. 48.*

Stony Point, NY, *description and location, pp. 1-2;British forces take, p. 4-6; peninsula at high tide, p. 5.*

    Battle of, *strategic background, pp. 2-4; British fortifications, pp. 5-6; British ordinance at, p. 6-; British garrison, pp. 6-7; Americans gather intelligence, pp. 8, 10-12; strategic and tactical*

W

Washington, George (General), *reconnoiters Stony Point with General Wayne, p. 1; breaks camp at Middle brook, NJ, and proceeds to West Point, p. 4; refrains from attack after raids on Connecticut coast, p. 5; writes Joseph Reed regarding British activity at Stony Point, p. 8; asks Major Henry Lee jr. for intelligence, p. 8; decision to use Light Infantry for attack, p. 9; opinions of Wayne, pp. 9-10; first instructions to Wayne as commander of Light Infantry, pp.10-11; McLane reports to regarding fortifications at Stony Point, p. 12; adopts British strategy in attacking Stony and Verplanck's Points, p. 13; sends Col. Putnam to reconnoiter at Stony Point, p. 15; communicates plan for attack to Wayne, pp. 15-16; orders two cannons as ruse, p. 17; advises against postponement of attack, p. 17; praise for Major Lombart de Noirmont, p. 23; Wayne's initial report to, p. 32; explains failure to take Verplanck's Point, p. 34; inspects Stony Point after battle and decides to abandon, p. 35; describes removal of captured cannon, p. 36; decision regarding Lt. Col. Johnson's request, p. 39; Wayne's report to of July 17, 1779, p. 43; praise for Wayne, pp. 43-44; praises Lt. Col. Fleury, p. 46; awarded medal by Congress, p. 46; Posey complains to, p. 47; requests information and covering party for reconnaissance of second British fort at Stony Point, pp. 56-57; advises Wayne to throw up a small work at King's Ferry after British withdrawal, p. 58; success of ruse of ordering cannon, pp. 69-70; British military's low opinion of, p. 71;why Wayne chosen to lead attack, p. 73; legend of sword ordered by for Peter Francisco, p. 75.*

Wayne, Anthony (Brigadier General), *reconnoiters Stony Point with General Washington, p. 1;background, military experience, Washington's opinion of his character, pp. 9-10; Washington writes first instructions to regarding Stony and Verplanck's Points, pp. 10-11; first reconnaissance of Stony Point, p. 12; Washington communicates his plan to, pp. 15-16; suggests postponement of attack; p. 17; inspects Light Infantry July 15, 1779, p. 18; orders Light Infantry to march south from Sandy Beach, p. 19; conducts final reconnaissance, July 15, 1779, p. 20; writes letter on eve of battle, p. 20; informs troops of object and nature of attack,, p. 21; alterations to Washington's plan of attack, pp. 21-22; leads main column during attack, p. 22; order of battle, p. 22; final instructions, including rewards, pp. 23-24; initial report to Washington of success, p. 32; Auchmuty's letter to regarding British wounded, p. 37; response, pp. 37-38; Lt. Col. Johnson writes to regarding British prisoners, pp. 38-39; forwards to Washington,, p. 39; report to Washington of July 17, 1779, p.43; Washington*

BIBLIOGRAPHY

Boatner, Mark Mayo III, Encyclopedia of the American Revolution, David McKay Company, New York, 1976.

Clinton, Sir Henry, The American Rebellion, Sir Henry Clinton's Narrative of His Campaigns, 1775-1782, with an Appendix of Original Documents, Willcox, William B., ed., Yale University Press, New Haven, 1954.

Dawson, Henry B., The Assault on Stony Point, H.O. Houghton, Cambridge, 1863.

"Diary and Papers of Captain Allan McLane," New-York Historical Society, Manuscript Department, New York, 1779

Johnston, Henry P., The Storming of Stony Point on the Hudson, James T. White, New York, 1900; reprinted 1971, DaCapo Press, New York, NY.

Loprieno, Don, "The Court-Martial of Lieutenant Colonel Henry Johnson: Continuing Research on the Battle of Stony Point," South of the Mountains, Journal of the Historical Society of Rockland County (N.Y.), January-March 1997.

Lossing, Benson J., The Pictorial Field-Book of the Revolution, Harper & Brothers, New York, 1852, vol. 2,

Nelson, Paul David, Anthony Wayne: Soldier of the Early Republic, Indiana University Press, Bloomington, Indiana, 1985.

"Pension Application of Robin Starr, 2nd Connecticut Regiment," National Archives, File S36810, Volume 2, Page 898,Washington, 1818.

Quarles, Benjamin, The Negro in the American Revolution, University of North Carolina Press, Chapel Hill, 1961.

Rankin, Hugh F., An Officer Out of His Time: Correspondence of Major Patrick Ferguson, 1779-1780, Reprinted in Sources of American Independence, Volume II, Howard H. Peckham, editor, Chicago and London, 1978.

Stille, Charles J., Major- General Anthony Wayne and the Pennsylvania Line in the Continental Army, Kennikat Press, Port Washington, New York, first published 1893, reissued 1968.

The Court-Martial of Lieutenant Colonel Henry Johnson, Public Records Office, London, 1781.

II.

The Prisoners: Captivity and Confinement

SELECTED LETTERS OF LIEUTENANT WILLIAM MARSHALL

Lieutenant (later Captain) William Marshall was a member of the 63rd Regiment of Foot, and on June 26, 1779, Marshall was appointed Acting Engineer in charge of the British defenses at Stony Point. A few weeks later, when the American Light Infantry assaulted the British fortifications in the early morning hours of July 16, Marshall was captured "on the Table of the Hill near where an Old Rebel Block House had stood," as he later tells us in the court-martial of Lieutenant Colonel Henry Johnson, the garrison commander, which was held in New York City in January, 1781. Marshall was an important voice in those proceedings, testifying on four successive days, the most of any witness. On the same day of the battle, he was among those who were marched off to their eventual destination of Lancaster, Pennsylvania, where he may have drawn a *Sketch of the Works at Stoney Point*. His name appears on a list of 23 officers sent on parole to Easton, Pennsylvania (and thence to Lancaster) prepared by the American Deputy Commissary of Prisoners, Abraham Skinner, on July 20, 1779 at Goshen, New York, a stop along the line of march.

Little is known about Marshall personally, but records indicate that he became a Lieutenant in December, 1775, was promoted to Captain on September 18, 1780 (though still referred to as "Lieutenant" in Lieutenant Colonel Johnson's trial a few months later) and, having survived the war, was reduced to half-pay in 1789 after apparently retiring from military service. From his extant correspondence, we also know that Marshall was in Lancaster until at least March 13, 1780, the date of his last letter from that location, and probably remained there until his release, there being no reason to suppose that he was separated from his fellow officers who had been captured at Stony Point. His map, which is the collections of the Historical Society of Pennsylvania, is undated, but since he signed his name using the rank of Captain, it seems likely that he completed the map between September, 1780 -- the date of his promotion -- and late November of the same year, when he was exchanged and left Lancaster for New York. As a prisoner for more than a year, he would have had ample time for such a project.

His letters are also in the collections of the Historical Society of Pennsylvania, and all are addressed to the same individual: "Tench Coxe, merchant at Philadelphia, " who was serving as a financial agent for the captured British officers in Lancaster. The first letter is dated November 11, 1779, a little more than three months after Marshall's arrival in town on August 3, so presumably before that correspondence, he had sufficient assets to pay his expenses. In his initial communication, Marshall refers to a letter of credit that had previously been arranged with a "merchant at Philadelphia" but apparently Marshall did not know which merchant. The letter of credit confirmed that Marshall had a credit with the issuer, in this case Tench Coxe (the "merchant"), and that Coxe would pay drafts drawn by Marshall against the letter of credit. Coxe, however, had taken the initiative and written to Marshall, and probably confirmed that the letter had in fact been delivered to him, thus making Marshall's further efforts to ascertain the apparently previously unknown merchant unnecessary, as Marshall himself indicates. In the present correspondence, Marshall encloses a bill for which he would like "silver dollars," very likely Spanish Milled Dollars, a coin widely circulated at the time. The bill -- precursor to a modern check -- is payable to a Major Worts, presumably an American officer of Lancaster, who will then give the cash to Marshall. Thus, Coxe functions as a banker as well as a merchant. Marshall also requests candles, cloth and tea, the cost of which will presumably be deducted from the amount indicated in the letter of credit. Marshall conveys greetings to Coxe from Lt. Col. Webster, for whom Coxe may have performed similar services. Finally, Marshall provides the Philadelphian with his current address –"at Mr. Kontz's the bottom of Queens Street, Lancaster."

This first letter establishes Marshall's priorities: to obtain necessary goods, particularly those that are difficult to find or simply unavailable in Lancaster, and to convert bills into cash since an officer on parole had to pay for room and board. These concerns are a recurrent theme running through the remainder of his letters to Coxe.

Lancaster 11th Nov 1779

Sir,

I acknowledge the receipt of your letter of the 7th instant and take the earliest opportunity of answering it. Captain McKennon of the 63rd regiment sometimes since wrote to me from New York, and mentioned having enclosed a letter of credit on a merchant at Philadelphia which by some accident was lost. I have wrote to him again on that business desiring a renewal of the same but since the receipt of yours his answer is of small consequence. I have enclosed drawn a bill upon you for 20 pounds sterling British which will be of no small service at this crisis; it is payable to Major Worts of this town who will return in a few days, if you could oblige me with some silver dollars in payment I should be much obliged to you. You may at times have an opportunity of remitting me some few articles from Philadelphia. I could wish for as much blue cloth as would make a coat and a small piece of scarlet velvet for the cape as it is at this time of little consequence the wearing of my uniform scarlet cloth being so immoderately dear. A pound of good tea would be very acceptable and a few pounds of spermacetti candles if not too dear, as there are not any to be had in this town. What ever expense you may be at on my account I will readily at any time settle and shall always acknowledge myself obliged to you for your trouble. Colonel Johnston [sic] is well and desires his compliments.

I remain sir your most obedient humble servant

William Marshall 63rd Regiment, Assistant Engineer

Address: Lt. Marshall at Mr. Kontz's the bottom of Queens Street, Lancaster

In his next letter, dated November 24th, a note of exasperation is evident in Marshall's refusal to accept paper money (Continental and state currency) in lieu of the silver dollars he had requested. No doubt he was fully aware that the purchasing power of paper was considerably less than that of coin. He also rejects what Coxe may have suggested; that is, that he draw on funds in England rather than his military pay in New York.

Lancaster 24th Nov 1779

Sir,

I acknowledge the receipt of your letter & my bill inclosed. With respect to the credit I had on Mr. Goold [?] at New York it is now certainly meant that the amount was to be paid in <u>hard cash</u>. I always understood it in that light I gave Major Wortz instructions accordingly. I would not by any means receive my money in <u>Paper</u>, & as it is inconvenient for you to pay me otherwise, the credit can be of no manner of use; neither would I wish to draw upon <u>England</u> while I have money paying in New York.

I remain Sir, your obedient Humble Servant
William Marshall
Lieutenant 63rd & Acting Engineer

By the following letter, dated January 18, the problem appears to have been resolved since Marshall thanks Coxe for the cash delivered by Major Worts and for the cloth, though the spermacetti candles have not yet arrived. Marshall then indicates the possibility that he will soon return to New York -- the hope of every British prisoner -- and therefore will not need "to draw any more Bills." Marshall was either misinformed or overly sanguine because his hope proved false: he would remain a captive until the end of the year.

Sir,

A weeks [sic] *since I acknowledged the receipt of the cash you sent me by Major Wortz of this town. The cloth came safe, tho'I have not as yet got the spermacetti candles you purchased; should be much Obliged to you to get them forwarded as speedily as possible, there being a probability of my soon going into New York. I have not occasion to draw any more bills therefore shall not trouble you on that head, but am extremely obliged to you for the business you have executed on my acct. remaining.*

> *Sir your most obliged humble servant*
> *William Marshall*
> *Lieutenant 63rd & Acting Engineer*

A week later (January 25), Marshall realizes that "there is a chance of remaining some time longer" and informs Coxe that he will continue to need his assistance in converting additional bills into cash in the manner of the previous bill which, despite his reluctance to accept paper currency, was paid half in paper, half in specie, as this letter makes clear. Given his situation, Marshall was hardly in a position to bargain or be particular about the method of payment. Coxe may have expressed some uncertainly about the validity of the bills since Marshall assures him that there "is not the least doubt but that whatever bills I may send you will be paid on their getting into New York, & am convinced there can be but little difficulty in sending them for payment", and even offers to have them endorsed by an officer of the Royal Artillery or draw on funds in England, something that he had previously written – on November 24 - he would not do.

Sir,

In my former letter to you I mentioned the probability of my soon going into New York, but I now understand there is a chance of remaining some time longer, therefore must be under the necessity of drawing some more cash, & as you are the only person I can correspond with on this side of our lines, must trouble you on that business. I would wish to draw on a person residing, at New York for thirty or forty Guineas [a guinea is 21 shillings] *on my own account, & can procure other bills to the amount of ninety guineas more if you could manage to get them sold, by taking half in paper & the rest in gold at the <u>Current-Exchange</u> allowing for the sale of the bills in the same way you obliged me with the last draught for credit on Mr. Goold. There is not the least doubt but that whatever bills I may send you will be paid on their getting into New York, & am convinced there can be but little difficulty in sending them for payment. Your answer will much obliged,*

> *Your most obliged Humble Servant*
> *William Marshall*
> *Lieutenant 63rd & Acting Engineer*

NB If there should be occasion I can get them endorsed by a captain of the Royal Artillery. Perhaps I may to get one bill upon England but not on my own account.

Two weeks later, not having heard from Coxe, Marshall surmised that his correspondence never reached Philadelphia, and wrote again to restate the contents of the missing letter. This time, until Marshall could procure additional bills from New York, he requested Coxe to find "some person in Philadelphia" who would be willing to accept a bill from the British

Commissary in New York -- in effect, negotiating a loan to Marshall's account through Coxe "allowing a reasonable premium for the time of this laying out of the cash." Marshall is clearly frustrated by his lack of resources, compounded by the fact, also expressed in this letter, that he has received no answer from New York in response to his need for more credit. Coxe also seems to be continually concerned and perhaps uneasy about the prospects for re-payment, and this new proposal by Marshall may be an attempt to reassure him. In any case, Marshall has no one else to turn to and says as much: "I am sorry to be troublesome to you on this occasion but in my present situation have not the smallest correspondence with any other person."

Lancaster February 10, 1780

Sir,

I have for the [illegible because of tears and folds in the original] *with expectation of having an answer from you on the purport of a letter I sent you a fortnight ago, perhaps by some accident it did not come to hand & for fear that should have been the cause, I must beg leave to acquaint you that I shall very soon be obliged to draw upon New York for a fresh supply of money, & have two or three gentlemen of my acquaintance in the same situation. If you could oblige me by getting some person in Philadelphia to take a bill upon Commissary Grant of New York for about thirty or forty Guineas on my acct. paying the money half in specie & the rest in Paper at the current exchange allowing a reasonable premium for the time of this laying out of the cash, I would be willing to negotiate the business without delay, & can procure good bills to the amount of ninety Guineas more on the same terms. I am sorry to be troublesome to you on this occasion but in my present situation have not the smallest correspondence with any other person & altho' I have repeatedly wrote into York for a further credit I have not had any answer. The person I mean to draw upon is pay master to the R. Artillery & Engineer.*

> *I remain Sir,*
> *Your most Obedient Humble Servant*
> *William Marshall*
> *Lieutenant 63rd & Acct. Engineer*

N.B. I have not as yet received the spermacetti candles you purchased for me some time since.

In early March, Marshall wrote his penultimate letter to Coxe (his final correspondence, dated March 11, is not reprinted here but focuses on the same financial concerns) in which it appears that bills have now been received from New York, and that Coxe is now attempting to sell these bills to a third party along the lines of Marshall's suggestion made in the previous letter. In the spirit of compromise that circumstances had forced him to adopt, Marshall was again willing to accept payment half in paper, knowing that it would purchase less than hard currency, and now would cost him more because of the necessity of selling his bills, an addition that could only increase the expense of the whole transaction. Coxe must have still expressed some trepidation about the financial security of his arrangement with Marshall, for once again, the harried officer confirms that while he "cannot possibly make it convenient to get them [the bills] endorsed by a pay master or field-officer, but am fully assured of the certainty of their being punctually paid as I have drawn for no more than the amount of any pay to the past of this month. . ." As their correspondence, or what survives of it, draws to a close, Marshall informs Coxe of a change of address. He now resides with Mr. George Saunderson, still on Queen Street in Lancaster, but no longer, apparently, at the bottom. Whether Coxe ever was fully repaid or whether Lt. Marshall ever got his candles are matters for speculation.

Sir,

I now acknowledge the receipt of your letter by Mr. Barton & as you will be obliging to endeavour to procure me some money by the sale of my bills, I have inclosed sent you a set drawn payable to your order for the amount of forty pounds sterling. I cannot possibly make it convenient to get them endorsed by a pay master or field-officer, but am fully assured of the certainty of their being punctually paid as I have drawn for no more than the amount of any pay to the past of this month. I have not yet been able to collect any bills from the gentleman I mentioned in my letter but will send them as soon as I hear again from you. As for the manner in which you may settle this business it must rest mostly at your discretion only observing to procure half the amount of the bills in specie & the rest in paper at the current exchange, allowing a reasonable discount.

I remain Sir,
your most obliged humble servant
William Marshall
Lieutenant 63rd & Acting Engineer

NB   You will oblige me to acknowledge the receipt of this as early as possible my address is, Lt. Marshall at Mr. Geo Saunderson. Queen Street Lancaster.

Obtaining credit and funds in wartime was a primary concern of captive officers, as Marshall's letters attest. But there were other problems and restrictions about which Marshall says nothing. Of course, an officer who has been given parole is subject to a number of limitations, some of which were spelled out by Sir Henry Clinton in a letter of September 23, 1780, to General Washington proposing a commissary of prisoners of war to visit areas where these prisoners (non-commissioned officers and privates) were being confined. When the commissaries were behind enemies' lines, they should "consider themselves on parole, neither to send verbal or written Intelligence to their own Party, or divulge anything that may be prejudicial to the Party with whom they reside, nor receive or forward any Letters but such as have been inspected by the Officers appointed for that Purpose and under no Pretence whatever to interfere with public affairs or Politicks. . ." This was not a new regulation and would certainly have governed Marshall and his fellow officers. In any case, Marshall would have been unlikely to attempt the expression of any political or military opinions to a merchant whose role was strictly professional, and may not have written to anyone else, since he himself states "in my present situation [I] have not the smallest correspondence with any other person."

Fortunately, another, more complete account of the plight of British officers survives in the diary of Ensign Thomas Hughes, reprinted in the Papers of the Lancaster Historical Society. Hughes (1759-1790), of the 53rd Regiment, was captured at Ticonderoga in 1777 and granted parole. He stayed for a time in Boston, and Pepperell, Massachusetts, and on May 22, 1779, arrived in Lancaster where he was required to stay within a mile of his quarters, a limitation that probably would also have applied to Lt. Marshall. Nonetheless, Hughes' situation and that of his fellow officers, was far better than the conditions that non-commissioned officers and ordinary soldiers had to endure. Often confined to prison, they could languish for months without hope of exchange. A typical example was Joseph Swain of the Royal Artillery, who had been captured during the attack on Stony Point. On February 5, 1781, a reference was made to him during the court-martial of Lt. Col. Henry Johnson, indicating that he was still a prisoner in the "Philadelphia gaol," more than a year and a half later.

A week after he arrived in Lancaster, Hughes was still looking for accommodations, writing in his diary that he had "been looking out these several days for lodgings but cannot procure any – the inhabitants say they are afraid to take in British officers, as they shall be accounted Tories." A few days later, on June 4, Ensign Hughes finally found a place, but like Lt. Marshall and many others in the same situation, he was having financial concerns, commenting that he was "entirely out of cash and cannot find a person to give us money for a bill." On August 3, 1779, as Hughes noted in his diary, Lt. Col. Johnson and other captured officers, including Lt. Marshall, arrived in Lancaster, having marched from Stony Point on July 16.

Naturally, all these officers wanted to be exchanged as quickly as possible, but hope of an early return to their own lines was dashed by news recorded by Hughes in early October: "All hopes of a speedy exchange are now over - the Commissaries [of prisoners] having quarreled on some trifling subject which may occasion our stay here all winter." Their captivity would, in fact, extend even beyond the winter and into the late fall of the next year.

Obtaining money to settle debts, combined with inflation and the unpredictable arrival of military pay, continued to be a problem for Hughes and other officers. On October 30, 1779, he observes that "the want of cash obliges us to borrow paper money to be paid for in solid coin – we are allowed 25 paper dollars for one silver dollar . . . as this reduces us to half pay, wrote Sir Henry Clinton to complain of our situation and desire pay may be regularly sent us." By January 21, the financial situation had apparently not improved since Hughes lamented that he had "not a farthing in my pocket, do not know where to apply for any loan and thirty guineas in debt. . ." By mid-February, bills and specie and paper money were still vital issues for the British officers, and now they became even more important because, as Hughes recorded in his diary, "Congress have issued orders that no prisoner of war shall be exchanged until his debts are paid – this is a good sign . . ." thereby combining the hope of release with the necessity of settling accounts.

However, life in Lancaster was not without its bright spots. Ensign Hughes, for example, describes attending a Moravian wedding, traveling to the Susquehanna River "with a party of girls," and visiting some iron mills in a nearby town, all three journeys approved by the authorities and all well outside the one-mile limit, which was later increased to three, a benefit that might also have been extended to Lt. Marshall and the other officers.

The rules that applied to prisoners were not always obeyed, and there were tensions between the officers and local citizens. On November 30, 1779 -- St. Andrew's Day -- Hughes described a fight in a tavern between some American militia and several "of our Caledonian lads." The following day, the British officers involved were ordered confined to their room until a hearing could be held to determine fault. The reason for the quarrel is not given, but it could easily have been an imprudent remark about politics or the latest military action. On June 26, 1780, Lt. William Horndon, one of three artillery officers captured at Stony Point, "was beat publicly in the streets this morn by the adjutant of the militia for using freedom with that gentleman's wife – [Deputy Commissary of Prisoners] Atlee will not interfere in the quarrel so Horndon must put up with the drubbing." Hughes also describes an officer who was jailed because he was refused leave and "flung up his parole."

The captured officers also disagreed among themselves. Hughes recorded a duel between Lt. Isaac Carey of the 17th Regiment and Ensign Richard Swords of the Loyal Americans. "After discharging pistols without effect, the seconds interfered and it was made up – it was occasioned by a drunken quarrel in which blows past [sic]."

On July 15, Hughes wrote in his diary about a recent order by the Board of War "that every British officer should wear his proper uniform and that whoever after this was found in a coloured coat should be taken up and put to prison. This has put most of us to an inconveniency as it is amazing difficult to procure cloth." This was certainly true since Lt. Marshall referred to scarlet cloth as "being so immoderately dear" in his first letter to Tench Coxe on November 11 of the previous year. The probable reason for the order was to provide quick identification, but how the officers were expected to comply is not clear.

As the fall of 1780 arrived, word of Benedict Arnold's treason was the latest topic in Lancaster, followed closely by ongoing discussions among the prisoners about the perennial subject of their eventual release. Finally, on October 21, Hughes reported that "we are already exchanged," though no official word had been received. In fact, unknown to Hughes at the time, his name -- as well as that of Lt. Col. Johnson, Lt. Marshall and the other officers taken at Stony Point -- appeared in a letter by Sir Henry Clinton to Lord Germaine listing exchanged prisoners since October 25. It was not until November 18 that the good news was confirmed, and Hughes must have been elated to write of "the agreeable intelligence of our being all to be exchanged, and . . we may go to New York when it suits our conveniency and we can get our debts settled – this last will give me some trouble."

It probably gave Lt. Marshall some trouble as well, though his surviving correspondence to Tench Coxe ends seven months earlier. On November 21, Ensign Hughes settled his affairs "by drawing a bill on New York at 12 per cent discount," and the following day set out for Elizabeth, New Jersey, by way of Bound Brook, en route to New York. Though it is not known when Marshall left Lancaster, it was very likely around the same time, no doubt as soon after November 18 as he could manage, not wanting to stay any longer than necessary. He must have arrived in New York later that month or early in December, not to appear again in historical records until January, 1781 as a key witness in Lt. Col. Johnson's court-martial. What little we know of the man himself is from that trial and the letters he wrote in an effort, common to many, to survive as best he could.

Though it contains some inaccuracies, this 1784 map by William Faden shows the relationship of the fortifications at Stony

North

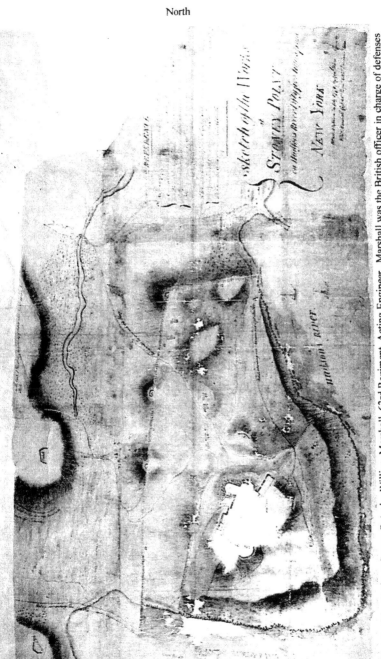

South

Sketch of the Works at Stoney Point by William Marshall, 63rd Regiment, Acting Engineer. Marshall was the British officer in charge of defenses at Stony Point, and was captured during the battle. He may have drawn this map when he was a prisoner in Lancaster, Pennsylvania.

Collections of the Historical Society of Pennsylvania

North

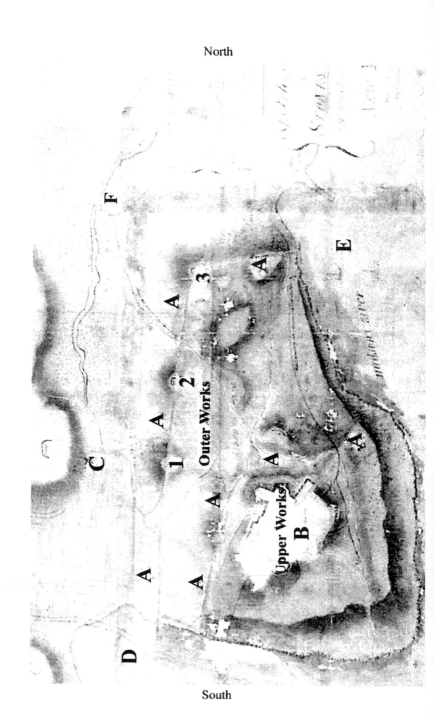

South

Sketch of the Works at Stoney Point

By William Marshall, Acting Engineer, 63rd Regiment

Key for Entire Map

A=abatis, one in the Outer Works, a second in the Upper Works.

B= the table of the hill, the most level part of the Upper Works.

C= location of the causeway spanning the creek which often flooded at high tide. Major Murfree's men broke away from Col. Butler's column at this spot to fire muskets and divert the British defenders.

D= location of the gunboat, missing from its post on the night of the battle. This shallow area of Haverstraw Bay is also where the south end of the abatis in the Outer Works extended into the water, and where the main column of American Light Infantry waded across from a sandy beach.

E= location of the *Vulture*, missing from its post on the night of the battle. It was anchored instead in the middle of the Hudson between the two peninsulas, possibly because of high winds.

F= Jaeger Bridge where Lt. Ross and his men first heard the enemy.

1, 2, 3= location of three fleches, each built on top of a rocky outcropping and skirted at its base by the abatis of the Outer Works. Each fleche was open at the rear and was made of earth, coated with fascines. They were designed to accommodate artillery, and their profiles, according to Marshall's testimony in the court-martial of Lieutenant Colonel Henry Johnson, were twelve feet at the base, tapering to a height of eight feet.

North

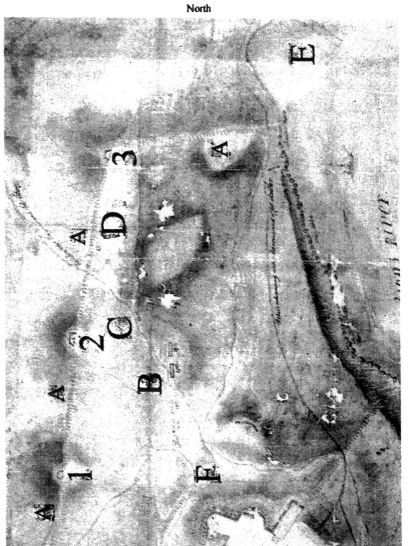

South

The Outer Works - detail from a *Sketch of the Works at Stoney Point* by William Marshall

Sketch of the Works at Stoney Point

By William Marshall, Acting Engineer, 63rd Regiment

Key for Outer Works

A= outer abatis

B= four companies of the 17th Regiment. In the event of an attack, these men were to line the outer abatis.

C= approximate location of a 3 pounder gun on a field carriage but not in battery. This gun, one of only two that fired during the battle, killed or wounded a number of men in the forlorn hope of Col. Butler's column.

D= location of two Grenadier companies of the 71st Regiment, under the command of Capt. Lawrence Robert Campbell. Like the four nearby companies of the 17th Regiment, they were ordered to defend the Outer Works

E= King's Ferry landing, west bank. The ferry operated between Stony Point and Verplanck's Point, and was a vital communications link between New York and the New England states.

F= main entrance to the Upper Works, protected by overlapping segments of the inner abatis (see key to Outer Works). This narrow opening was largely ignored by the American Light Infantry who focused instead on penetrating or going around the abatis near its flanks.

1= fleche #1 contained the other gun that fired during the battle -- a short brass 12-pounder gun confined by an embrasure. This battery, under the command of Lt. William Horndon, boomed repeatedly in the dark to no apparent effect. The American main column swept around it undeterred on their way toward the Upper Works.

2=fleche #2 contained two Coehorn mortars, neither one of which was fired during the attack. Lightballs fired from these weapons might have illuminated the darkness, but none was brought up or used.

3= fleche #3 mounted two Royal mortars and a brass 12 pounder gun. According to Lt. William Nairne of the 71st Regiment, this position was overrun and the artillerymen captured by the advancing Americans.

North

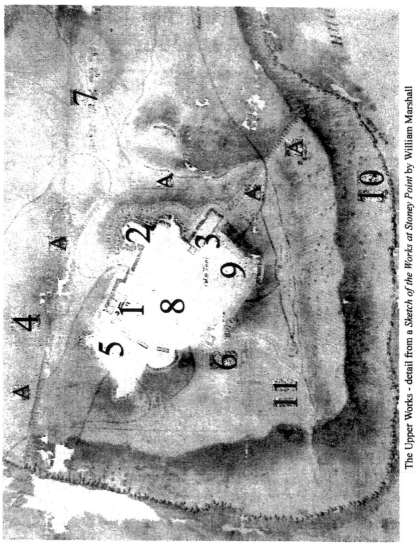

South

The Upper Works - detail from a *Sketch of the Works at Stoney Point* by William Marshall
Collection of the Historical Society of Pennsylvania

Sketch of the Works at Stoney Point

By William Marshall, Acting Engineer, 63rd Regiment

<u>Key for Upper Works</u>

A= inner abatis

1 = left flank battery containing an 18 and a 24 pounder gun, each on its own platform and confined by embrasures.

2= flagstaff battery containing an iron 12 pounder mounted en barbette. This is also where Lt. Col. Francois Fleury struck the British flag.

3=right flank battery containing an 18 and 24 pounder gun on a single platform with embrasures. According to Lt. William Armstrong of the 17th Regiment whose company was posted close by, the American north column under Col. Butler entered the Upper Works through the embrasures of this battery in addition to flanking the north side of the inner abatis.

4= battery containing an eight-inch Howitzer mounted en barbette. This weapon was directed towards the shallow south flank of Haverstraw Bay and had sufficient shot and shell to decimate the main American column, but the Light Infantry captured the weapon before the artillerymen could load or fire.

5= location of the troops in the Upper Works – four companies of the 17th Regiment and a detachment of Loyal Americans.

6= location of the American blockhouse, destroyed when the British captured Stony Point, May 31, 1779.

7= four more companies of the 17th Regiment (see Key to Outer Works).

8= location of a 10-inch land mortar.

9= location of a long brass 12 pounder gun in the New Work, unfinished at the time of the battle but intended to fire at enemy vessels in the river below and help protect Verplanck's Point on the east bank.

10=the area called "the precipice" by the British where the north end of the inner abatis ended high above the shoreline.

11= powder magazine

View of "the angle" - the shallow part of Haverstraw Bay on the south shore of Stony Point. It was this area that the American right column waded through, going around the outer abatis and ascending to the high ground of the Upper Works.

View from the east toward "the table of the hill," the most level ground of the Upper Works. The stone structure on the far right is situated at the approximate location of the right flank battery, and was constructed in the early twentieth century.

View looking east from the Outer Works toward the Upper Works in the distance. The Flagstaff Battery was located near the top center of the ridge in the background, and the inner abatis ran along the base of the same formation.

View from the south toward the left flank battery in the Upper Works. The two guns here, intended for long range daytime targets, were kept unloaded at night. The Howitzer battery was located on the left at the base of the same ridge.

List of British Officers and Men Captured at the Battle of Stony Point, July 16, 1779

LIST OF OFFICERS ON PAROLE WHO WERE SENT FROM STONY POINT TO EASTON

Rank	Name	Regiment
Lt. Colonel	Henry Johnson	17th Regiment
Captain	John Darby	17th Regiment
Captain	Robert Clayton	17th Regiment
Captain	William Tiffin	Artillery
Captain	Morris Robinson	Loyal Americans
Lieutenant	William Armstrong	17th Regiment
Lieutenant	Isaac Carey	17th Regiment
Lieutenant	William T.H. Williams	17th Regiment
Lieutenant	William Simpson	17th Regiment
Lieutenant	William John Mawhood	17th Regiment
Lieutenant	John Hayman	17th Regiment
Lieutenant	R. Duncanson	71st Regiment
Lieutenant	William Nairne	71st Regiment
Lieutenant	John Ross	71st Regiment
Lieutenant	Robert Grant	71st Regiment
Lieutenant	William Horndon	Artillery
Lieutenant	William Marshall	63rd Regiment
Ensign	Frederick P. Robinson	17th Regiment
Ensign	Henry Hamilton	17th Regiment
Ensign	Richard Swords	Loyal Americans
Ensign	William Huggeford	Loyal Americans
Asst. Surgeon	Richard Auchmuty	17th Regiment
Conductor	Isaac Enslow	Artillery

Source: Abraham Skinner to Robert H. Harrison, July 20, 1779; George Washington Papers at the Library of Congress.

LIST OF BRITISH SOLDIERS TAKEN PRISONER
AT STONY POINT 16 JULY 1779

Royal Artillery

William Leicester – driver
Samuel Rownall
Robert Stevenson
Richard Wallace
Joseph Swain
Robert White
Richard Mathews
Joseph Newton
Albert Forrister
John Reach
Mark Jenkins
William McCarter
George Mitchell
John Ireland
Duncan McPherson
Joseph Rawson
Hugh Spires
John Small
William Hodds
David Cooper
John Robertston
John Kennis
Nathaniel Jones – wounded

John Currie
George Seton – wounded and left
at Hackets[town]
John Adams
James Watson
William Greenlow
John McDougal
Patrick Philips
James Grounston
William Atkin
Alexander Whitlow
George Russell
Jonathan Carlin
Norman Robinson
William Collins
George Howie
Richard Gregory
Abraham Nichols
James Atkins
Samuel Morganstrayd

Total 43

17th Regiment

Sgt. Richardson
Sgt. Jackson
Sgt. Smith
Cpl. Abbott
Cpl. West
Cpl. Bone
Drummer Gale
Drummer Rowe
William Clark
Anthony Close
Hugh Frill
William Hamilton

William Key
James Lockyear
Richard Long
Robert Long
Michael Lockrey
Samuel Lynch
Joseph May
Jonathan Rushford
John Townsend
James Turner
Richard Tamser
George Watson
Septimus Wilson

Total 25

Sgt. Naylor
Sgt. Miller
Cpl. Newton
Cpl. Baine
Drummer Cheshire
Frederick Betfield
William Barker
Robert Bursler
James Douglass
Carl Dingle
George Dolton
Peter Federham
Samuel Fletcher
Conrad Habonight
Michael Hagar
John Hudson
Michael Miller

John Million
John McElveen
John Nevitt
William Peterson
William Page
Christian Settleben
Phillip Shamberg
Ignatius Schnider
John Stokes
Martin Trost
John Watts
Carl Widerman
John Wade
James Wylock
Richard Walton
John Ryder

Total 33

Sgt. Davis
Sgt. Gillott
Cpl. Radford
Cpl. Quin
Drummer Powell
Thomas Battsell
Cornelius Brown
John Brewer
Thomas Bouran
William Brackley
Thomas Bracknall
George Clift
James Holinsworth
John Hooper
Uriah Jackson
Alexander McKay

John McKenzie
Eurebeus Moon
Jonathan Nixon
Thomas Nurmery
Richard Rice
Thomas Savage
John Simpson
Elias Simmondson
John Tunks
Joseph Twist
Joseph Wood
Joshua Waddington
Robert Westgarth
Robert Henderson

Total 30

Sgt. Andrews
Sgt. Hunspages
Cpl. McFarlan
Cpl. Atkinson
Cpl. Davis
Drummer Platt
Drummer Clark
Thomas Ayres
William Brownall
Richard Cartwright
Nicholas Champ
Thomas Champion
Thomas Combes
William Combes
Joseph Davis
Robert Drysdale
John Greene

David Greene
Thomas Goddard
John Howard
James Kennedy
James Lancaster
James Logan
William McLaughlin
William Pitkin
James Richie
David Robinson
William Shurrman
Peter Sellers
John Slee
Henry Wedlow

Total 31

Sgt. Allen
Sgt. Gray
Carp. Cameron
Corp. Ash
Drummer Kennedy
James Belekey
William Browne
John Clarke
Smith Clough
James Eaton
William Gordon
John Garrison
Edward Green
Mark Green
Eliphalet Humpage
John Hacket
Edward Lane

Owen Mealy
Michael Madigan
Charles McGrigor
Ishmael Monday
William Norman
William Naylor
John Pitkins
Henry Simms
John Swain
John Scott
Thomas Thornton
Thmas Walker
Samuel Wootton
Richard Woodward
George Harrison

Total 32

Sgt. Webb
Sgt. Boll
Sgt. Gibson
Cpl. Hughes
Cpl. Higginson
Cpl. Pugh
Drummer Collins
Drummer Buttler
Patrick Curry
Anthony Danby
William Doddin
William Dick
William Frost
Richard Griesly
James Heyden
Dennis Huggins

Thomas Kitson
Patrick Kelly
William Kirk
Mathew Law
Charles Ludlum
Barney McCormick
William Parker
George Parr
William Reynolds
Leonard Raper
John Smith
Thomas Symistre
William Teesdale
John Dalton

Total 30

Sgt. Workman
Corp. Puzoy
Corp. Brooks
Corp. Drysdale
Drummer Hudson
Daniel Amos
James Aldridge
William Blandale
Henry Collenridge
Thomas Crowder
William Croaker
William Donald
Michael Davis
Joseph Davie
John Fitzgerald
Joseph Ginman
William Gordon

Mathew Gilmore
Peter Hinds
Thomas Hyde
William Loversuch
George Low
William Mitchell
Daniel McCollam
Daniel Monro
Alexander McKinly
George Norton
James Poulston
William Oliver
William Simms
James Thornhill
Thomas Wattson
John Wright

Total 33

125

Sgt. McAllister
Corp. Ireton
Drummer Sherriff
Drummer Rich
Robert abrahams
Richard Bearman
James Bromley
Thomas Duplidge
Robert Hustone
John Hombro
Nicholas Higginbottom
Michael Knowls

John Neyland
James Pringle
Patrick Pierce
Patrick Rabbit
Aylmer Reed
Christopher Simmson
Thomas Silvy
Francie Sawyer
Hugh Dawbie

Total 21

First Company 71st

John McKenzie, Sr.
Sgt. Simms
John McKenzie, Jr.
Cpl. Cochran
Peter McIntire
Cpl. Cummins
William McKay
Allen Boyd
William Mackey
John Balfour
Peter Mc Courtney
Henry Brown
John Michael
George Bruce
Alexander McLean
Robert Barclay
Kenneth McKenzie
James Bell
James McDonald
John Cameron
Alexander McLacklin
James Christie
James McKenzie
Colin Cameron
Donald McLean
John McArthur
Donald Coates
Alexander Ross
David Dennit
Arthur Rose
Lawrence Duff
John Ridey
Mathew Finlay
Laughlin Sinclair
Donald Frazier
Peter Stewart
Simon Frazier
Donald Stewart
James Glaze
John Tayer
James Key
David Turner
Charles Jake
David Tulloch
John Johnson
Alexander Willson
John Hay
John Walker
John Foggery
Andrew Wachant
George Laying
Peter Williamson
Gilbert Layeon
Donald McLeod
Donald McDonald

Total 57

Donald McDonald
Donald Murrey

126

Second Company

Sgt. Burns
Sgt. Stewart
Cpl. Edgell
Cpl. Ferguson
Cpl. McArthury
Cpl. Towey
Corp. McCormack
James Main
William McLeod
Malcolm McKeller
Robert Little
Robert Buchannon
Donald Frazer
John Mackey
David Kerswell
Malcolm McDougal
James McLean
Archibald Gray
Hugh McCollam
John McCollam
Peter McGrigor
Hondree Coming
Alexander Monro

George Mackey
Donald Coggle
James Jelford
John Field
Duncan Bell
James Muatt
John Craig
James Folletts
Richard Thornton
William Monro
John McLachlen
John Caris
Alexander McIntosh
Charles Frazier
James Mitchell
William Dunsmore
Joseph McDonald
Alexander Allen – left at Sussex
John McLean

Total 42

Loyal
Americans

Sgt. Pringle
Sgt. Conkling
Joshua Northin
John Harrison
John Tunis
John Jenkins
Morris Peters
Abraham Lewis – deserter sent back to camp
Frederick Aker
Martin Stover
Richard Spragg
John McCord
James Hill
Abraham Potts
Jacob Wood
Peter Weaver
John Welch
Ezra Mead
Nathan Mead
Patrick McNeil
John Smith
Jacob Dupoy
John Ogden
William Riddle – deserter sent back
Andrew Squires
Abraham Williams
Richard Williams
John Slocum
Thomas Marly

Reuben Morgan
John Shear
John Stevenson
John Nicholson
Edward Murtis
John Basley
Abraham Wood
Henry Ackerman
Henry Jacobs
Elias Williams – run
Andrew Miller
John Hopper
Nathan Stevenson
Jacob Craft
Samuel Light
William Ackerman
Uriah Jacobs
John Edward
David Reed
John Lovett
Jeremiah Jones
Bartholomew Travis
Peter Outhouse
Daniel Lounsbury

Total 53

Artificers

Timothy Fielding, <u>late at Fort [blank] a deserter</u>
Samuel Burnell
John Shannon
Joseph Paytan
William Fife
Levi Van Kleck
James Powell – <u>deserter</u>
Richard Prickett
William Kelly
John Grant

Total 10

Thomas White – of Lord Rawdon's

Number of prisoners received agreeable to this list, 441.
Deserters from American Army and sent Adjutant General, 3.
Made their escape, 1.
Left at Sussex, 1
Left at Hackettstown, 1
Delivered Commissary of Prisoners, Philadelphia, 435.

Source: List of privates and non-commissioned officer taken at Stony Point and who were marched through Goshen, 20 July 1779, for Easton. Historical Society of Pennsylvania, Thomas Bradford Papers, Land and Naval Prisoners, p. 24.

III.

The Court-Martial of Lieutenant Colonel Henry Johnson

NOTES ON THE LEGAL ASPECTS
OF THE COURT-MARTIAL OF LT. COL. HENRY JOHNSON

By Page Lockhart

The Deputy Judge Advocate appearing for the Crown in Lt. Col. Johnson's court-martial was Captain Stephen Payne Adye of the Royal Regiment of Artillery. Adye was the author of *A Treatise on Courts-Martial*, first published in 1769. The *Treatise* became the leading authority on the subject and went through eight editions, the last being published in 1810. Adye was not a lawyer by training but, as the *Treatise* illustrates, had studied both historical and current legal sources. His work was intended as a guide to military officers in applying the Articles of War which set forth the various offenses and punishments, as well as regulating such procedural matters as the number of officers needed to form a court-martial, the hours during which it could operate, and so on. Adye highlights the critical role played by the Judge Advocate, "who may be said to be the main spring of a court-martial, for on him the court depends for information concerning the legality as well as regularity of their conduct, and therefore if he errs, all may go wrong."[1] According the Adye, the Judge Advocate must inform the court in points of law, act as clerk (that is, make sure that an accurate record is made), prosecute the case, and assist the prisoner in his defense; therefore, "[i]mpartiality which is necessary to every member of a court-martial, is particularly so to him; he should be remarkably careful not to let one part of his business prejudice him in the conduct of another..."[2] It was, of course, particularly critical that the Judge Advocate be impartial since during this historical period the defendant was not represented by counsel.

[1] *A Treatise on Courts-Martial,* Stephen Payne Adye, R. Aitken, Philadelphia, 1779, p. 44.
[2] *Ibid.*, p. 47.

Martial law and courts-martial were authorized by the "Act for punishing Mutiny and Desertion," a statute enacted during the Restoration when a standing army was created for the first time in England. In his *Treatise*, Adye takes the position that the Act "has only laid down such rules for the proceedings of courts-martial, as were intended to differ from the usual methods in the ordinary courts of law; it is therefore natural to suppose that where the act is silent, it should be understood that the manner of proceeding at courts-martial, be regulated by that of the other established courts of judicature."[3]   Adye then goes on to discuss those aspects of procedure which are not contained in the Articles of War, but which are basic to due process, such as the need to notify the defendant of the place and time of trial and provide him with a copy of the charges against him.

There are some general comments to be made about the purely legal aspect of Lt. Col. Johnson's court-martial. One is that, as opposed to a modern trial transcript, the Johnson court-martial contains only the testimony of the witnesses. Other discussions which, it can be inferred from the context must have taken place, are not included. For example, there is no mention in the transcript of the number and order of witnesses, although this would have had to be discussed in order for the trial to proceed in an orderly way. Another point of interest from a legal perspective is that Adye's presentation resembles a civil-law inquiry more than it does an adversarial prosecution, probably because of his duty to be impartial, as noted above. For instance, he repeatedly asks witnesses about the whereabouts and control of the Gun Boat, and occasionally gets different answers to the same questions. A modern prosecutor would present only the information that supports his case, although a prosecutor would have the obligation to disclose exculpatory evidence to the defense.

---

[3] *Ibid.*, p. 44.

Also, Adye makes an opening statement, but no closing argument, perhaps because this court-martial does not concern a crime, as some did, but only a purely military question: "[h]ow far Lt. Colo. Johnson was culpable in suffering that Post [Stony Point] to be lost." Finally, Adye's training as an artillery officer is apparent, and particularly useful in this case, as he closely questions the artillery officers who appear as witnesses regarding the location and bearing of the various cannon.

Although he makes no closing argument, he shapes the testimony by focusing on two basic questions: what did Lt. Col. Johnson do before the battle to make the post secure against attack, and once the attack had begun, what action did Lt. Col. Johnson take to defend his post? Answering the first question requires a determination of the kind of attack Johnson should reasonably have expected based on the information he had at the time, and an inquiry into the nature of the defenses, including the deployment of what modern military personnel call "assets" (troops, guns, vessels), and the construction of fortifications. Answering the second question necessitates an inquiry into Johnson's activities after the first shots were fired.

It is also interesting that Johnson's court-martial had to be reconstituted after several witnesses had testified, because one of the members of the court became too ill to continue. Adye deals with this by having the witnesses who have already testified read over their testimony, reaffirm it and then respond to any additional questions desired by the court as newly constituted. In his *Treatise*, however, Adye holds a different view:

> *It may not be improper here to remark that although a president and 12 members are sufficient to constitute a legal court, yet it is frequently judged necessary to assemble and swear in more, in order... to guard against accidents arising from sickness or other causes of the*

non attendance of some of them. Courts-martial, ...upon the delinquency of one or more of their members, taken upon themselves to admit new ones during the course of trial and have then proceeded as if they had, from the commencement, taken their seats as such; judging it necessary only to read over the evidence already gone through in ...the new members... presence; but proceedings of courts-martial, thus conducted, can never meet with the approbation or confirmation of His Majesty or those in authority with him.[4]

This quote appears in the 1786 edition, but not in the 1779 edition. The reason for its inclusion in the later version is not known, but it is entirely possible that Adye may have had second thoughts about the procedure in Johnson's court-martial, which took place in 1781.

The verdict rendered by Lt. Col. Johnson's court-martial, after being confirmed by the Commander-in-Chief, was transmitted to the Judge Advocate in London, Sir Charles Gould, who reviewed it to ensure that the findings and sentence were legal. He then submitted the verdict to the King for a second confirmation. Other than this process of review and confirmation, there was no right of appeal.

Page Lockhart is a practicing lawyer with trial experience and an interest in the history and development of legal procedure. Her notes on the transcript of the proceedings that follow are identified by her initials.

---

[4] *A Treatise on Courts-Martial,* Stephen Payne Adye, R. Aitken, Philadelphia, 1786.

LIST OF WITNESSES

THE COURT-MARTIAL
OF LIEUTENANT COLONEL HENRY JOHNSON

Transcript of Trial and Testimony of Witnesses

Annotated with Military Notes and Legal Comments

Spelling and punctuation of the original trial record have been retained;
however, in order to conform to modern usage, the language has been changed
from third person to first person.

At a General Court Martial held at New York in the Province of New York on Tuesday, January the 2nd and continued by Adjournments to [1] by Virtue of a Warrant bearing date the 1st Inst. from His Excellency Sir Henry Clinton, Knight of the most Honourable Order of the Bath, General, and Commander in Chief of all His Majesty's Forces within the Colonies laying on the Atlantic Ocean, from Nova Scotia to West Florida, inclusive etc. etc. etc.

[1] Apparently, the end date of the court-martial was inadvertently left blank. The last day of testimony was February 20, 1781.

MAJOR GENERAL WILLIAM PHILLIPS
PRESIDENT[2]

[2] Section XV, Article II, of the Articles of War stipulated that a general court-martial held in Great Britain or Ireland consist of no fewer than thirteen members, including the President, and applied to British officers serving in America.

Brigr. Genl. John Leland
Brigr. Genl. Samuel Birch
Lt. Col. Jno. Gunning, 82d Regt.
Lt. Col. Robt. Abercrombie, 37th Regt
Lt. Col. John Yorke, 22d Regt.
Major Valentine Gardner, 16th Regt.
Capt. Kenneth Mackenzie, 37th Regt.
Capt. Willm Gore, 33rd Regt.
Capt. Ludovick Colquhoun, 74th Regt.
Capt. James Fraser, 76th Regt.
Capt. George Nugent, 57th Regt.
Capt. George Abson, R. Artillery

Stephen Payne Adye, Esqr. D. Judge Advocate [3]

[3] Stephen Payne Adye, though not a trained lawyer, was a captain of artillery who had served as Deputy Judge Advocate since 1766, and was the author of a *Treatise on Courts-martial*, the first work in English on military justice in nearly a hundred years. (PL)

The President, Members and D. Judge Advocate being duly Sworn, Lieut. Colo. Henry Johnson of His Majesty's 17th Regt of Foot, came Prisoner before the Court, accused of having suffered the Post of Stoney

Point, with the Troops in Garrison, the Artillery and Stores to fall into the Hands of the Enemy, on the Night of the 15th or Morning of the 16th of July 1779, when he (Lt. Colo. Johnson) was Commanding Officer at the said Post. [4]

The D. Judge Advocate open'd the Prosecution on the Part of the Crown[5] with the following Address to the Court, viz.

Gentlemen,

That the Post of Stoney Point, with the Troops in Garrison, Artillery etc. fell into the Hands of the Enemy as stated in the Accusation, is a fact; too well known & authenticated to be denied or controverted by Lt. Colo. Johnson himself - The Matter therefore that calls for your Enquiry and Decision is, How far Lt. Colo. Johnson was culpable in suffering that Post to be lost - In order to investigate this, as fully as possible I shall first produce Witnesses, to speak to the Measures taken by Lt. Col. Johnson, for the Preservation of His Post, previous to the Attack, and secondly, such as are most likely to give you information relative to his Conduct and Endeavours, to repel the Enemy, during the Attack - I shall then close the Prosecution with the usual Reservation of being allowed to animadvert on the Evidence and to reply to any new matter that Lt. Colo.

[4] Lt. Col. Johnson was not accused of violating a specific Article of War, being charged instead with suffering "the Post of Stony Point, with the Troops in Garrison, the Artillery and the Stores, to fall into the Hands of the Enemy. . ."

[5] Deputy Judge Advocate Adye as prosecutor probably prepared for the trial by interviewing as many of the officers concerned as he could, and other soldiers whose testimony seemed necessary. As the testimony develops, it is clear that he has formed some preliminary theories about Lt. Col. Johnson's errors of omission or commission, as he pursues certain issues, such as the location of the Gun Boat. (PL)

Johnson may start in the course of his Defence, which it is absolutely impossible for a Prosecutor to anticipate.

The Court then Adjourn'd till next Morning at 11 o'Clock. [6]

Wednesday, Jany 3d, 1781.

The Court being Met pursuant to Adjournment

<u>Ensign Henry Hamilton</u> Adjutant to the 17th Regt. of Foot, being duly sworn, was examin'd.

Q. What Was the strength of the Garrison at Stoney Point on the Night of the Attack?

A. Four hundred and Seventeen Rank & File, besides Officers & Non Commission'd Officers.

Q. What were the Alarm Posts, [7] and what Orders did Lt. Colo Johnson give in case of an Alarm?

A. On or about the 11th of July, Colo. Johnson, having received Intelligence from Deserters and others, that the Rebels meant to attack Stoney Point, he in consequence thereof Assembled the Captains of Corps then under his Command, namely, Capt. Traille of the R. Artillery, Capt. Tew of the 17th Regt., Capt. Campbell of the 71st Regt. and Capt. Robinson of the Loyal American Regt., and communicated to them the Intelligence he had received, and pointed out

[6] Section XV, Article IX of the Articles of War mandated the hours of the court: between 8 AM and 3 PM, "except in cases which require an immediate example". The transcript of the first day's proceedings does not include the usual discussion that probably occurred, referred to by present-day lawyers as "house-keeping" – that is, establishing the manner in which the trial will proceed (number of witnesses, list of exhibits, and so on). The omission of this process from the record makes it seem that nothing was accomplished on the first day. (PL)

[7] Deputy Judge Advocate Adye sets the scene by calling as his first witness Ensign Hamilton, who, as adjutant or chief administrative officer, would be knowledgeable about orders, numbers of men, and deployment of troops. The alarm posts he describes that were established by Lt. Col. Johnson were apparently based on incomplete or inaccurate information supplied by "Deserters and others"; they resulted in a division of his command which seriously reduced the garrison's ability to defend the fortifications.

139

to them the places they were to occupy with their Men in cases of Alarm; and also mentioned what Numbers were to be furnished by each, as in lying Picquets, which were to be mounted every Evening at Gun firing, which Picquets were Posted agreeable to the Detail No. 1. [8] Four companies of the 17th Regt., and the 2 Comps. of the 71st Grenad. lined the outward Abbatis[9], four Companies of the 17th Regt. and the Detachment of the Loyal Americans which the Witness looked upon as a Company, lined the Upper Works[10], the Artillery to their Guns.

Q. Was the Gun Boat which was usually on the left[11] Flank, at her Station the Night of the Attack?

A. It was not.

Q. Under whose Orders was this Gun Boat supposed to be?

A. As it was so frequently taken away I cannot say under whose Orders she was.

Q. Had not the Gun Boat been taken away several Nights previous to the Attack?

A. Yes, very often. [12]

Q. Was there not a detachment of the Garrison of Stoney Point, posted on board this Gun Boat?

A. There was usually one, but there was none that Night.

Q. Did you not often hear Lt. Colo. Johnson express his dissatisfaction at the Gun Boat

[8] See No. 1 in the appendix.

[9] As indicated earlier in endnote # 7 I in section I, an abatis (or abbatis) is a wall of fallen trees whose sharpened branches are oriented toward the enemy.

[10] The two sets of British fortifications are not always called by the same name. "Upper Works" is sometimes "Inner Works," and "Advanced Works" is sometimes "Lower Works." or "Outer Works."

[11] "Left" and "right" are, of course, relative terms, so it should be remembered that the British defenses were oriented toward the west or landward side of Stony Point and the Americans attacked towards the east or river side– therefore the British left flank is opposite the American right.

[12] This is the first time – but not the last – that Deputy Judge Advocate Adye will raise the issue of the missing Gun Boat, which should have guarded the shallow south flank through which the main American force waded. Its absence deprived the garrison of an important means of defense and may well have altered the outcome of the battle.

being taken away?

A. I have often seen him displeas'd at it.

Q. Do you know whether the Gun Boat was at its station the Night before the Attack?

A. I believe that it was not.

Q. Do you know where the Gun Boat was on the Night of the attack?

A. I do not.

Q. Upon the Gun Boat being taken away, was there any Guard or Picquet posted on the left Flank or any steps taken to secure that Flank?

A. The Boat was so frequently taken away that there was no Alteration made in the usual Guards.

Q. Where was the Vulture Sloop of War on the Night of the Attack? [13]

A. She lay off Stoney Point.

Q. What was her Position?

A. She lay off the Bluff Point.

Q. Where is the right Column of the Enemy supposed to have enter'd?

A. I cannot say.

Q. Supposing them to have enter'd between the first and second Abbatis, had the Gun Boat been at her station, do you think it possible for a Column of Men to have waded thro' the Water, without being heard by those in the Gun Boat? [14]

A. Had the Gun Boat been at her station, and the People in her Vigilant, I do not think it possible for a Column of Men to have waded thro' the water without being heard, notwithstanding the Darkness of the Night.

[13] The *Vulture* was also absent from its post on the night of the battle, possibly because of high winds described by later witnesses. Bluff Point is a small peninsula on the other side of the Hudson, south of Verplanck's Point.

[14] The American right column – 700 men commanded by Col. Christian Febiger - was the main attack force and would probably have lost the vital element of surprise had the gunboat been at its assigned location.

Q. What height had the Enemy to climb after having come on shore between the first and second Abbatis?

A. They had some Rocks to climb, but the height I cannot pretend to say.

Q. What Orders were given to those in the Gun Boat?

A. To keep a good look out and in case of the Enemy approaching to fire or hail the Garrison.

Q. What was the nearest Guard or Picquet to the Gun Boat?

A. There was a Serjeants Picquet without the Second Abbatis, at about 100 Yards distance, which could have heard them hail, & I have often hail'd the Gun Boat from the Body of the Work.

Q.Were there any Beacons prepared, in order to be lighted in case of an Attack on a dark Night, not only to give light to the Garrison itself, but to give Notice to the Vulture and Verplank's Point? [15]

A. I do not know of any.

Q. Was there a Parole and Countersign usually given as also a <u>Mot de Ralliement</u>? [16]

A. I do not know of any being given; Lt. Colo. Johnson would not allow of a Countersign, either the Night of the Attack or on any other. [17]

Q. Was there any Alteration made in the disposition of the Troops after the Garrison was reduced?

A. Yes, there was a total change, four

[15] It seems likely that the adjutant would know these preparations had there been any, but apparently a night attack had not been considered.

[16] "Mot de Ralliement" is French for rallying cry.

[17] The absences of passwords at night indicated Lt. Col. Johnson's concern for security.

companys of the 17th Regt. were moved from the outside of the Outer Abbatis to the upper works, and four more Companys moved up between the two Abbatis'; the 17th Regt., whilst the 63rd & 64th Regts. were at Stoney Point, had lain without the outward Abbatis. [18]

Q. How were the four Companys within the inner abbatis Posted?

A. They were Posted in the Upper works, under the Command of Capt. Clayton.

Q. Did not Colo. Johnson give Orders for the advanced Picquets to withdraw the Moment they were attack'd?

A. I do not remember the Words of the Order, but the purport of it was, that they were to withdraw within the outward Abbatis.

Q. Do you know of any other Intimation Lt. Colo. Johnson received of the Enemy's Intention to attack him, besides that of the 11th of July which he has already spoke of?

A. I understood that there were two Men came in on the Night of the Attack.

Q. Did Colo. Johnson give any Orders in consequence of these Men coming in, and what were those Orders? [19]

A. Yes, he gave out the Order mark'd No. 2.

Q. Do you know what Information those Men gave Lt. Colo. Johnson?

A. From the Order that Lt. Colo. Johnson afterwards gave out, I supposed that the Rebels meant to attack Stoney Point, but I did

[18] The British troops that captured Stony Point from the Americans on May 31, 1779, comprised a temporary garrison of the 63rd and 64th regiments which were replaced by the eight companies of the 17th regiment. Four of these companies were ordered - apparently by Lt Col. Johnson - to defend the Outer Works, thereby reducing the defensive strength in the Upper Works, the main fortification.

[19] Lt. Col. Johnson's order directed the men "to Lay with all their Cloaths on at Night, Except Coats which with their Arms, Ammunition & Accoutrements is to be Carefully put up in such a manner as they can get them upon the Shortest Notice." For the complete text, see #1 in the appendix.

not hear Colo. Johnson speak to these Men.

Q. Had you any reason to suppose from Conversation with Colo. Johnson or from any other Circumstances that that was the Night the Enemy intended to make the Attack?

A. No. [20]

Q. Was the Creek practicable for Infantry at all times of the Tide?

A. Many parts of it were. [21]

Q. Where did the Column of the Enemy that Attacked in Front, come in?

A. I cannot answer that Question with exactness.

Q. Upon the Attack commencing was there any signal made to Verplanks Point?

A. I know of none.

Q. (by the Court) Do you know by whose Orders the Gun Boat was removed, either the Night of the Attack or any Night previous to it?

A. I do not.

Q. Did you act as Fort Major[22] or only as Adjutant to the 17th Regt.?

A. I kept a Detail of all the Infantry in Garrison, but did not interfere with the Artillery.

Q. Do you know whether Lt. Colo. Johnson endeavor'd to find out by whose Orders the Gun Boat was taken away, and whether he remonstrated against it?

A. I do not know.

Q. Was the situation of the Vulture Sloop such as to be of Assistance to the Garrison in

[20.] The previous order notwithstanding, Ensign Hamilton did not anticipate a night attack.

[21.] The creek crossed the peninsula in front of and below the Outer Works. A causeway spanned it at fleche #1.

[22] In British military parlance, a principal fortified place had, among other titles and functions, a Fort Major who was not always a major in actual rank. One of a Fort Major's responsibilities would have included preparing a "Detail" of the garrison. "Interfere" in this context means Ensign Hamilton did not account for the artillery's number or location.

case of an Attack? [23]

A. I cannot judge.

Q. Was the Gun Boat at Her Station at Sunsett on the Evening of the Attack?

A. As nearly as I recollect, she was taken away the day before. [24]

Q. Were those places of the Creek that were practicable at high Water, the best for passing at low Water?

A. I think not.

Q. Did the Picquet of a Serjeant, Corporal, & 15 Men posted on the left of the outward Abbatis, discover the Approach of the Enemy's right Column?

A. I do not know.

Q. Do you know where the first Alarm was given?

A. In front.

Q. Do you think the Number of Men order'd for the defence of the outer Line, were sufficient to have lined the whole outward Abbatis?

A. I do not know, as I am not certain as to the distance; and it depended upon the disposition to be made by the Capt. Commandg there.

Q. Do you know under whose Orders the Capt. of the Vulture was?

A. I do not.

Q. Would not the Gun Boat had it been at its station, have annoyed the Enemy considerably in their March?

A. It would.

[23] Stony Point rises some 150 feet above the Hudson; the *Vulture* would have been firing a short distance above her waterline in the dark towards targets it could not see, and might very well have killed or wounded some of the defenders.

[24] Other questions remain unanswered about the gunboat – where exactly was it on the night of the battle, how often it had been taken away, why had Lt. Col. Johnson not complained about its absence (other than to Ensign Hamilton), and who was in command of the vessel?

Q. Would not the Vulture, had she lain with her Broadside to the part where the right Column of the Enemy enter'd, have prov'd a formidable Battery against them?

A. I can't tell.

Q. Had you ever had an Opportunity of knowing what was the strength of the Enemy who attack'd them?

A. I had heard from some of their own people that they were about 1800. [25]

Q. What was your line of Duty on the Night of the Attack, so as not to be able to say where the Enemy penetrated?

A. At the first Alarm I was in the Upper Works with Lt. Colo. Johnson, who gave Orders to the Men to stand to their Arms, and I think to repair to their Posts; I went first to the lower Works, and then to the Upper Works, to see that the Men were at their Posts; that in endeavouring to return to the lower Works, where Lt. Colo. Johnson then was, I fell into the Hands of a Body of the Enemy on the left flank; that I made my escape from these, but attempting to return to the lower Work by the right flank I fell in with another party of the Enemy, by whom I was made Prisoner.

Q. What length of time intervened between the Alarm, & the Period of your being taken?

A. I think about four or five & twenty Minutes.

Q. Was Lt. Colo. Johnson Commanding Officer, or was he subject to the Order of Lt.

[25]The actual number was approximately 1,150, not including the reserve.

Col. Webster? [26]

A. I do not know. [27]

Q. Whether any part of the Work constructed for the Defence of Stoney Point, were closed on all sides?

A. They were not, I think.

Q. What were the Picquets by day, & by Night. [28]

A. By day, there were two Serjeants, four Corporals, and 36 Privates as advanced Picquets; at Night there were 1 Subaltern, 5 Serjeants, 5 Corporals, 1 Drumr. & 76 Privates as outlying Picquets, and a Capt. and Subaltern of the Day to visit them. Besides these there were 3 Serjts., 3 Corporals, and 33 Privates on Guard by day and Night, and an inlying Picquet of 3 Subalts, 6 Serjts., 6 Corpls., and 86 Privates and they were posted as follows -- At the Howitzer Battery 1 Serjt, 1 Corpl, & 12 Privates, in No.1 (out work) 1 Subn., 1 Serjt. 1 Corpl & 16 Privates; in No. 2 1 Serjt, 1 Corporal, and 12 Men; at one fleche 1 Corpl and 6 Men, at No. 3 (out work) 1 Serjt and 8 Men; at another fleche 1 Sub. 1 Serjt. 1 Corpl. & 16 Men, and at a third fleche the same Number. [29]

Capt. Willm. John Darby of the 17th Regt. of Foot, being duly Sworn, was Examin'd.

Q. Were you not the Captain of the Day when Stoney Point was Attacked and carried by the Enemy?

A. I was.

[26]Lt. Col. James Webster of the 33rd Regiment was Commanding Officer of both posts. At the time of the court-martial, Lt. Col. Webster, described by Sir Henry Clinton as" an officer of great experience and on whom [he] reposed the most implicit confidence," was serving under Cornwallis in the American south. Webster was mortally wounded at the battle of Guilford Courthouse on March 15, 1781, less than a month after the conclusion of the trial.

[27]It seems odd that Ensign Hamilton does not know who was the commanding officer at Stony Point, and has some doubt ("I think") about the works being enclosed.

[28]The number of pickets (42) posted beyond the Outer Works in daytime was increased to 88 at night, inadvertently adding to the difficulty of redeploying these troops in the dark without confusing them with the enemy.

[29]Besides fleches 1,2, and 3 on the Outer Works, there were also 3 infantry fleches, one containing 7 men and two containing 19 men each. The exact location of these fleches (v-shaped fortifications open at the rear) is unknown.

147

Q. Do you know whether the Gun Boat was at her station on the Night of the Attack?

A. It was not.

Q. Did you, as Captain of the Day, report this to Lt. Colo. Johnson?

A. No; It was not under my Directions as Captain of the Day.

Q. Do you know under whose Orders the Gun Boat was?

A. I do not.

Q. Do you know where the Right Column of the Enemy penetrated?

A. I can't pretend to say.

Q. Had you not reason to think it was between the two Abbatis?

A. No; I had reason to think that they did not penetrate there.

Q. What was the usual station of the Gun Boat?

A. On the left flank in Haverstraw Bay; I cannot ascertain the exact spot.

Q. Had the Gun Boat been at her usual station on the Night of the Attack, do you he think it would have been possible for a Column of Troops to have waded thro' the Water, and have landed either between the two Abbatis or within the inner one, without being heard by those in the Gun Boat?

A. I think that they must have heard it, had they been Vigilant. [30]

Q. Supposing right Column of the Enemy to have enter'd, between the two Abbatis; what sort of ground had they to pass over, before

[30]Capt. Darby confirms Ensign Hamilton's testimony about the missing gunboat and that, had it been at its post, it would have heard the American column wading through the water. Also, like Hamilton, he does not know who commands the gunboat. One possible reason for Darby not taking the initiative in reporting the vessel missing is that it was often not there; another is that he may have felt at the time that its absence was not important at night.

they reached the body of the Work?

A, They had a hill to ascend, which was rather rugged.

Q. Supposing them to have landed within the inner Abbatis, what sort of Ground had they to go over?

A. Very rugged and steep ground. [31]

Q. Was the Gun Boat at her Station the Night before the Attack?

A. I believe not -- Nay, I am pretty sure that she was not.

Q. Upon the Gun Boat being taken away, was there any additional Guard or Picquet posted on the left Flank? [32]

A. There was always a Picquet on the left flank but no additional one posted that Night.

Q. Where was that Picquet Posted?

A. Near Haverstraw Bay, on the outside of the Outer Abbatis.

Q. Did the Right Column of the Enemy penetrate without alarming this Picquet?

A. They did not, the Picquet fired.

Q. From whence came the first Alarm of an Enemy approaching?

A. I think from the Officers Picquet at the Bridge, [33] as they fired and his Drum beat to Arms.

Q. Were the Different Barriers shut, the Bridge pulled up, and the Picquet beyond it withdrawn on the Night of the Attack?

A. The different openings in the Abbatis were left open for the Picquets to retire through; the Bridge had been taken up some

[31] This question, of course, was also asked of Ensign Hamilton and results in basically the same answer: the terrain was rocky and steep.

[32] This question was asked of Ensign Hamilton as well, and concerns the picket located outside the Outer Works between fleche #1 and the shoreline on the south flank. Cpl. Simon Davies, assigned to this picket, testified later in the proceedings.

[33] Lt. John Ross of the 71st Regiment commanded this picket – identified variously as the officer's or subaltern's picket – which was located at the bridge outside fleche #3.

days before, and an Abbatis thrown across it, and no Picquet was Posted beyond it.

Q. Did you know of Colo. Johnson having had intelligence of the Enemy's intentions on the Evening of the 15th July?

A. I know that there were two Men come in, whom I sent to Colo. Johnson, but I do not know what intelligence they brought. [34]

Q. Did you ever hear Lt. Col. Johnson express any doubts with respect to the insufficiency of the Post, as to its defences or Garrison?

A. I do not recollect it, he may have talked of the Works wanting enclosing.

Q. Were there any Beacons prepared in order to be lighted, in case of an Attack in the Night, not only to give light to the Garrison itself, but also to give Notice to the Vulture and to Verplanks Point? [35]

A. Not to my knowledge.

Q. Where were you posted during the Attack?

A. At a Rock between the two Abbatis.

Q. Do you recollect the 3 Pder & 12 Pder in the advanced work firing? [36]

A. Yes.

Q. Did the flash of those Guns give you an opportunity of seeing the Enemy?

A. No; I was not near enough to observe them.

The Court Adjourned till Next Morning at 11 O'Clock

[34] What these men conveyed to Lt. Col. Johnson is not a matter of record, but if it was that the Americans intended to attack that night, Capt. Darby, as Captain of the Day, probably would have been so informed.

[35] Deputy Judge Advocate Adye has asked this question before, a pattern he will continue throughout the trial. Getting the same reply to the same question from different witnesses simply confirms the truth of the answer.

[36] The 3 pounder, the only artillery piece not in battery, was located between the works, and the 12 pounder was located in fleche #1 in the Outer Works.

Thursday, January 4, 1781

The Court being Met Pursuant to Adjournt.

Capt. Willm. John Darby was again examined,

Q. Did the Creek make Stoney Point an Island at all or anytime of the tide?

A. I do not know; it was a very small Creek.

Q. Was there a Parole and Countersign, or Mot de Ralliement, given on the Night of the Attack, or any Night previous to it?

A. There was not, [37] I had given Orders to the Picquets that upon any one of them being Attack'd they were all to fall Back to their Alarm Posts.

Q. Did you as Captain of the Day, give any particular Orders to the Subalterns Picquet at the Bridge, & what were those Orders?

A. Only the same Orders as to the other Picquets.

Q. Did the two Abbatis run any Distance into the Water?

A. The outer one on the side of Haverstraw Bay did, but neither of them on the side of Kings Ferry. [38]

Q, (By the Court). What were your reasons to suppose that the Enemy did not enter on the left Flank between the two Abbatis?

A. Because my Post was there, and I did not see the Enemy push up that way.

Q. Could a body of the Enemy have passed under the Bank, between the two Abbatis, without your observing them?

[37] Capt. Darby confirms Ensign Hamilton's testimony that passwords were not allowed at night, part of Lt. Col. Johnson's security precautions.

[38] King's Ferry, an important river crossing which linked New York to the New England states, is on the north side of Stony Point. While Capt. Darby is correct in stating that neither abatis ran into the water at that location, it is also true that the inner abatis ended on top of a precipice and did not extend to the shore below.

A. In the day time they could not, but I did not see them on the Night of the Attack. [39]

Q. Were there any Sentries or Picquets between your Post & the Water to the left?

A. No.

Q. What was the distance between your Post and the Water side to the left?

A. I suppose an hundred Yards or thereabouts.

Q. How long was the Post maintained after the Attack commenced?

A. I suppose from Twenty to five & twenty Minutes. [40]

Q. Did you see Colo. Johnson during the Attack?

A. No, -- but I heard him.

Q. Did he hear Colo. Johnson give any Orders during the Attack & what were those Orders?

A. I first heard him order the Men to fire & afterwards to stop firing as one of the Picquets which was coming in call'd out that they were friends. [41]

Q. Did all the Picquets retire according to Orders upon the Attack commencing?

A. I can't say whether they all retired; I saw the Serjeants Picquet that was Posted between the Subalterns Picquet at the Bridge, & that on the left.

Q. Do you know in what manner the Picquet on the left retired?

A. No, but I suppose they did retire, as he had given Orders for all the Picquets to do so; I

[39] The right column of American Light Infantry, having crossed the shallow water of Haverstraw Bay, ascended the rocky slope and entered the Upper Works near the Howitzer battery, well past Capt. Darby's post.

[40] Capt. Darby's estimate of the battle's duration agrees with that of Ensign Hamilton.

[41] As Ensign Hamilton has previously stated, Lt. Col. Johnson played an active role in defending the Outer Works where he had rushed after the first shots were fired. The fact that some of the pickets identified themselves as "friends" as they entered the abatis openings in the darkness gives a hint of the confusion to come.

myself went out to the center picquet.

Q. In what part of the Works did you hear Lt. Colo. Johnson giving Orders during the Attack?

A. It was near the 3 Pdr between the two Abbatis. [42]

Q. Do you know of Lt. Colo. Johnson having at any time Remonstrated against the Gun Boat being taken away?

A. Not to my knowledge.

Q. Do you know how the other three Companies of the 17th Regt. besides his own, which were intended for the defence of the outward Abbatis were posted?

A. I know what were their Established Alarm Posts, but I cannot say what Orders they may have receiv'd from Colo. Johnson on the Night of the Attack, I saw Capt. Tew at his Alarm Post and spoke to him.

Q. What were the Alarm Posts of those three Companies?

A. Along the line of Abbatis, and on the different Works.

Q. Were any part of the Works on Stoney Point enclosed? [43]

A. Not any.

Q. Do you think that if there had been an enclosed Redoubt in the upper work, & another in the lower one, the Enemy would have succeeded that Night?

A. It was always my opinion that had there been a closed work, and it had been occupied, we might have defended it, but that

[42] According to a *Sketch of the Works at Stoney Point* by Lt. (later Capt.) William Marshall, Acting Engineer of British Defenses, the 3 pounder was located between the two works and between fleches #2 and #3.

[43] The question of whether the works were enclosed will be returned to periodically throughout the court-martial. Capt. Darby states here what must have obvious to many of the defenders, at least in retrospect.

is mere matter of opinion.

Q. Had you receive any particular Orders for the Management of your Company that Night?

A. Not any, except that I met Lt. Carey, who was an Officer of my Company retiring and Mr. Carey told me that he had receiv'd Colo. Johnson's Orders to retire into the Upper work. [44]

Q. Did you understand that it was intended to enclose the works on Stoney Point?

A. I never knew it Officially.

Q. Do you know for what purpose Tools, and Chevaux de frize [45] were applyed for by Lt. Colo. Johnson?

A. I suppose for closing the work; the Chevaux de frize was made use of towards that purpose.

Q. Were the Chevaux de frize made use of on the left Flank, towards Haverstraw Bay, or where?

A. They were made use of on the right flank.

Q. Where were you made prisoner?

A. Within the upper Abbatis, as I was going into the upper work, [46] in consequence of the Order I receiv'd by Lt. Carey.

Capt. Robert Clayton of the 17th Regt. of Foot, being duly Sworn, was examin'd,

Q. Where were you and your Company Posted on the Night of the Attack of Stoney Point?

A. My own Company was Posted at the

[44] Lt. Col. Johnson probably concluded at this point that the Upper Works was the focus of the enemy assault, and that the garrison should concentrate its defense there.

[45] The Chevaux de Frise (or "frize") were brought across the Hudson from Verplanck's Point, where the British occupied a captured American fort. A number of these barriers – see endnote #35 in section I - could be linked together to form a portable wall of spikes, providing a partial, albeit temporary, enclosure on the other side of the Upper Works between the right flank battery and the new battery, unfinished at the time of the battle.

[46] The entrance to the upper work was a steep, narrow opening overlapped by two ends of the inner abatis and located in between the left flank battery and the flagstaff battery.

entrance of the Upper Work, but I, as Eldest Officer[47] commanded that whole line of Defence, in which were posted four Companies of the 17th Regt. and a Detachment of the Loyal American Regiment.

Q. What did the Number of Men, under your Command for the defence of the upper works Amount to?

A. 1 Capt. 5 Subs. 5 Serjts. I believe 10 Drummers and 92 Rank & file[48] -- I do not include the Colonels Guard, the Gun Boat Guard, nor the Detachments on the Howitzer Battery & fleche.

Q. Where did you, as Commanding Officer of the inner line of Defence, take Post, on the Night of the Attack?

A. Upon the Battery on the left hand near Haverstraw Bay, where there were one 24 & one 18 Pdr.

Q. Do you recollect the usual station of the Gun Boat in Haverstraw Bay?

A. Nearly opposite the Corporals Picquet on the left Flank.

Q. Had the Gun Boat been at that station the Night of the Attack, was it possible for a Column of Troops, to have waded thro' the Water and penetrated between the first and second Abbatis without those in the Gun Boat hearing them?

A. I think it was possible from the high Wind and darkness of the Night. [49]

Q. Was it possible for a Column of Troops to

[47] "Eldest officer," as used here, refers to date of commission.

[48] Capt. Clayton calculates the total strength of the garrison in the Upper Works as 113, which is somewhat at variance with the figures of Ensign Hamilton, the Adjutant, who concluded that there were 128 - in either case, not enough men to repel the two American columns with a total of approximately 1000 men.

[49] Here, Capt. Clayton's opinion about the effectiveness of the Gun Boat differs from the views of the two previous witnesses, Ensign Hamilton and Capt. Darby, who felt its presence would have hindered the approach of an enemy force.

have Waded through the Water in Haverstraw Bay, so as to have turned the left flank, without their being heard by those in the Battery where you took Post?

A. I think it was possible the Night of the Attack on Account of the High Wind. [50]

Q. Do you recollect whether the Wind blew towards the shore or from it?

A. I believe from the Shore.

Q. What distance was this Battery where you took Post from the nearest shore of Haverstraw Bay?

A. About seventy or eighty yards.

Q. Were there any Sentries posted between this Battery and the left of the inner Abbatis?

A. Not to my knowledge.

Q. Were the 24 & 18 Pdrs on that Battery fired during the Attack?

A. They were not, from want of Ammunition; there being no Powder there. [51]

Q. Who was the Artillery Officer on that Battery?

A. There was a Person of the Artillery there, but I did not then know him to be an Officer, from the Darkness of the Night, but since I have return'd from Captivity I find it to have been Lt. Roberts.

Q. Supposing the Enemy to have penetrated between the two Abbatis, would not the 24 Pdr have Galled them & probably impeded their March had the Alarm of their Approach been given in time? [52]

A. I do not imagine that it would, as it did

[50] Capt. Clayton is the first witness to comment on the "High Wind," which tended to muffle the sound of advancing troops. In his response to the previous question, he refers not only to the wind but also to the darkness of the night as well.

[51] As later witnesses confirmed, these guns were directed at long-range daytime targets, and had no ammunition close by at night.

[52] Because the two 24 pounders in the Upper Works were confined by embrasures and situated on hills, these guns could neither be turned nor lowered.

156

not point to that part, nor could it be turned that way, or fired upon the lower Abbatis from the steepness of the height on which it stood.

Q. Did you observe the Enemy upon the left Flank before they got to the Spot where you yourself were Posted?

A. I did not observe them until I myself was taken. [53]

Q. Was Lt. Colo. Johnson in the Upper Work at any time during the Attack?

A. He was not; there were some few Shots fired before Colo. Johnson went down to the lower Work; I received my Orders, between the Entrance, and the Howitzer Battery.

Q. What were the Orders you received from Lt. Colo. Johnson during the Attack?

A. After a few Shots being fired in Front I met Lt. Colo. Johnson and walked with him, as far as the Howitzer Battery, during which time I received my Orders. Those Orders were, to send an Officer and about 20 Men to line the Abbatis, between the 24 Pdr on the right flank, & the Water, and I accordingly order'd Lt. Armstrong with the Major's Company, which amounted to nearly that Number to repair thither - Lt. Colo. Johnson further directed me to send a Non-Commissioned Officer and 10 or 12 Men to take Post on the lower fleche, upon the left facing Haverstraw Bay; Capt. Robinson with the rest of His Detachment which, consisted of 13 Men of the Loyal Americans, remained

[53] Capt. Clayton's simple statement gives some indication of how difficult it was to see the Americans in the darkness until they were very near.

in the upper fleche; my Company with 2 others of the 17th Regimt. were posted from the Entrance of the upper work, to the point on the rock near Haverstraw Bay. These 3 Companies together consisted of 38 Men exclusive of Non-Comm'd Officers. [54]

Q. Do you know whether the Officer who Commanded in the upper fleche or the Non-Commissioned Officer in the lower fleche upon the left flank, discover'd the Enemy before they got close to their Posts?

A. I do not.

Q. Do you know whether there were Sentries Advanced from those two Posts?

A. I believe not, as the lower fleche was immediately upon the Rocks.

Q. How long after the firing commenced, did you receive the Orders you have recited, from Lt. Colo. Johnson?

A. About five, six, or seven Minutes.

Q. How long was the Post maintained after the Attack commenced?

A. About half an Hour intervened between the first Shot being fired, and the Garrison falling into the Enemys hands. [55]

Q. Did the Enemy get possession of the upper works without resistance?

A. There was firing on the right and some few Shots on the left; those from the left were fired upon the front.

Q. Where did the Enemy penetrate on the left? [56]

A. I cannot speak from my own knowledge,

[54] When the attack began, as Capt. Clayton tells us, Lt. Col. Johnson went to the Outer Works to rally his men and directed Clayton to defend the right flank in the open area between the right flank battery and the water. Clayton ordered Lt. William Armstrong and one company to that location. Other troops were dispatched to a rail fleche on the left flank near the shallow waters of Haverstraw Bay. The remaining three companies were deployed from the main entrance of the Upper Works along the left flank to "the point on the rock" near Haverstraw Bay.

[55] Like the previous two witnesses, Capt. Clayton estimates that the battle lasted approximately a half hour.

[56] The American right column penetrated the abatis of the Upper Works not far from the Howitzer battery, but having entered at that point, some of the 700 man force might have swept around from behind Capt. Clayton's position.

but they came upon me from the Rear.

Q. Do you recollect where the Vulture Man of War was stationed on the Night of the Attack? [57]

A. Off the Point of the Rock.

Q. Do you know the number of Rebels that seized upon your Post at the upper Works?

A. I do not.

Q. Did you know of the Rebels having Marched a Column upon the left before they seized upon your Post?

A. I did not, but I heard a Clashing of Arms in front, between the upper Abbatis, & the flag Staff, and a Report prevail'd then that all our Men were retiring towards the upper work. [58]

The Court adjourned by direction of the Commander-In-Chief 'till further orders Wednesday, Jany 24th, 1781 [59]

The President and Eleven of the Members met pursuant to Order, but Lt. Colo. Gunning being unable from sickness to attend and Major Stewart of the 63rd Regt. being appointed a Member in his Room, & the Court thereby become a Newly constituted one; the Presidt, Members, and Judge Advocate were Consequently sworn and it was then proposed by the D. Judge Advocate on the Part of the Crown & acceded to by Lt. Colo. Johnson that the testimony of each Witness as given before the Court, as

[57] Like the location of the Gun Boat, the whereabouts of the *Vulture* is a recurring question.

[58] Capt. Clayton may be referring to the defenders' response to the approach of the American left column under the command of Col. Richard Butler.

[59] At the end of testimony on January 4, the Court did not meet for a period of twenty days, possibly because of the illness of Lt. Col. Gunning and the difficulty of finding a suitable replacement. That must remain conjecture, however, since no reason other than "by direction of the Commander-in-Chief" is given for the adjournment.

formerly constituted should be read to them, they being previously sworn, and these several testimonies with any alterations or illustrations the Witnesses themselves might chuse to make, or such additional Questions as the Members and interested Parties chuse to ask & the Witnesses answer, be recorded and looked upon as the Minutes of the Court, as at present constituted. [60]

The President, Members, & D. Judge Advocate being accordingly sworn & taking their places as follows.

Major General William Phillips, President
Brigr. Genl John Leland
Brigr. Genl. Saml. Birch
Lt. Colo Robt. Abercrombie, 37th Regt.
Lt. Colo. Jno. Yorke, 33rd Regt.
Majr. Valentine Gardiner, 16 Regt.
Major Chas. Stewart, 63rd Regt.
Capt. Kenneth Mackenzie, 37th Regt
Capt. Willm. Gore, 33rd Regt.
Capt. Lodovick. Colquhoun, 76th Regt
Capt. James Fraser, 76th Regt.
Capt. George Nugent, 57th Regt
Capt. George Abson, R. Artillery

Stephen Payne Adye Esqr. D. Judge Advocate

Ensn. Henry Hamilton, Adjt. to the 17th Regt. of Foot, being duly sworn, the Evidence, already given by him was read to, & acknowledged by him, and he was then further question'd:
Q. What were the Number of Men appointed

[60] This procedure contradicts what Deputy Judge Advocate Adye himself states in his Treatise on Courts-Martial (see previous discussion under "Notes on Legal Aspects") by requiring only that the witnesses read over their previous testimony, reaffirm it, and respond to any further questions that arise by the court as newly constituted. Lt. Col. Johnson made no objection to this arrangement, no doubt in the interest of time. (PL)

for the Defence of the outward Abbatis and the three Works intended to defend that Abbatis?

A. Three Capts, eleven Subalterns, eight Serjts, eleven Drummers, and an hundred & Eighty seven rank & file, exclusive of the outlying Picquets. [61]

Q. (By Lt. Colo. Johnson) What Numbers were appointed for the defence of the upper works?

A. Two Capts, 5 Subalterns, 11 Serjts, 10 Drummers, and 149 Rank & file.

Ensign Hamilton then laid before the Court the distribution of the Troops at Stoney Point No. 3. [62]

Capt. Clayton, of the 17th Regt. of Foot Attending, he was duly sworn, and his former evidence being read to and acknowledged by him, he was further examined,

Q. Might not the 8 Inch Howitzer have galled the Enemy advancing upon the left flank, had case shot been fired from it?

A. I believe it might.

Q. Was that Howitzer either Order'd to be fired or fired during the Attack?

A. I do not remember that it was fired or Order'd to be fired. [63]

Q. Was it under your Command?

A. I had no directions respecting it.

Q. Who had the immediate direction of the Howitzer Battery?

A. I do not know.

[61] The figures Ensign Hamilton provides – and as the adjutant, he would know - are telling: 220 men have been deployed to defend the Outer Works, but only 177 inside the main fortification. This arrangement would have been effective only if the troops on the Outer Works had had time to withdraw to the Upper Works, a strategy more likely to succeed under daylight conditions than during an unexpected nighttime attack.

[62] See No.3 in the appendix for Ensign Hamilton's chart indicating the distribution of troops.

[63] Capt. Clayton's position during the initial phase of the battle, as he himself said, was in the left flank battery, which was located on a ridge just above the Howitzer battery below, and about ten yards from it. Nonetheless, Captain Clayton did not remember whether the Howitzer was fired and did not know who was in charge of that battery, even though, in the absence of Lt. Col Johnson, Captain Clayton would have had "command over artillery" in those works.

Q. Whether during the time that Lt. Colo. Johnson was in the lower works, and you considered yourself to be Commanding Officer of the upper works, did you look upon yourself to have any Command over the Artillery in those Works?

A. I certainly must, in the Absence of Lt. Colo. Johnson.

Q. Were there any Guns in the upper work made use of during the Attack?

A. I believe that the 12 Pdr at the Flag Staff was fired some few times, but I am not positive. [64]

[64]Capt. Clayton was mistaken on this point: other witnesses testified later in the trial that only the 3 pounder between the Works, and the 12 pounder at fleche # 1 were fired during the battle.

Lt. John Ross of the 71st Regt. of Foot, being duly Sworn deposed: that I was Posted with a Picquet of 30 Men at a Place commonly called the Jaeger Post, on the 15th of July, 1779; that about 12 o'Clock at Night one of the Centries that I had Posted fired a Shot, upon which I sent a Corporal & some Men down, to know what was the cause of it, and they brought up the Man that had fired, who seemed to be of opinion that there was a body of the Enemy in front, the Corporal and the rest of the Men were of the same Opinion; [65] another Sentry posted at the same place then fired a Shot, and I then got the Picquet collected together, and order'd the Drummer to beat to Arms, [66] that a little after, the visiting Officer, Lt. Cumming came up to me and advised me to retire with my Picquet, for that the Enemy were assuredly in motion

[65]Lt. Ross's men, on picket duty by the bridge crossing the stream in front of the Outer Works, were the first to encounter the attacking Americans, either members of Major Murfree's detachment which had been ordered to mount "a perpetual and galling fire" to divert the British defenders, or the American left column under Col. Richard Butler.

[66]In an age when the drum communicated signals between an officer and his men, "to Arms" was a loud, continuous roll.

back and forward, in different places; I told him that I saw No Enemy; the Night being extremely dark and very Windy, [67] made me suppose that what the Men reported to me to have heard, was occasioned by the Wind rustling amongst the Bushes, and that the Orders I had received from the Picquet was to retire only in case of danger; that I had hardly said this, when I heard a Volley of Small Arms from the part of our own Works, where Capt. Tew commanded, and where I was to retire through; upon this I got all the Sentries collected, and retired by the 3 Pdr. [68] and Capt. Tew desired me to fall in with my Company and to line the Abbatis; that I had just got within the Works when I receiv'd the Push of a Bayonet from a Man who knocked me down the Hill with the Butt end of his firelock, imagining that this was one of our own Men, who had done it thro' a mistake I damn'd him for a Scoundrel, whereupon several Shots were immediately fired from behind us and Capt. Tew immediately ordered Lt. Cumming to go up and see, who those were that were firing, as we did not know whether they were Rebels or our own Men, that immediately after, Orders came to Captain Tew (as I understood from Lt. Colo. Johnson) to cease firing and collect all the Men he could, as the Enemy were getting into the upper works, [69] with which order Capt. Tew complied, but could not collect above 15 or 16 Men, and Attempted to get

[67] Lt. Ross is the second witness to mention the high wind, which in this case causes some uncertainty and delay in responding to the attack. Combined with the darkness, it helped the Americans retain the element of surprise.

[68] It must have been unnerving for Lt. Ross and his men to be in front of musket fire directed by other defenders, and probably accounts for his decision to withdraw inside the Outer Works.

[69] Lt. Col. Johnson probably realized at this point that the Upper Works were now the focus of the American assault, and tried to redeploy his troops to that location – a virtually impossible task given the darkness and confusion of the night and the difficulty of distinguishing the British defenders from the Light Infantry, particularly in the area between the Works.

into the upper work by the Main Entry, but of three of the Men who went before, two of them were killed and the third return'd & told me that the Enemy were in that Entry, that upon my going a little Nearer, I could see their Arms and we then wheel'd to our left, and got in by the right of the Work; there a body of the Rebels presented themselves as we went in there and desired us to surrender on which Capt. Tew made use of some hasty expression, which I do not remember, but Captain Tew was immediately fired on and killed, [70] I then went off with one or two Men in expectation of finding some of our own people, but saw none but Rebels; I at last met with Lt. Colo. Johnson, to whom I mentioned his situation, that I was very much hurt and faintish at the time and beg'd to know if I could get into My Marquise, [71] but I understood that all was over at this time, hearing only a Shot now & then.

Q. At what time of Night do you suppose you received the Order from the Captn. of the Picquet, to retire in case of danger?

A. I received the Order when I mounted the Picquet.

Q. Have you ever Mounted that Picquet before the Night of the 15th July?

A. Yes.

Q. Did you, during your being on this Duty on the 15th receive any other Orders than the Ordinary ones given on former Occasions?

A. So far as I can recollect, I did not; my

[70] Capt. Francis Tew of the 17th Regt. was the only officer on either side killed in the battle and was probably the unintended victim of British musketry since the American Light Infantry were under strict orders not to load or fire.

[71] "Marquise" (or "marquee") refers to an officer's tent.

Orders than were, as on former Occasions, to retire by the 3 Pdr. in case of danger. [72]

Q. Was the Bridge thrown over the Marsh in your Front, taken up that Night?

A. It certainly must have been, as I never saw a bridge there.

Q Where was the Sentry who fired the first Shot from your Picquet, posted?

A. On the same side of where the Bridge had been, as my Picquet had been.

Q. Was the Marsh in Front fordable at either high or low Water?

A. I do not know, as I never tried it.

Q. Do you know whether part of the Enemy came over that Marsh?

A. Yes. I know that they did come over this Marsh, and from thence I should suppose it was fordable. [73]

Q. What length of time intervened between the first Shot being fired, by a Sentry of your Picquet, & your going up and finding the Enemy in Possession of the upper work?

A. I think it must have been near an hour, it could not have wanted above ten Minutes of it.

Q. Where were you taken, and how long after meeting Lt. Colo. Johnson?

A. I was taken in the upper work immediately after meeting Lt. Colo. Johnson.

Q. You have said that on meeting Lt. Colo. Johnson, you understood all was over, did this Opinion arise from Lt. Colo. Johnson telling you all was over, or from what you

[72] As noted earlier, the 3 pounder was located between the Works, approximately halfway between fleches #2 and #3.

[73] The marsh through which the two American columns entered extended entirely across the peninsula and was deeper than expected, delaying the American assault for some 20 minutes, according to Gen. Wayne's letter to Washington dated July 17, 1779.

saw and heard yourself?

A. From what I saw and heard myself.

Q. Did you give any Orders for any other Picquet to retire besides your own?

A. No. I had no others under my Command.

Q. Who did it prove to be that knock'd you down the Hill?

A. It proved to be one of the Rebels, who Lieut. Cumming[74] knock'd down with his Sword.

Q. Were the Rebels then in Possession of any part of the outward Abbatis?

A. Not that I knew of; I supposed them to be some Stragglers, who had got in, but I know not how.

Q. How long was it from hearing the Volley fired from behind, when you were with Capt. Tew, to that of your finding that all was over?

A. About Twenty Minutes. [75]

Q. As Capt. Tew collected only 15 or 16 Men, who went up with him, do you know what became of the remaining Men of Capt. Tew's Command?

A. As their Tents were in the Way going up, I suppose they may have straggled into them, but this I Offer as mere Matter of Opinion.

Q. Do you know who brought the Order from Lt. Colo. Johnson to Capt. Tew to go up to the upper work?

A. I do not.

Q. Was there any firing in your going up from the upper Work, previous to Capt. Tew

[74]Lt. Patrick Cumming of the 71st Regt. was later wounded and captured. On the 17th of July he was transported, along with other wounded officers, on board British ships bound for New York.

[75]A few questions earlier, Lt. Ross stated that an hour had elapsed from the beginning of the battle to the capture of the fortifications. This second estimate is more in keeping with the recollection of earlier witnesses.

making use of the hasty expression you have mention'd?

A. No.

The Court Adjourned 'till next Morning at 11 o'Clock

Thursday, January 25th 1781

The Court being Met pursuant to Adjournment

Capt. Willm. John Darby of the 17th Regt. of Foot, being duly sworn and his former evidence read to, & confirm'd by him, he was further examin'd,

Q. Were the Picquets posted at particular fords or easy passages of the Creek, or intended only to have such relation to each other as might naturally assist in case of an Attack?

A. There were six different Picquets posted along the Creek, [76] including a Corporal & 9 Men detached from one of them, across the Creek upon the left, that I imagined were stationed there to give the Alarm, in case of the Enemy approaching & to retire, in consequence of which I gave those Orders.

Q. Did you as Captain of the Day go upon the Alarm, to the Picquets or take Post with your own Company?

A. I first went to the center Picquet [77] & came in with it, and afterwards took Post at the Alarm Post of my Company.

Q. Did you, previous to your going to your

[76] As Ensign Hamilton testified earlier, 88 men and officers were assigned to night picket duty.

[77] This would be Lt. Ross's picket posted by the bridge, though it was located more to the right than to the center.

167

Alarm Post, give any particular Orders to the
Picquets?

A. No, I naturally supposed, that they would
all go to their respective Alarm Posts, I heard
Lt. Colo. Johnson's Voice & suppos'd he
would give his Orders. [78]

Q. What Number of Officers, and Men did
the six Picquets consist of?

A. One Subaltern, five Serjeants, One
Drummer, and Eighty One Rank & File. [79]

Q. What Number of Sentries were Posted
from these Picquets, and were they so Posted,
as to form a Line of Communication, one
with another? [80]

A. According to the best of recollection, there
were Nineteen Sentries during the Night,
forming a Chain from right to left.

Q. What was the length of that Chain of
Sentries?

A. I do not know.

Q. (by Lt. Colo. Johnson) Could a Body of
Men have passed the Chain of Sentries
without being noticed? [81]

A. The Enemy certainly could not have
passed at any time unnoticed.

Q. by the Court. Did you hear any Noise that
gave you reason to suspect, that the Enemy
were coming round upon the left?

A. No.

Q. Did you go to the Howitzer Battery, and
what were your reasons for so doing?

A. I went to the Howitzer Battery, & my
motive for doing so was, that as the Enemy

[78] It seems odd that Captain
Darby would not issue specific
orders to the pickets, rather than
assume ("I naturally supposed")
that they would retire to their
alarm posts.

[79] Capt. Darby's figures match
those given previously by
Ensign Hamilton.

[80] Sentries were detached from
their pickets to which they
would return in the event of
alarm or attack.

[81] This is only the second time in
the trial that Lt. Col. Johnson
asks a question; Capt. Darby's
reply confirms Lt. Col. Johnson
deployment of sentries, with the
implication that any enemy
attack would be readily detected.

did not push up in my Front, I suspected they might Attempt to turn our left Flank, & I was of Opinion that the Howitzer, if fired, might be of considerable use, & not hearing it fire, occasion'd my going there. [82]

Q. Was there any Officer of Artillery at the Howitzer Battery?

A. Not then; there was only one Man there, who called to me that the Enemy were all in the Works, or Words to that purpose, upon which as I was returning to my own Alarm Post, I received an Order by Lt. Carey from Colo. Johnson, to fall back into the upper Works.

Q. Was the Howitzer fired at any time during the Attack?

A. I think that it was not.

Q. (By Lt. Colo. Johnson) Had you not posted a part of the inlying Picquet at the Howitzer Battery as their Alarm Post, & what Number? [83]

A. I had Posted a Non-Commission'd Officer & 10 or 12 Men there.

Capt. Willm. Tiffen of the Royal Artillery, being duly Sworn, deposed: that about 12 o'Clock on the Night of the 15th July, I was alarm'd by my Servant, who informed me that there was some firing in front, I immediately came out of my Tent, when I heard some one calling out for the Artillery; as the greatest part of the Men of the Artillery were encamped upon my right, I ran

[82]The importance of the Howitzer battery, directed as it was toward the shallow water on the south flank, is not lost on Capt. Darby. Even though "the Enemy were all in the Works" it could have impeded their progress.

[83]The second question Lt. Col Johnson asks of Capt. Darby, like the previous one about sentries, underscores the defensive measures that were in place. The men listed by Capt. Darby were infantry soldiers, not the artillerymen assigned to the Howitzer.

immediately to the Tents to see that the Men were turned out, and finding none there, I went immediately to the 18 Pdr. on the left of the upper Work, [84] there I found Lt. Roberts of the Artillery, who perceiving me on the Battery, said, as you are here, if you please, I will go to another Battery -- that in about 8 or 10 Minutes I was taken Prisoner by the Enemy; [85] that previous to this, about two Minutes, some one or more called out, for God's sake don't fire, it is our own Picquet coming in; the firing on the Right & I believe some in the front, continued for five or six Minutes after I was taken.

Q. Did you Command the Artillery on the Night of the Attack of Stoney Point?

A. Yes.

Q. How long had you commanded the Artillery there, previous to the attack?

A. Capt. Traille, whom I relieved, left the Post about 3 o'Clock in the Morning of the 15th July. [86]

Q. What were the Orders and instructions you received from Capt. Traille relative to the distribution of the Artillery Men, and the use of the Guns in Case of the Attack?

A. I received no written Orders from Capt. Traille and the only Verbal ones I can recollect were, as we were walking round the different Batteries, that the Guns were to be loaded every Night, [87] & pointed to certain places, that in case of an Attack a Rocket, or two Rockets, (I do not recollect which) were

[84] Capt. Tiffen is referring to the left flank battery – 18 and 24 pounder guns, each on a separate platform, and confined by embrasures.

[85] Capt. Tiffen's precipitate capture - most likely by the vanguard of the main column - attests to the swift movement of the Americans through the water on the south flank and past or through both abatis.

[86] A little more than twenty -one hours later, the Americans attacked Stony Point.

[87] As he later makes clear, Captain Tiffen did not include the ordnance in the Upper Works when he states that "the guns were to be loaded every Night."

to be fired, and this Signal was left to the care of one McPherson, a Gunner and the two Lieutenants Roberts, and Horndon, alternately visited the Advanced Works every Night that this is all I can recollect, except that Capt. Traille order'd the Conductor[88] to make out a Return of the Stores, which could not be given to me, till the Night of the Attack, as it consisted of four or five Sheets of Paper, and referr'd me to Lt. Roberts who acted as Adjutant for any further Information I might want.

Q. Was the Signal Rocket, or Rockets fired on the Night of the Attack? [89]

A. I do not know that they were.

Q. As Capt. Traille told him that the Guns were every Night Pointed to particular Objects, can you point out those particular Objects?

A. It is an event of so long standing, and I had been so little a time in the Garrison, that I cannot recollect.

Q. Do you recollect to what Object the 8 Inch Howitzer was Pointed?

A. It was Pointed towards the causeway in Haverstraw Bay. [90]

Q. What was the Distance between the Howitzer Battery and Haverstraw Bay?

A. I do not know.

Q. Do you not suppose that had the Howitzer fired in the direction it was pointed that it would have done considerable execution upon a Column of the Enemy marching by

[88]Conductors are artillery assistants who receive and deliver supplies, and are responsible for magazines when assigned to garrison duty.

[89]There is no record of any rocket(s) being fired during the battle.

[90]The captain's memory has apparently failed him here: there was no causeway in Haverstraw Bay.

that Rout?

A. Had they come that way, it certainly would. [91]

Q. Do you know that a Column of the Enemy did come that way?

A. I do not.

Q. Was the Howitzer fired during the Attack?

A. I believe not.

Q. Were you upon the Howitzer Battery during the Attack?

A. No.

Q. Did you receive any Orders from Lt. Colo. Johnson previous to the Attack?

A. No.

Q. Did you see Lt. Colo. Johnson, or receive any Orders from him, or any other Person, during the Attack?

A. No. [92]

Q. How long did the Attack continue?

A. The Attack may have began some time before I was Alarmed; from the Time of my coming out of my Tent to my being taken, it might be about fifteen Minutes.

Q. Upon your going to the 18 Pdr. Battery where you found Lt. Roberts, whom else did you with there?

A. I found One Man of the Artillery and a Drummer; there was a Detachment of Infantry, and as I believe of the 17th Regt.

Q. Were any of the Artillery fired during the Attack, and from whence?

A. The 3 Pdr. and the light 12 Pdr. in No. 1 were fired. [93]

[91] There is no doubt in Captain Tiffen's view, nor in that of any witness thus far, that the Howitzer could have done great damage to the 700 Americans of the main assault column.

[92] Although the night attack was unexpected and quickly launched, it is peculiar that the commanding officer of artillery, newly arrived as he may be, is not consulted or directed by Lt. Col. Johnson "or any other person."

[93] Both guns were in or close to the Outer Works and were the only artillery pieces fired that night, an observation that is corroborated by other witnesses whose testimony follows. The question "were the guns loaded" that Deputy Judge Advocate Adye asks next refers to these two weapons.

Q. Were the Guns loaded on the Night of ye Attack?

A. I believe they were; I did not see them loaded nor did I receive any report of it.

Q. Who Commanded the Artillery on the Howitzer Battery?

A. The distribution of the Men had not been then been given to me, I can only say that it was a Non-Commissioned Officer, as I was told.

Q. Do you know why there was no Powder on the different Batteries, particularly on that where there was an 18 & 24 Pdr. and to which you yourself went on the Night of the Attack? [94]

A. There were no Travelling Magazines, as is usual, and it would have been imprudent to have lodged Powder under Canvas, as the Tents were so near; [95] besides it was not expected that there would be occasion for those particular Guns on a Night Attack; the outer works, as well as the Howitzer Battery, were supplied with such proportion of Ammunition as Capt. Traille thought necessary to be deposited there.

Q. What do you comprehend under the term of Advanced Works?

A. The fleches No. 1, 2, & 3 & the line of the outward Abbatis.

Q. Do you know the reason why the Howitzer was not fired?

A. No.

Q. Whether you, as an Officer of Artillery,

[94] These "different Batteries" were all in the Upper Works and had no ammunition close by.

[95] The reference is to the infantry tents of four companies of the 17th Regiment and a detachment of Loyal Americans.

173

are of Opinion that the 18 & 24 Pdrs. could not have been an Annoyance to the Enemy in a Night Attack?

A. Not knowing the situation of the Enemy, I cannot say; I should suppose not, speaking to this particular Attack, for they might have probably hurt some of our own people in the Advanced Works. [96]

Q. What was the strength of the Detachment of Artillery at Stoney Point?

A. One Capt. two Subaltns. 5 Bombardiers One drummer & 39 Privates, total 48. [97]

Q. What Number of Guns were there at Stoney Point, and their Calibre, and how disposed of?

A. Of Brass - Heavy 12 Pdrs. Two -- Light 12 Pdr one -- Pdr. one, 8 Inch Howitzer one, 10 In. Mortar one, 5 1/2 Inch two, 4 2/5 two – Iron, Heavy 24 Pdrs two, 18 Pdrs. Two, 12 Pdrs. One, Total 15 -- of Brass One Heavy 12 Pdr. was near the Engineers Tent; on the Table of the Hill, intended for a Battery that was not completed, and one Heavy 12 Pdr. in the fleche No. 3, one light 12 Pdr. in the fleche No. 1, one light 3 Pdr. in the Abbatis near No. 2, two 5 1/2 Inch Mortars in No. 2, and one 4 2/5 in No. 3 these last pieces were in the outer Works. One 8 Inch Howitzer on what was called the Howitzer Battery, as also One 4 2/5 Mortar; One 10 In. Mortar on the Table of the Hill, Of Iron, One 12 Pdr. on the Flag Staff Battery, and two 24 Pdrs. and two 18 Pdrs. on the inner work. [98]

[96] Any artillery fired from the Upper Works would certainly have run the risk of producing casualties among British troops on the "Advanced Works" in front.

[97] These numbers are not included in Ensign Hamilton's distribution of troops (see #3 in the appendix) since the Royal Artillery was a separate branch of the service.

[98] Despite the passage of time and Capt. Tiffen's brief tenure of less than a day as artillery commander at Stony Point, his recollection of the number (15) and type of cannon is quite accurate with two minor exceptions: the two 5 1/2 mortars were in fleche #3 instead of #2; and both 4 2/5 mortars (Coehorns) were in #2, rather than one Coehorn being in #3 and the other in the Howitzer battery.

174

Q. (by Lt. Colo. Johnson) What Number of Rounds of Ammunition, were fired from the 12 Pdr. in No. 1 and the 3 Pdr. near No. 2? [99]

A. Lt. Horndon reported to me that he fired away all the ammunition he had, from the 12 Pdr. which consisted of 25 Rounds; the 3 Pdr. fired much more, but I cannot ascertain the Number, I have heard between fifty and Sixty Rounds.

Q. (by the Court) Had you ever such correct Information and Orders, and had you known every Minute Particular of the Post, was there time between the Alarm, and the Post being possessed by the Enemy to have used the Artillery to Effect?

A. I believe not to greater than it was. [100]

Q. Had there been any firing from near you, directed towards the front, previous to your hearing somebody (as you have said) call out don't fire?

A. Yes, I think I heard some upon my left.

Q. Do you know the reason of your being sent to relieve Capt. Traille?

A. I believe it was on Account of his illness.

Q. Do you believe that it was on Account of his illness that Capt. Traille referr'd you to Lt. Roberts for further information relative to the Post etc.?

A. I believe that it was.

The Court Adjourn'd till 10 O'Clock the Next Morning

Friday, Jany 26th 1781

[99] Lt. Col. Johnson's question is interesting in that he inquires about the rate of fire but not its effect.

[100] However, as Captain Tiffen agreed earlier, the Howitzer "would have done considerable execution."

The Court Being Met pursuant to
Adjournment

<u>Lt. Willm. Horndon</u> of the Royal Artillery, [101] being duly Sworn, deposed: that I was the Officer of Artillery on the 15th July, who, in case of Alarm, was to take charge of the Guns in the Works along the Outward Abbatis; that I visited them at the time in the Evening, order'd by Captain Traille, after which I retired to my Tent, but previous to my laying down, gave Orders to the Non-Commissioned Officer of the Guard, to call me in case of Alarm, and in any rate at 1 o'Clock; that as soon as the first Shot was fired, the Non-commissioned Officer called me Accordingly, and I immediately repair'd to the work on the left of the outward line of Defence, where there was a Brass Light 12 Pdr. , [102] that soon after I arrived there I heard a great firing of Musquetry from right to left, & Consequently began firing the 12 Pdr. to a particular Object, to which I was Order'd to point that Gun, in case of an Alarm, that by the light occasioned by the flash of the Gun I could perceive a Body of them coming thro' the Water; upon the left, that I attempted to bring the Gun to bear upon them, but could not effect it, the Embrazure being too confined; that the Number of Men on the Battery where I was, having by stragglers coming in, increased to Twenty Seven, exclusive of my own four of Artillery,

[101] There were three artillery officers at Stony Point: Captain William Tiffen, Lieutenant William Horndon, and Lieutenant John Roberts. Horndon and Roberts alternated command of the guns in the Outer Works and the Upper Works.

[102] Lt. Horndon is describing fleche #1, and the "great firing of Musquetry" to which he refers may have been the diversion created by Major Hardy Murfree's two companies. Horndon's 12 pounder in fleche #1 was mounted in a defensive work high on a rocky outcropping, with the American right column going round it en route to crossing the shallow water on the south flank, and were probably too far away to be illuminated by muzzle flashes, despite the testimony here. The embrasure prevented the gun from being brought to bear on the left, and the musket fire could have had only minimal effect in the dark and at that range.

two of which I had sent for a supply of Ammunition, with them I commenced a fire of Musquetry; I am ignorant of the Number of Rounds they fired, but I heard afterwards that they fired twenty seven Rounds; that soon after we heard a Huzza[103] in the upper Work, from which I conceived that the Enemy were in Possession of those Works, and was the more convinced of it, from the Men I had sent for Ammunition, not returning; that perceiving that the Enemy had white feathers as I then thought, tho' they proved afterwards to be only paper, in their Hats, I order'd a Non-Commissioned Officer of the 17th Regt. with two Grenadiers of the 71st Regt. to turn their Coats and go and examine the Abbatis upon my right, and left, my intention being to escape if possible to the Bluff Point opposite which a British Ship[104] lay to make Signals; that these Men returned & informed me that the Abbatis was lined with Rebel Troops, that I then sent Serjt. Bluer of the 17th Regt. to the upper work who returned with information that the Post was in the hands of the Rebels upon which I went into the upper Work and met a Col. Fleury, [105] who demanded my Sword from me, and I accordingly gave it to him, and upon Colo. Fleury demanding to know where my Men were, I directed him to the 12 Pdr. Battery and he there took them Prisoners.

Q. To what Object was the light 12 Pdr.

[103]The "Huzza" or cheer that Lt. Horndon reports was also heard by other witnesses; that, combined with the failure of his men to return with more ammunition, led him to suspect that all was over. Nonetheless, he conducted reconnaissance to ascertain the situation and determine whether or not the battle was lost.

[104]This would be the *Vulture*.

[105]Lt. Horndon refers to Lt. Col. Francois Teissedre de Fleury, the French volunteer who commanded the vanguard of the American right column.

order'd to be pointed in case of Alarm?

A. To a Causeway, over the Creek.

Q. Did you see any of the Enemy coming along the Causeway to which this 12 Pdr. was pointed?

A. I did not, for this reason I altered the direction of the Gun, and pointed it Alternately to the right, and left, in order to scour the swamp in front. [106]

Q. Do you know by what different passages the Enemy penetrated?

A. I do not.

Q. Did you see a Column of the Enemy, advancing in your front, across the Marsh or Swamp?

A. No.

Q. How long do you imagine the Attack continued, before the Post was Carried?

A. From the time that I heard the first firing to my hearing the Huzza in the upper Work, I suppose it was about five & twenty Minutes.

Q. To what Object was the Howitzer pointed to every Night?

A. I believe it was pointed to throw Shells upon the Sea Shore near the Bay, I never laid it myself, being then a Young Officer, Capt. Traille gave his Orders to Lt. Roberts to regulate these Matters. [107]

Q. What Number of Rounds did you fire from the 12 Pdr. on the Battery where you took Post?

A. I do not know; I fired so many as induced me to send for a fresh supply of Ammunition.

[106] The fire was directed to the area where Major Murfree and his men were firing muskets to divert the British defenders, but was not effective since not a single casualty was sustained by these two companies.

[107] It is curious that Lt. Horndon, seeing that his gun could not be turned to fire on the Light Infantry below and to his left, did not alert the Howitzer - though there may not have been enough time - unless he assumed that it would soon lob shells against the enemy crossing the water.

178

Q. Did you give any Orders to the Men at the 3 Pdr. behind the outward Abbatis? [108]

A. No, they continued to fire and expended all their Ammunition, except One Round, as I imagine, as I found no more in the Box, the next Morning.

Q. What Number of Rounds do you Conjecture the 3 Pdr. fired?

A. Sixty Nine, I supposed, as Seventy was the Number of Rounds usually carried.

Q. Had the Work at which you took Post, on the Night of the Attack been en barbette, [109] or an embrazure been open'd to the left, would the Gun have annoy'd the Enemy you saw in the Water?

A. Very much. [110]

Q. What Guns appeared to you to have been intended for the Defence of the left Flank?

A. I supposed the Howitzer to have been the principal piece intended for that purpose; I apprehend that the 12 Pdr. of the Flag Staff Battery might also have been turned that way; [111] the 18 & 24 Pdrs. were in Embrazures, and seemed intended for distant Objects and could not, I think, have been brought to bear upon the Column of the Enemy I saw coming through the Water.

Q. Was the 3 Pdr. en barbette or in an embrazure?

A. It was in no Work at all, but intended for the defence of the Opening of the Abbatis.

Q. Do you know to what Object the fire of the 3 Pdr. was directed on the Night of the

[108.] The 3 pounder was the only other artillery piece fired during the attack; at fairly close range in the dark, the ammunition used was probably canister. This gun killed or wounded a number of Americans in the forlorn hope of Col. Butler's column and slowed their advance to the Upper Works.

[109] As noted previously in the battle narrative of section I, "en barbette" indicates that a cannon is mounted to fire over a low wall rather than being confined by embrasures.

[110] It would appear to be the result of good planning rather than good luck that the American main assault column – the one with the most troops – proceeded past a battery whose gun could not turn.

[111] The iron 12 pounder gun in the Flag Staff battery, though mounted en barbette, was on the other side of the peninsula, too far away to be useful, as other witnesses later testified.

179

Attack?

A. I do not know the immediate Spot to which the 3 Pdr. was pointed, but I learned afterwards from Lt. Gibbons[112] of the Rebel Army, who commanded the forlorn Hope, that seventeen out of the Twenty, of which his Party consisted, were knock'd down by the first fire from the 3 Pdr.

Q. Who Commanded under you at the 3 Pdr?

A. I do not recollect.

Q. Can you describe the place and situation in which you discover'd a Column of the Enemy wading thro' the Water?

A. I saw some of them without the outward Abbatis, but none within, they were in the Water or upon the Beach.

Q. Where do you imagine the right Column of the Enemy penetrated?

A. I do not know.

Q. Were they within the reach of Case Shot from the Gun where you were?

A. I think they certainly were, & that I should have fired Case Shot at them, could I have brought the 12 Pdr. to bear upon them, but not being able to Effect this, I order'd the Infantry to direct their fire that way.[113]

Q. When you discover'd the Enemy coming upon your left, did you make any Report of it to Lt. Colo. Johnson or any other Officer of the Garrison?

A. I did not, as every person knew what Alarm Post to repair to, in case of an Attack, I did not think it Necessary.

[112]Lt. Horndon refers to Lt. John Gibbon of Pennsylvania. The reader is referred to endnote #43 in section I for background regarding Gibbon's claim of 17 men "knock'd down."

[113] One can almost sense the frustration in Lt. Horndon's response, knowing that, except for the embrasure, the gun would have been able to turn and might have made a difference.

Q. Did you see Lt. Colo. Johnson during the attack?

A. No.

Q. At the time that you discover'd a Column of the Enemy passing through the Water, were any part of the Enemy's Troops in Possession of the Works?

A. I do not know. [114]

Q. Do you know of any Rockets being fired or other Signal made upon the Attack?

A. I do not. [115]

Q. Do you know of any particular Signals being Ordered to be made in case of an Attack?

A. No, if there were any, they was not imparted to me.

Q. Can you describe the Ground between your Post and the Water on the left?

A. I cannot. [116]

Lt. William Fyers of the Corps of Engineers being duly sworn and desired to give his Testimony relative to a Sketch [117] of Stoney Point, sign'd by him which was laid before the Court, deposed: that I called it a Sketch because it was not an actual Survey made by myself; many of the Works & distances were surveyed by Lt. Simpson of the 17th Regt. and I paced several of the distances myself and found them to be very exact; from my own knowledge of the Ground I have reason to think it very accurately laid down in general; that the Works in the upper part of

[114] Though he had heard a Huzza and the men he sent for ammunition ominously did not return, Lt.. Horndon, of course, would have had no direct knowledge of the military situation.

[115] Even if rockets were fired to signal the *Vulture* and the other British garrison at Verplanck's Point less than a mile away, the high winds and the quick pace of the battle would have likely prevented any aid – and the garrison at Verplanck's was at the time the object of a feint, or false attack, by Col. Rufus Putnam.

[116] Why Lt. Horndon could not do so is a mystery since he was there every other night on duty and must have been there occasionally in daylight as well.

[117] As Lt. Fyers later states, he left Stony Point before the battle, but had produced a "Sketch" based on a survey drawn by Lt. Simpson who was there until the fortifications were captured. The sketch was unfortunately not found with the court-martial record.

the Hill, I traced on the Ground myself and sketched the Ground in general on the spot.

Q. What sort of Ground was it on the shore to the left, between the inner Abbatis and the Angle of Haverstraw Bay? [118]

A. According to the best of my recollection it was Rockey as represented in the sketch before the Court.

Q. Was the Shore steep?

A. The Rocks were steep, near the inward Abbatis, but diminish'd Gradually towards the Angle of the Bay, which was very accessible.

Q. Was the Road that was made at Stoney Point for bringing up the Cannon for the Attack of Verplanks Point afterwards broke up? [119]

A. Not whilst I remain'd there.

Q. What state were the Abbatis in, when you left Stoney Point, and when did you leave it?

A. The two Abbatis laid down in the Sketch were laid, and part of them pinn'd down, but I can't say how much when I left it as I recollect I left Stoney Point about the 20th of June.

Q. How far did the two Abbatis run into the Water on the left flank at the time you left Stoney Point?

A. The Outward Abbatis ran to the low Water Mark; I do not recollect whether it was laid at Spring Tide or not. The inner Abattis went no farther than the Precipice, According to the best of my recollection.

[118] The "Angle" is the shallow part of Haverstraw Bay of Stony Point as the peninsula curves along the south shoreline.

[119] Deputy Judge Advocate Adye refers to the British capture of Verplanck's Point on June 1, 1779.

Q. (by Lt. Colo. Johnson) Whether the Ground to which the inner Abbatis extended on the left, which you term a Precipice, was a direct perpendicular or merely a steep, Craggy Ground?

A. It was Steep, Craggy rock, According to the best of my recollection. [120]

Q. Was it accessible to Troops?

A. I cannot say that I particularly explored it there may have been places Accessible in the day, which were not so in the Night, that may have been accessible to a few Men, tho' not to a Column of Armed Men.

Q. What Depth of water was there under this Precipice, where the inner Abbatis ended, at low Water?

A. At low Water there was a Dry Beach. [121]

Q. What depth of Water was there in Haverstraw Bay, from the low Water Mark, & was it fordable?

A. I never sounded it. [122]

Lt. Willm. Horndon of the Royal Artillery was again examin'd

Q. How long had you been at Stoney Point previous to the Attack?

A. I arrived there the 31st of May or 1st of June.

Q. Was it Fordable in the Bay, beyond the extent of the left of the outward Abbatis?

A. It was, I have bathed there, and often seen Men walk a great way farther out than I was myself.

[120] The outward abatis (on the south flank) was waded around by the American right column, and the area between the precipice and the shoreline below on the north was entered by the American left column under Col. Butler, despite the fact that it was "Steep, Craggy rock."

[121] Even though there was a dry beach at low water, the water was still deeper on the north side of the peninsula, and there was no "angle" as there was on the south.

[122] From the perspective of hindsight, Lt. Fyers might have agreed that the water should have been sounded – here and all along the shoreline - as part of the intelligence necessary for an effective defense.

Q. How far have you gone beyond the left of the Abbatis?

A. I have gone I suppose about One hundred. and fifty Yards from the Shore, [123] I do not know how far the Abbatis ran into the water.

Q. Was it high or low Water that you forded beyond the Abbatis?

A. I do not know.

Q. Was it high Water or low Water at the time of the Attack?

A. I can't tell.

Q. Was it a Muddy Bottom or a Sandy or Stoney One?

A. I do not recollect.

The Court Adjourned till next Morning 11 o'Clock

Saturday, Jany 27th 1781

The Court being Met pursuant to Adjournment

Capt. Lawrence Robert Campbell of the Grenadiers of the 71st Regt. of Foot, being duly sworn, deposed: that according to the best of my recollection, the Post of Stoney Point was Attacked between 12 & 1 o'Clock in the Morning of the 16th July; the two Companies of Grenadiers, which I had the Command of, immediately repair'd to the Post which had been previously pointed out by Lt. Colo. Johnson; [124] that they had no sooner taken their Ground, than there commenced a very heavy fire from the

[123] Lt. Horndon's testimony indicates that, by contrast, the south side of Stony Point (by the "angle") is very shallow for a considerable distance.

[124] In the event of an attack or alarm, Capt. Campbell and his men had been ordered to line the outer abatis.

184

Rebels, upon their Party & that of Capt. Tew, who was immediately on my left, [125] which lasted I think from the best of my knowledge, from twenty to thirty Minutes, about the expiration of that time I got Wounded, and was going towards the Hospital [126] on the Rock, in the Upper Works; that when I had nearly Arrived there I saw a Number of the Garrison that had been stationed at that particular part, and having stopt them, I asked the reason of their running from it, and was informed that, that Work had been carried by Storm, & on this intelligence I return'd and was told that there were one or two flat Bottom'd Boats at the Ferry, under a Guard, still remaining, that I repair'd thither and got into one & was carried on board a Transport; [127] that I had not got far from the Shore when I perceived that the Enemy had turned the Cannon in the upper Works, upon the Shipping laying in the River; what happen'd afterwards he cannot say; these are the most Material Circumstances relative to the defence of the Post that came within my knowledge.

Q. Where was the Post Assign'd by Colo. Johnson to the two Companies of Grenadiers under your Command?

A. I was Order'd to line the outward Abbatis with my right to the Rock, impending over King's Ferry, and my left extending to the road near which the 3 Pdr. was posted. [128]

Q. Had the Enemy penetrated the outward

[125] Captain Tew's troops were deployed by fleche #2 in the Outer Works.

[126] The location of what was undoubtedly a field hospital is not precisely known.

[127] Though wounded in both legs as he later testified, Capt. Campbell was nonetheless able to escape - one of only two British officers to avoid capture during the battle.

[128] Capt. Campbell's troops were deployed along the outer abatis from the King's Ferry to approximately half way between fleches #2 and #3.

Abbatis on the right before you were
Wounded and left them?

A. Some parties, I believe, had rushed in but
not any great Body of Men.

Q. Do you know where the Column of the
Enemy Opposed to you, penetrated the
Abbatis?

A. I cannot say, as I do not know that they
did penetrate that way.

Q. Was the heavy fire from the enemy that
you have mentioned, upon the right of the
outward Abbatis where you Commanded?

A. Yes. [129]

Q. Had you ever the Opportunity, either from
what you yourself saw and heard during the
Attack, or from any other Circumstances, of
knowing the disposition in which the Enemy
made the Attack?

A. I can't say I did.

Q. Could you from the flash of the Enemy's
Fire which was opposed to you, judge which
way they were endeavoring to advance?

A. I could judge from their fire that One
Column was advancing towards the right,
where I commanded, and I paid particular
Attention to that Column, but I also imagined
from the firing that I saw to my left that the
Enemy were likewise advancing that way.

Q. Where do you suppose that those small
parties of the Enemy, which you just now
mentioned, to have rushed in, had penetrated,
and what do you suppose were their
Numbers?

[129]Capt. Campbell very probably
refers to shots from British
defenders. See the later
testimony of Cpl. John Ash.

186

A. They had penetrated in different Parts of the outward Abbatis; what I saw did not exceed about three or four in Number.

Q. Where were you at the time of your being Wounded?

A. Near the Work No. 3.

Q. Were you wounded by a Ball or Bayonet?

A. By a Ball. [130]

Q. Did you hear any firing in the upper Work previous to your being Wounded?

A. I heard a Considerable fire to the left, but whether it came from the Upper Works or the left of the lower Abbatis, I cannot say, as it was at a considerable distance.

Q. Can you speak with any precision of the distance from the right to the left of the outward Abba is, or of the distance between the two Abbatis?

A. No, I cannot.

Q. Were the two Companies of Grenadiers under your Command formed one or two Deep?

A. I order'd them to be formed One deep, [131] in order to extend the line, and had several intervals between, occasioned by the length of line they had to occupy, this alludes to the intervals between the fleches [132] for there was an Officer with a Party of from 15 to 20 Men in a temporary fleche made of rails, and a party of a Serjt and 12 or 14 Men on the right, near the Water side & upon a path way, which led from King's Ferry.

Q. Did Lt. Ross with his Picquet join you

[130] Capt. Campbell's wounds were probably from a British musket ball because the American columns attacked with unloaded firearms, and Major Murfree's men were relatively far away from the Outer Works.

[131] The necessity of forming one line rather than two may have indicated that Capt. Campbell lacked sufficient troops to man the Outer Works adequately.

[132] The fleches Capt. Campbell refers to should not be confused with fleches 1, 2 and 3 along the Outer Works. Rail fleches were V-shaped fortifications made of logs and designed for infantry.

187

after retiring?

A. He may have joined the Party, but it being excessively Dark, I did not see him.

Q. What Number of Men did the two Companies under your Command consist of and parade under Arms on the Night of the Attack?

A. According to the best of my knowledge at this distance of time about One hundred.

Q. In what state was the outward Abbatis on the Night of the Attack, and was it pinned down? [133]

A. I think that it was in a very good state, and pinned down; but I cannot speak positively.

Q. What was the Nature of the Ground within Musquet Shot, in front of your Post?

A. Towards the right it was exceedingly Steep and rugged, from the Temporary fleche to No. 3 with Stumps of Trees, [134]Rocks & brushwood which served to cover the Enemy's Approach, till they were nearly close to the Abbatis; from No. 3 to the left flank of my Post it was a more open Country, and a more Gentle slope.

Q. Did you receive any Orders from Lt. Colo. Johnson during the Attack and what were those Orders?

A. I received Orders from Lt. Colo. Johnson previous to the Attack, to be in readiness for it, but none during the Attack.

Q. Did you receive those Orders in the Evening of the Attack, and were those Orders such as induced him to expect the Enemy

[133]The abatis would have been pinned by attaching collars called "staples" around tree branches and trunks and driving them into the ground.

[134]The British had cut down the trees in front of their defenses to create a field of fire, and to deprive the enemy of cover, which would account for the "Stumps" mentioned here.

meant to Attack that Night in particular?

A. Yes. I received the Orders about Nine o'Clock that Evening, the Orders were to be in readiness at a Minutes Warning, in case of an Attack, from which I was induced to think an Attack was intended that Night. [135]

Q. Did you see or hear Lt. Colo. Johnson during the Attack?

A. I saw Lt. Colo. Johnson pretty early in the Attack, to my left, about the Center of the outward Abbatis. I heard him speak and seemingly giving Orders, but could not understand distinctly what he said.

Q. Do you imagine that the small Parties of the Enemy that you have described to have crept in through the outward Abbatis, could have effected it without forcing the single files of your Party?

A. I think they could, I saw several of them Bayoneted Afterwards, who had pushed through and had got too far to retire.

Q. Why do you distinguish the fleche made of rails, upon the right of your Post, from the other three Works of the outward Abbatis, by calling it temporary?

A. My only reason was, that it was made after the other Works were finished, by the particular Order of Lt. Colo. Johnson, and was made of temporary Materials. [136]

Q. Did the Rebels who got through the outward Abbatis, pull up any part of it, previous thereto, in order to accelerate their Entrance?

[135] There is no record of what Lt. Col. Johnson may have said to Capt. Campbell and other officers on the night of July 15th, but his order No. 1 (see appendix) does not specify a night attack, though it does stipulate that the men are to be ready "upon the shortest notice".

[136] This infantry fleche may have been Lt. Col. Johnson's attempt to provide extra defense on the flanks because the Works were open.

189

A. Not to my knowledge.

Q. (By Lt. Col. Johnson) How near were the Enemy to the Abbatis, in your front, on the Night of the Attack, before you could clearly distinguish them?

A. In the difficult part of the Front, which I have already described, I believe, they came very near, without being distinguished. But in the more open part they were discovered at a greater distance, tho' not very far.

Q. Were not the Openings in the Abbatis in your front, closed on the Night of the Attack?

A. I believe that they were. [137]

Q. Were either of the Works that the two Companies under your Command Occupied, closed in?

A. They were not. [138]

Q. What part of your body, or limbs, were you Wounded?

A. I receiv'd two Wounds, one above the Right Knee, & the other thro' the left leg.

Q. Were your Wounds so bad as to disable you from getting off without Assistance?

A. They were not so bad at first, but that with some Assistance I could walk a little.

Lt. William Armstrong of the 17th Regt. of Foot being duly Sworn, deposed: that on the Evening of the 15th July, I heard the Company I commanded receive Orders to lay in their Cloaths & Accoutrements, as two Spies sent out by Lt. Colo. Johnson, had come in and given intelligence that the

[137] In previous testimony, Capt. Darby had stated they were open.

[138] "The Works " referred to are fleche #3 and the temporary infantry fleche ordered by Lt. Col. Johnson.

Enemy was moving down in force towards us; these orders I heard given also to the other Companies, posted in the inner Work, where I, with the Company under my Command, was also Posted; that I did not understand from the intelligence that the Spies brought in that the Enemy meant to make the Attack that Night; [139] but merely that they were moving down towards us with heavy Cannon; that between 11 & 12 o'Clock at Night, I heard one or two Shots fired by the advanced Sentries, which I thought belonged to the Subalterns Picquet, [140] that I immediately went up to the Company, from which I was at that time about thirty Yards distant, & by the time I joined them, I found most of the Men paraded and standing to their Arms in front of their Tents, and after finding all of them present I remained with them for some Minutes in that situation, when Capt. Clayton came to me and gave me Orders to take Post on the Abbatis, on the right of the upper Work; I accordingly went and took Post there; the firing then commenced on the outer line on the left of the 3 Pdr. and as there did not seem any necessity for my remaining in that situation, I took upon myself the liberty of moving the Company, to cover the entry thro' the inner Abbatis, [141] as from the small Number of Men in the inner Work, the whole line could not be manned, and took Post between the Flag Staff and the Battery on the right Flank;

[139] Lt. Armstrong and Capt. Campbell drew opposite conclusions from the same order – Armstrong anticipated a daylight attack, Campbell, a nighttime attack. Only Armstrong expected "heavy cannon".

[140] This was Lt. Ross's picket posted at the bridge in front of fleche #.3.

[141] The "inner Abbatis" consisted of two overlapping segments with the main entrance to the Upper Works in between, and it was here that Lt. Armstrong posted his company.

191

that I then order'd the Men to load, and to stand to the Parapet with Order'd Arms, the firing was then very severe in front, & from the Noise, for it was so dark that I could not distinguish any thing by sight, [142] I had reason to think that there was a large Body of the Enemy then entering the opening in the inner Abbatis, immediately in his Front, and which I had posted myself to defend; that I then ordered the Company to fire, and they accordingly fired five or six Rounds a Man, but hearing Colo. Johnson speaking in front, I halted the fire for fear I should kill our own People whom I supposed to be amongst them; that I could distinguish Colo. Johnson rallying a Party of Men and ordering them to charge the Rebels; soon after one of the Men of the Company who had belonged to the Picquet, and had not been before under his immediate Command, came up to me, and informed me that the Rebels were in our Rear, that just as he had delivered this information two Men, who from having large pieces of White paper in their Hats, [143] I suppos'd them to be Rebels, came up close to me; these I Ordered the Company to Bayonet, & immediately order'd the Company to fire into our rear, Just as I had utter'd these Words I received a Contusion in the head from a Ball, which rendered me insensible, and in that situation I was taken Prisoner.

[142] As confirmed by previous witnesses, the darkness and the confusion would have made it extremely difficult to tell the defenders from the enemy.

[143] These were the "visible badge(s) of distinction" proposed by Washington in his letter to Wayne on July 10, and previously noted in the testimony of Lt. Horndon. Their purpose was to identify the Light Infantry to each other and avoid the confusion the British were now experiencing.

The Court Adjourn'd till Monday Morning
11 o'Clock
Monday, January 29th 1781

The court met pursuant to Adjournment but
were Obliged to Adjourn again on Account
of the Non Attendance of a principal
Witness, [144] who was ill, and accordingly
adjourn'd until next Morning at 11 o'Clock.
Tuesday, January 30th 1781
The Court being Met pursuant to
Adjournment

[144] The "principal Witness" is
unidentified, though it probably
was Lt. Armstrong.

Lt. Armstrong already sworn was again
examined.
Q. Do you know the disposition of the
Enemy on the Night of the Attack, or in how
many Columns they penetrated?
A. In a Conversation I had with some of the
Rebel Officers next Morning after the Night
of the Attack, they told me that they Attack'd
in three Columns. [145]
Q. Can you from your own observation, or
what you afterwards heard, inform the Court
of the Route those three Columns took?
A. The one that came upon our left, which
was consequently the right Column of the
Enemy, came along the Beach where the
Serjeant's Picquet was, and turn'd the left
point of the outward Abbatis, which
projected into the Water, [146] when they
divided into two Parties, as I suppose from
the information I receiv'd; that party which

[145] The "third" column to which
Lt. Armstrong refers must have
been Major Murfree and his two
North Carolina companies which
had been ordered to create a
diversion – but they were not a
column.

[146] Lt. Armstrong is describing
the American right column,
consisting of 700 men, including
General Wayne, and led by Col.
Christian Febiger of Virginia.
As Lt. Armstrong states, they
entered the Upper Works
through the abatis near the
Howitzer battery. Once inside,
they also came up from behind
and through the main entrance
where Armstrong's company
had been posted.

193

enter'd on our left came thro' the inward Abbatis at about ten Yards to the left of the Howitzer Battery; I saw the Opening in the Morning; this Party then came round the left of the Heavy Battery, in the interval between the detachment of Loyal Americans and the 17th Regt., and thereby got in the Rear, I was also informed that some of them had penetrated so far in the rear before they ascended the Hill, that they came up by the Magazine; that other part of this right Column of the Enemy came in at the Opening which I posted myself to cover, the center Column [147] of the Enemy I have reason to think was repulsed and did not get in, untill the upper works were taken possession on; their left Column penetrated the outward Abbatis, by a foot Path, near the fleche made of Rails, or came round the point of it, which as it was low Water at the time they might easily do, [148] but could not afterwards ascend, except by single Men, and that with great difficulty, it being a Precipice; they then ascended the Hill and came through the two Embrazures of the right Hand Battery, and I have reason to think that they were the Party that killed Capt. Tew [149] when he was Order'd by Lt. Colo. Johnson to charge them. Q. Do you speak from your own knowledge when you say, that it was low Water at the time of the Attack?

A. It must have been low Water, as Major Stewart [150] who commanded the Rebel Light

[147] The "center column" again refers to Major Murfree's men whose goal was distraction, not assault.

[148] At least part of the American left column under Col. Butler bypassed the outer abatis by going around its north end near King's Ferry, climbed up the precipice where the inner abatis ended above the water, and came through the right flank battery whose guns had been silent.

[149] It seems more likely that it was Lt. Armstrong's men who fired upon Capt. Tew by mistake since, as noted previously, the Americans attacked with unloaded muskets and fixed bayonets.

[150] Major John Stewart of Maryland led the vanguard of the American left column, not the American right column, and waded around the abatis by King's Ferry, as previously described.

194

Infantry, & led their right Column, came round the point of the Abbatis which projected into Haverstraw Bay and was not wet above the Middle of his Leg.

Q. What was the usual Station of the Gun Boat in Haverstraw Bay? [151]

A. It was in a line with the outward Abbatis, I can't speak Absolutely as to the distance, but at low Water, it must have been at a great distance, at least half a Mile, on Account of the Shallowness of the Water.

Q. Supposing the Gun Boat to have lain as near the point of the Abbatis, as it was possible, on the Night of the Attack, do you think a Column of Troops could have Marched thro' the Water round the point of the Abbatis and not have been heard by those in the Gun Boat?

A. I cannot say whether they could have been heard, but the Gun Boat must have lain at so great a distance as it's fire could not have been of any consequence or impede the March of a Column in the least, indeed, I recollect it blew so hard that Night that I think it was impossible for those in the Boat to have heard them. [152]

Q. How nigh to the point of the Abbatis could the Gun Boat lay at high Water?

A. It might have been made fast to it.

Q. What sort of Ground had the Enemy to pass after coming on shore between the two Abbatis on the left?

A. After turning the Abbatis, there were

[151] The familiar question about the Gun Boat refers to the other side of Haverstraw Bay where the American right column under Col. Febiger approached. The importance of the Gun Boat as a vital means of defense was obviously very apparent to Deputy Judge Advocate Adye.

[152] Lt. Armstrong did not share the view, expressed by others, that the Gun Boat might have been able to stop or disrupt the American attack in that location. Indeed, as he states, the high wind would have made it "impossible" for the Gun Boat to hear them.

195

about ten Yards that were rather difficult of Ascent, [153] but afterwards an easy gradual Ascent up to the inward Abbatis, & after that it was almost a Plain.

Q. Was there any body of Men so Posted, as either to Oppose or give an Alarm of the Approach of an Enemy, between the place you suppose them to have come on shore at, & the inward Abbatis?

A. I know of none but Capt. Darby's Post. [154]

Q. Could not a Column of the Enemy have advanced from the point at which they came on shore to the inward Abbatis, without falling in with, or being Observ'd by Capt. Darby's Post?

A. They might have done it upon the left, but then the party in the Howitzer Battery were ready to receive. [155]

Q. Is it from your own knowledge, that you say it was easy to go round the Right of the outward Abbatis at low Water?

A. Yes, there were several large Stones there, to step upon; I have gone round it at low Water myself.

Q. Can you speak from your own knowledge, what sort of Bottom it was in the fordable part of Haverstraw Bay?

A. I have often been bathing there, it was a Sandy Bottom.

Q. Could Field Pieces with the Boxes taken off be brought round that way?

A. I hardly think it was possible for Field Pieces to be taken round that way.

[153] Another recurring question concerns the terrain which is generally rocky and steep, conditions that might impede troops but certainly did not halt the American advance.

[154] Captain Darby's post was "on the left flank between the two abbatis."

[155] However, Lt. Armstrong has previously testified that the American right column entered the inner abatis "about ten yards to the left of the Howitzer Battery."

Q. Did the Party posted in the Howitzer Battery [156] discover the Column of the Enemy that penetrated the inward Abbatis, within ten Yards of that Battery?

A. I think they must as I could plainly distinguish the fire of the party Posted there.

Q. Do you know whether the Howitzer was fired at the same time?

A. I believe that it was not.

Q. Were there any Troops to your Right during the Attack, after you had moved from your first Position?

A. I do not know that there were.

Q. What length of time intervened between your hearing the first firing and your receiving the Contusion, by which you were render'd insensible?

A. Between Twenty & five & Twenty Minutes.

Q. Do you know of any line of Men being Posted along the inner Abbatis, from the left of the Howitzer Battery to the Shore of the Bay?

A. I do not know of any Men being Posted there. [157]

Q. Where was the Ordinary Alarm Post of the Company which you Commanded?

A. In the front of the Company's Tents, in the rear of the Battery of the left, there to Assemble and wait for Orders.

Q. Have you any reason to imagine that the left hand Column of the Enemy penetrated the outward Abbatis, at the Point describ'd,

[156] According to Ensign Hamilton, there were 14 infantrymen from the 17th Regiment stationed in the Howitzer battery at night.

[157] Capt. Clayton testified earlier that Lt. Col Johnson had directed him to send 10 or 12 men to man the rail fleche "upon the left facing Haverstraw Bay," so there was a small defensive force in that area.

197

previous to the Troops in the lower Works, moving by Lt. Colo. Johnsons Order, in support of the upper Works?

A. I imagine that they did not, from this reason: that Lt. Colo. Johnson had got into the inner Work, and charged those who got in at the two Embrazures, in the right Battery of this upper Work.

Q. Do you suppose that the Rebels who got in thro' these Embrazures, would have been repulsed, [158]had not the left and rear of what is term'd the upper Works been turn'd?

A. I do.

Q. How high was the right hand point of the outward Abbatis from the Water below?

A. There was a Precipice of, I suppose, five or six Yards.

Q. (by Lt. Colo. Johnson) What was the distance between the two Abbatis in the front of the Howitzer Battery?

A. I suppose it to be between Eighty and One Hundred Yards.

Q. Was there any other Works besides the Howitzer Battery to oppose the Enemy between the two Abbatis, if there was, by whose orders were those Works constructed?

A. There was a little Breast work of Rails [159] between the two Abbatis, and another within the inward Abbatis, about ten Yards to the Right of the Howitzer Battery, both of which were erected by Order of Colo. Johnson, and intended to prevent a Column of the Enemy from coming up to our left; and the Parties in

[158]Considering that the attacking force outnumbered the defenders more than two to one and had the dual advantages of surprise and darkness, it seems likely than any repulse would have been only temporary.

[159]These infantry fleches were among those mentioned earlier by Ensign Hamilton and Captain Clayton. According to Ensign Hamilton, two had a complement of 19 men each, and one had 7.

both these Works fired upon the right
Column of the Enemy on the Night of the
Attack. [160]

Q. Could not the Troops, posted in the left
hand fleche (No. 1) of the outward Abbatis as
well as the other Works already mention'd
have Annoyed the Enemy, in moving up
thro' the Interval between the two Abbatis, in
front of the Howitzer Battery?

A. They could.

Q. Whether you had any other Opportunity,
besides what arises from your Observation,
of knowing how long the Action continued?

A. The Morning after, I had a good deal of
Conversation with some of the Rebel
Officers, relative to the Mode of Attack, and
the time it continued; one of them of the
Rank of Major, whose Name I do not
recollect at present, and who that Night
belonged to the reserve of their Army, told
me that he had the Curiosity to take out his
Watch when the first Shot was fired, and
from that time till the Musquetry ceased, it
was exactly thirty-three Minutes. [161]

Lt. William Simpson of the 17th Regt. of
Foot [162] being duly sworn deposed: that the
first I knew of the Attack, was from my
Servant, who came into my Tent about 12
o'Clock at Night, and informed me, that
several Shots were fired at the advanced
Picquet, and that the Drum had beat to Arms,
upon which I immediately repair'd to my

[160] As Lt. Horndon has testified,
his men and the pickets who had
joined them, "commenced a
musketry fire," but with little
effect.

[161] This is the most exact
estimate of the battle's duration
thus far, and comes very close to
the opinion of other witnesses.

[162] As will be stated later in the
court-martial, Lt. Simpson also
served at least occasionally as an
assistant engineer, and Lt. Fyers
has already referred to a survey
that Lt. Simpson had made.

Alarm Post at the outward Abbatis, I belonging at the time to Capt. Tews Company; soon after a firing of Musquetry Commenced between the Rebels from without, & the Party I was with from within, as also from the 3 Pdr. - that about ten Minutes after, I heard a party of about 30 Men in Confusion on my right & rather in my rear, and went up to them, imagining them to be British troops, but found my Mistake by being Wounded and taken Prisoner; that soon after, I was made Prisoner by this Party, Lt. Colo. Johnson came up, having from the extream darkness of the Night, also mistaken them for our own People; [163] that as he came up, he endeavored to give them some Orders, which Orders, as far as I can recollect, were to face the damned Rascals, or Rebels, as they were coming up; upon which they challenged him, by saying Damn ye, who are you, and one or more of them I saw Charge the Colonel with their Bayonets, the Colonel perceiving his Error, narrowly escaped from that Party; that soon after he left them, they seemed to be in a great Confusion and under a smart fire, either from the upper Works, or from a party between the Upper and lower Works, as also from their own Party, on the Outside of the outer Abbatis, as they were firing at the time; that I had not then delivered my Sword to the Officer of this Party, which I believe, was the cause of the Officer striking me with his Fusil, &

[163] As has been noted several times before, confusion played an important role in the battle, a situation that inevitably created misidentification and a weakened defense. Lt. Simpson's account is an ample testament to the chaos produced by the night attack.

knocking me down; I cannot pretend to say, what afterwards became of that Party, as I was left alone, and upon going into the inner Works thro' the inner Abbatis, was made Prisoner with the rest of the Garrison.

Q. Do you know from your own Observation, or any Subsequent information you may have receiv'd in how many Columns the Enemy Attacked?

A. From information of the Rebel Officers, I have reason to believe that General Wayne came in with six or eight hundred men upon our left flank, [164] and forded the Water round the outward Abbatis; whether he came around the left point of the inward Abbatis or forced thro' it, I cannot say, but he might have forded around even the inner Abbatis, [165] as the Gun Boat was not at her Station, but I have reason to think that he came thro' the inner Abbatis, close to the Water side, & thereby gained not only our left flank but our rear; the Enemy likewise made a feint in front, and another real Attack upon the Right, close to the Water side.

Q. How long did the Attack continue from the time you repaired to your Alarm Post, till you were taken Prisoner in the upper Works?

A. I think that it was about twenty five Minutes.

Q. Had the Gun Boat been at her Station on the Night of the Attack, could the Enemy have come thro' the Water on the left Flank undiscovered? [166]

[164]Lt. Simpson refers to the 700 men of the American right column, commanded by Col. Febiger and accompanied by Gen. Wayne.

[165]However, the inner abatis was on much higher ground and the terrain was steep and rocky, as several witnesses have stated.

[166]Yet again, the question of the Gun Boat's location and effectiveness is raised. However, the name of the Gun Boat is never mentioned, nor is its length, or whether it was powered by sail alone or was a row galley. It probably had a relatively shallow draft to be assigned to the south side of Haverstraw Bay, and Ensign Hamilton indicates that 8 men were assigned, both day and night, as Gun Boat guards.

A. I think that it was totally impossible, that even a much less number than really did come that way, could not have approached thro' the Water, without being discovered, by those in the Gun Boat.

Q. Supposing the Gun Boat at her Station, could she have considerably annoyed the Enemy on their March?

A. I think that she could have given them a sufficient Alarm to have enabled us to make such a disposition as would have protected our left flank, tho' she could not have made such resistance as to prevent the Enemy getting forward.

Q. Do you know what Weight of Metal the Gun Boat carried? [167]

A. I do not; I think that there was One Gun only in her.

Q. Did you from your Station in the Center of the lower Abbatis, see the right Column of the Enemy on their March? [168]

A. I did not.

Q. Do you know where the Party of the Enemy, which took you Prisoner, penetrated, or from whence they came?

A. I do not; they seemed to have come from the right, I know that they did not penetrate in my front.

Q. As the Gun Boat was not her Station on the Night of the Attack, was there any change of disposition made?

A. Not that I know of.

Q. Did Lt. Col. Johnson ever, to your

[167]"Weight of Metal" refers to number and size of cannon.

[168]Lt. Simpson was part of Capt. Tew's company which lined the outer abatis from fleche #1 to approximately halfway between fleche #2 and #3.

knowledge, remonstrate against the Gun Boat being taken away?

A. Not that I know of. [169]

Q. Do you know by whose Orders the Gun Boat was removed the Night of the Attack?

A. I do not, neither do I know under whose Orders, the Gun Boat was. [170]

Q. Do you know the Station of the Vulture Sloop of War, on the Night of the Attack? [171]

A. She lay off the East Point of Stoney Point, nearly in the Middle of the River, between that & the Opposite Shore.

Q. Had the Vulture been Stationed as near as she could Lay, with her Broadside towards the fordable part of Haverstraw Bay, could she have Annoyed the Enemy with her Guns?

A. I think she could whilst they were fording the Bay.

Q. Was there any Signal made to the Vulture on the Night of the Attack?

A. None that I knew of, but I have heard from the Commanding Officer that the Vulture was intended as a defence to the right flank of Stoney Point & the Gun Boat for that of the left.

Q. Was there any Row Boat from the Vulture or else where as a Guard Boat in Haverstraw Bay, in General?

A. None that I know of.

Q. In the station of the Vulture, as described by you, how near would her Guns have borne on the right flank of the Upper & Lower Abbatis, or could they have borne upon them

[169]This familiar question, like others about the Gun Boat, underscores another important (though unasked) question: did Lt. Col. Johnson attempt officially to determine why the Gun Boat was absent, and, if not, why not?

[170]Deputy Judge Advocate Adye probably observed the precaution of sequestering witnesses (i.e., not allowing them to hear each other's testimony), but Lt. Simpson's answer suggests that he had already talked to witnesses who had previously testified, since he anticipated Adye's usual next question about the Gun Boat. (PL)

[171]One wonders why Deputy Judge Advocate Adye thought Lt. Simpson could answer this question (or the others that follow) since Simpson was in the middle of the Outer Works during the battle - nowhere near where the *Vulture* either was or should have been.

at all?

A. I do not imagine from the Station of the Vulture, on the Night of the Attack, that she could have been of any Service at all.

Q. Do you not think that the firing from Stoney Point, during the Attack might have been easily heard on board the Vulture & at Verplanks Point?

A. I am very certain that it must have been heard.

The Court Adjourned till next Morning at 11 o'Clock
Wednesday, January 31st 1781
The Court being Met pursuant to Adjournment

Lieut. John Ross, of the 71st Regimt. already sworn, was again examined

Q. After retiring within the outward Abbatis, did you fall in upon the right or left of Capt. Tew's Command? [172]

A. I believe upon his right.

Q. After forming behind the outward Abbatis did you see Captain Campbell?

A. No.

Q. From the Position you took, could you see or form any Judgment how the left Column of the Enemy entered?

A. I could not.

[172] As stated previously, it was Lt. Ross's picket that first encountered the Americans and gave the alarm by having the drummer beat "To Arms."

Lieut. John Roberts of the Royal Artillery being duly sworn, deposed that on or about the 30th of May, I went with a detachment of Artillery to Stoney Point, [173] & remained there till the Post was taken; that I was desired by Captain Traille to Act as Adjutant to that Detachment, & after the Army in General had retired, leaving Garrisons at Verplank's & Stoney Point, I was desired by Capt. Traille to make a distribution of Stores, & a Disposition of Men to each Battery, (except Ammunition being lodged upon the Upper Works) which was accordingly done, & every thing remained in this Situation till the Night of the Attack, that some days after the disposition of the Men to the different Batteries was Settled, those Men who were intended for the defence of the lower Line, were Ordered to remove from the General Encampment of the Detachment of Artillery, which was in the rear of all the Works, and take up their ground in the rear of the Center Advanced Work No.2, that they might be the more ready in case of an Attack; [174] that at about 12 o'Clock on the Night of the Attack, there was an Alarm given, by the Sentries firing, that as there was not above two Shots fired at first, imagining this might arise from the Sentries who might have fired inconsiderately (there having been several false Alarms before) [175] I waited about a Minute & a half at my Tent when I heard several more Shots fired, upon which I put on

[173] Lt. Roberts was the last of the three artillery officers at Stony Point to testify. Unlike Capt. Tiffen who had barely arrived before the battle, Roberts was posted to Stony Point in late May, and he may have been older and more experienced than Lt. Horndon who described himself as "a young officer.". It should also be remembered that Deputy Judge Advocate Adye was a captain of artillery himself and focuses here at considerable length on the defensive component which was intended to be the main deterrent of any enemy assault. Of particular interest is the Howitzer which Roberts may have laid.

[174] This redeployment of men moved them closer to the artillery they would be firing. Their original location was below the Upper Works near the point of the peninsula, too far away to get to their guns quickly.

[175] False alarms, of course, often mask real danger and delay a timely response.

my Coat and Shoes or Boots (I do not remember which), and ran to turn the Men out, and after doing this, I went to Capt. Tiffin, whom I found getting out of his Tent; I being the Officer of the inner Work that Night, than repaired to the Battery on the left flank, where there were an 18 and 24 Poundr. & where I found Capt. Clayton of the 17th Regiment; and a party of Men lining the Parapet; that Capt. Clayton seeing that I belonged to the Artillery (tho' I believe he did not know to be an Officer, from the Manner in which he spoke to me), said, for God's sake, why are not the Artillery here made use of, as the Enemy are in the hollow, [176] and crossing the Water; the hollow I understood Capt. Clayton meant, was the One a little in front, & to the left of the Advanced Abbatis; my Answer was that the Ammunition was not come up, there being no Ammunition kept on these Batteries; and had it been up, these Guns, I imagined, could not have been made use of; [177] that I then left the Platform of that Battery, on which I was, to hasten up the Ammunition, which I met the Men bringing up from the Laboratory Tent, [178] & on going to the other Platform of the same Battery I met Captain Tiffin; some Conversation passed between Capt. Tiffin and myself, in which Captain Tiffin asked if the Ammunition was come up & if the Men were at their Guns, my Answer was that I believed the Ammunition was come up & the

[176]The hollow that Capt. Clayton is referring to is "the angle"- the curve of water and land on the south side of Stony Point, mentioned previously by Lt. Fyers.

[177]The guns " could not have been made use of" because they were on a steep ridge and could not be depressed to fire below.

[178]The "Laboratory Tent" was an area for the preparation of gunpowder and artillery ammunition.

men at the Guns, as I had just left the other Platform, [179] and that as I found him (Capt. Tiffin) there, I would go to some other Battery, to which Capt. Tiffin replyed, that it was very well; that knowing the Guns on this Battery could be of no Service, I went towards the Howitzer Battery, knowing that the Howitzer could be of considerable Service against the Enemy, as they were coming up the Side of the Hill; that when I had got within 10 or 20 Yards of the Howitzer Battery, I found the Enemy were in Possession of it, at least I had great reason to imagine so, from the noise I heard within the Work; for I heard a Man, whom I have since found to be a Bombardier of Artillery, calling out & desiring that they would kill him rather than torture him; [180] I then waited some little time there, not being positive that the Enemy were in Possession of the Work, and during this time several people were passing and repassing, and after being there about a Minute and a half I heard a Body of them Approaching, and I then concluded that the Enemy were in Possession of the Howitzer Battery, and were pushing for the Upper Work, upon which I also bent my Steps that way, but fell over a Log of Wood, and several People fell over me before I recovered myself, and I have great reason to believe that the Enemy entered the upper Work at the Barrier [181] at the same time that I did; a stronger reason I have to think that the

[179] As previously noted, the left flank battery contained an 18 and 24 pounder, each on a separate platform.

[180] This is a puzzling remark because the Americans would not have had time to "torture" a prisoner, presumably to obtain information, when speed and surprise were so vital.

[181] The scene that Lt. Roberts describes occurred at the inner abatis. As Lt. Armstrong had testified previously, the American right column entered the Upper Works about ten yards from the Howitzer battery.

Enemy were in Possession of the Howitzer Battery at the time was, that a Soldier of the Artillery, who was one of those detached for the Howitzer Battery, whom I found in the inner Work, and who must have enter'd the inner Work at the same time with me or just before, told me that the Enemy were in possession of the Howitzer or had drove them from it, and further that they were within the Work; What I understood by the Enemy being within the Work, was that they were within the inner Works; that a very short time afterwards, I heard a Body or Column of Men on the right within the inner Abbatis (as far as I can form a judgment) & I heard the advanced Party of this Column, [182] calling out, <u>throw down Your Arms</u>, that I was then going down the hill in the rear of the Work, where the Encampment of the Artillery was, near where a Block house [183] had stood, when I found the Enemy had not only turned the flank, but had got into the rear; that finding I could not return to the Work again without being in danger of being taken Prisoner, I immediately made for a Spring, which I myself had made, and the passage to which was thro' a very intricate Path, and before I got to the Water side I heard a Huzza [184] on the top of the hill, which convinced me that the Enemy had got Possession, that I then thought of making my Escape, by wading thro' Haverstraw Bay & crossing the Country, imagining it a more certain Way,

[182] Lt. Roberts is probably referring to the vanguard of Col. Butler's column, which had also begun to enter the Upper Works.

[183] This was an American blockhouse, destroyed when the British captured Stony Point on May 31, 1779.

[184] Lt. Horndon, the artillery officer at fleche # 1 on the Outer Works, reported hearing the same "Huzza", and from it drew the same conclusion.

than going to the other side; & I accordingly took the Water and forded a considerable Way, I suppose near a half a Mile, with all my Cloaths on, but hearing the Vulture Sloop of War, which I could not see, from the darkness of the Night, fire a Gun, I undressed myself & Swam [185] to her, reaching her, whilst she was under way, after the Enemy had fired from Stoney Point, either at the Shipping or Verplank's Point.

Q. Were not the Artillery in the different Batteries, ordered to be loaded every Night, and pointed to particular Objects?

A. All except those on the inner Works viz. two 24 Prs. two 18 Prs. an Iron 12 Pr., a 10 Inch Mortar and a Brass heavy 12 Pr. [186]

Q. To what Object was the 8 inch Howitzer pointed in General?

A. At Night it was always depressed so as to point to the Bottom I before described, and to Haverstraw Bay.

Q. Do you know Where the right Column of the Enemy penetrated?

A. From the Noise & the Manner in which (hearing the fire of the British Troops) their fire was directed, I conceive that some of them must have come round the point of the outward Abbatis, and some of them must have pulled away the Outward Abbatis & got thro' it or over it. [187]

Q. Had those Shot been fired from the Howitzer in the direction it was in every Night pointed, would it not have had a very

[185] Lt. Roberts, the second officer to avoid capture - Capt. Campbell of the 71st Regiment, it will be recalled, was the other - had an unusual skill for the 18th century: the ability to swim. For that reason, as well as the dark, windy conditions, most of the garrison did not attempt escape by water.

[186] As Lt. Roberts explained later, these guns were intended for daytime defense only, and were therefore kept unloaded at night.

[187] Lt. Roberts refers here to the American right column which waded through Haverstraw Bay on the south flank.

seasonable effect and galled the Enemy in their Approach that way?

A. I conceive that it would.

Q. Was the Howitzer fired on the Night of the Attack? [188]

A. I do not think that it was.

Q. Was there Ammunition deposited on the Howitzer Battery during the Night?

A. There was.

Q. Do you imagine the Howitzer not being fired was Occasioned by the Rapid Success of the Enemy in taking Possession of the Howitzer Battery or from what other cause did it proceed?

A. I believe it was from the Rapid Movement of the Enemy, [189] & the Men of Artillery who were Attached to that Battery laying so far from it, as they lay the furthest off of any of the Troops in Garrison.

Q. How far did they lay from the Battery, & how long do you think they would have been coming up?

A. I cannot ascertain it, the Night was dark & the way difficult and rugged.

Q. What length of time intervened between your hearing the first Shots fired, when you turned out the Men, & your Attempting to get into the Howitzer Battery, and hearing a Man call to put him to death & not torture, from which you drew the conclusion that the Enemy were in Possession of that Battery?

A. Twelve or thirteen Minutes.

Q. What time intervened between your

[188] Asked almost as often as questions about the gunboat, queries regarding the Howitzer – the other half of the defensive system on the south flank –are just as important and as revealing.

[189] As far as can be determined, the Howitzer - whose strategic value was belied by having its crew "lay the furthest off of any . . in the Garrison" - is not mentioned in any American intelligence report or account, but considering the devastating effect it could have had on the attack, it seems likely that its location was noted for early capture.

210

hearing the first Shot and the Huzza on the Hill, as you were endeavouring to go to the Spring?

A. From fifteen to twenty Minutes.

Q. Did you, as Acting Adjutant of the Artillery, receive any particular Orders on the Evening of the 15th of July, previous to the Attack & what were those Orders? 190

A. I received None.

Q. What were the Orders in general given to the Artillery, relative to their Mode of laying at Night?

A. Those belonging to the outward Works lay in their Cloaths, the others did not; the Man of the Artillery whom I met coming from the Howitzer Battery, was without his Coat, I only knew him by his Voice.

Q. Were the Garrison Orders issued at 9 o'Clock on the Night of the 15th given to the Artillery? 191

A. They never came to me; No particular Order came that Night.

Q. Had you any reason to think that an Attack was intended that Night?

A. I had reason to think there would be an Attack in the Morning[192] and my reason was, that whilst Captain Tew & I were together in the Body of the Work, a little after dark in the Evening of the 15th, some person who was passing said that two Men had come in, who had reported that the Enemy intended to Attack the Post in the Morning, upon which I said, that as I was to be up early in the

[190] Ensign Hamilton, adjutant of the 17th Regiment, testified previously that on July 11, Captain Traille of the artillery and other captains of the corps were assigned alarm posts. Traille, however, was replaced by Captain Tiffen in the early morning of the day before the battle, and Tiffen may not have received this information. He does not mention it in his testimony, and states that he "received no written orders from Capt. Traille."

[191] The Garrison Orders (or After Orders) to which Lt. Roberts refers (see No.1 in the appendix) does not specifically include the artillery.

[192] Three officers thus far have testified about the time they thought the attack would occur: Capt. Campbell of the 71st Regiment indicated that he thought "an attack was intended that night," Lt. Armstrong of the 17th Regiment stated "I did not understand that the enemy meant to attack us that night but were merely moving "moving down towards us with heavy cannon," and Lt. Roberts expected it to begin "in the morning."

211

Morning, I would go early to Bed, and accordingly went to Bed, and heard nothing more of the Matter till the Attack began.

Q In what Manner were the usual Orders of the day or any other Orders conveyed to the Corps of Artillery?

A. The time for giving out the usual Orders of the day, was always notified by beat of Drum, that in case of any after Orders, I always had a Message from the Adjutant of the 17th Regt. upon which I either attended myself at the Adjutant's Tent, or sent the Serjeant Major of the Artillery to the Serjeant Major of the 17th Regt.

Q. Do you know how it happened that no after Orders were Conveyed to the Artillery on the Night of the Attack?

A. I do not.

The Court Adjourned till next Morning at 11 o'Clock

Thursday, Febry 1st 1781

The Court being Met pursuant to Adjournment

Lieut. John Roberts was again Examin'd.

Q. (by the court) Did you, as the Officer of Artillery on the Upper Works for that Night, consider the Howitzer Battery as under your Command?

A. I did not. [193]

Q. Who Commanded the Howitzer on the Night of the Attack?

[193] This organizational detail is significant. Even though the Howitzer was much closer to the Upper Works than the Outer Works, it was not under the command of the artillery Officer of the Upper Works. Though Lt. Roberts "always visited" the Howitzer when he was Officer of the Outer Works, apparently Lt. Horndon did not consider it part of his responsibility, since, in his testimony, he makes no mention that he "visited" the Howitzer on his way to fleche #1 when the battle began.

A. A Non-Commissioned Officer of the
Artillery. The Howitzer was always Visited
by me in the Evening when I was the Officer
of the Outward Works' but the Men attached
to that Battery lay within the inner Work.

Q. How long was it from the time the Enemy
were discovered in the Hollow, you have
Mentioned, to your finding them in
Possession of the Howitzer Battery?

A. It is impossible to Ascertain it with any
Certainty, but I should imagine that it might
be Six, Seven, eight, or Nine Minutes. [194]

Q. How often do you imagine that the
Howitzer could have been fired in this time?

A. As often as there were Minutes of time
intervened, as the Ammunition had been
particularly disposed of on the Battery, so as
to prevent any Mistake happening.

Q. What did the ammunition consist of, fixed
Shells or Case Shot? [195]

A. Both.

Q. Were any Precautions taken by fixing
Stakes, etc., as is usual, in order to bring the
Howitzer to point at the same Object again,
after the Natural & Common Alteration that
might have been occasioned by every Recoil?

A. No; had it been necessary to fire Shells to
150, 200, or 250 Yards, that Precaution, I
suppose, would have been taken, but as the
distance was so short, at which they were to
fire Case Shot, it could not make a difference
of above five or six Yards; it consequently
could not have missed its Object, particularly

[194] The Howitzer – a weapon
which, as indicated in section I
of the present volume, could lob
a 46 pound exploding shell a
range of 1200 yards – had the
capability of firing one shot per
minute at the American Right
Column, whose attempts to gain
cover would have been
considerably slowed by the
water through which they had to
wade.

[195] Either projectile – shell or
case shot (canister) – would have
been devastatingly effective
even in the dark at that range..

213

as the Battery was <u>en Barbette</u> & the Howitzer might have been traversed, without the danger of injuring an Embrazure.

Q. Was there a Slow Match burning upon the Howitzer Battery under the Charge of a Man of the Artillery? [196]

A. If I recollect right there was a Slow Match burning on that Battery; Not under charge of a Man of the Artillery, but under that of a Centinel of the Line.

Q. When you were Officer of the lower Works, was it customary to have a Slow Match burning there?

A. According to the best of my recollection, it was.

Q. What were your reasons for Asserting that the 18 and 24 Prs. on the left flank, could be of no Service on the Night of the Attack?

A. Because they could not be depressed to the Object, on Account of the projection of the brow of the Hill; they were intended for distant Objects, [197] & laid accordingly for a Hill in front; and as it was naturally supposed that they would not be wanted on a Night Attack, the Ammunition for them was not deposited on the Batteries, & the detachments of Artillery Men for these Guns were in a much smaller proportion than for the light Guns, upon the Idea that there would be always time enough to obtain Additionals from the Infantry.

Q. Were the two heavy Guns of the same Nature in the Battery in the front in the right

[196] "Slow Match" is a length of narrow rope soaked in a gunpowder mixture and used to light the priming powder in the vent or touch hole of an artillery piece, which, in turn, ignites the charge in the bore causing the weapon to fire.

[197] Ammunition was not on hand because these line-of-sight guns were useless at night when long range targets were impossible to see.

flank of the Upper Works, in the same Predicament?

A. They were intended for a similar Service; for the opposite Hills. [198]

Q. Could these four Guns be so depressed as to strike the lower Abbatis?

A. They could not, except in one particular Spot, to which one of them might; but to this Spot, which was, I think, on the right of No. 3, [199] it was very inaccessible, and very little probability of an Enemy Attacking there.

Q. Did not the Upper Line in general command the lower line with Musquetry and Artillery?

A. I do not conceive that it did in general, but only in some particular places, and for which reason an intermediate fleche was thrown up in front of the right flank, & other fleches were made of rails for Musquetry where the Upper line could not command it.

Q. Can you describe the Advantages & disadvantages of the Situation of the Iron 12 Pr. mounted en Barbette, at the Flag staff. [200]

A. This Gun was looked upon the Artillery, as intended to be made use of against distant Hills in front being en Barbette, & as it could be of no Service against the Outward Line from a rugged piece of Ground, prevented it bearing upon so near an Object.

Q. Could this gun, being en Barbette, bear on any part of the Ground between the two Abbatis, or of Haverstraw Bay so as to have Annoyed a Column of the Enemy Marching

[198] The right flank battery, like the left, had the same limitations, and both were intended for the same purpose: long-range daytime defense.

[199] Fleche #3 on the Outer Works was in fact one of the areas through which the American left column entered, as a later witness will testify.

[200] The Flag Staff battery, mounting an iron 12 pounder, was situated between the flank batteries in the Upper Works. It could be traversed because it was not confined by an embrasure, but like the other artillery nearby, it could not fire below because of the hill on which it had been placed.

that Way?

A. I don't conceive that this Gun could have been so depressed, as to have borne upon where the right Column of the Enemy came up, unless it had stood on an inclined Platform, but this I only offer as a Matter of Opinion, as I never tryed it; but it appeared to me that it might bear upon the Bay, at about an hundred & fifty Yards distance from the Shore.

Q. Was this Gun fired on the Night of the Attack?

A. I do not think that it was; and I am Confirmed in this Opinion [201] from the following fact; that Bombardier Leslie, who was Attached to this Gun, finding that he could not bring it to bear on the right Column of the Enemy, he left his own Gun & ran down to the Howitzer, in hopes of being of service there and was Wounded and taken Prisoner on this Battery.

Q. Were not the fleches No. 1, 2, & 3 in the outward Abbatis, commanded by the Upper Works?

A. I think that they were, being situated upon high Knolls.

Q. Had the outward Battery at the extremity of the right flank of the Upper Line, any Guns upon it?

A. It was an Unfinished Battery, on which the Brass 12 Pr. was to have been placed, to prevent Boats with Troops coming on the right flank; [202] this Gun on the Night of the

[201] Lt. Roberts concurs with Captain Tiffen, who testified previously. Capt. Tiffen stated that only the 12 pounder on fleche #1 and the 3 pounder deployed between the works fired during the battle. Since Tiffen was at the left flank battery in the Upper Works, he certainly would have heard the boom of the Flag Staff battery a few feet away.

[202] American fortifications at West Point were only twelve miles north and "Boats with Troops" might come down river.

Attack, stood on the right of this Unfinished
Battery, pointed to this Object &
Ammunition provided for it.

Q. From the state of the Upper Works, on the
Night of the Attack, could light Artillery
have been made use of from thence, so as to
have Annoyed the Enemy?

A. I do not conceive that it could.

Q. Do you know of any Consultations held
between Capt. Traille, the Chief Engineer &
Assist. Engineer, previous to Capt. Traille's
departure, relative to the defence of the
place?

A. I do not.

Q. Could the Artillery in the left hand fleche
of the lower Abbatis, called No. 1, fire
towards the left flank, or into Haverstraw
Bay?

A. I do not think that it could, as it was a
Work with an Embrazure, which Embrazure
only admitted the light 12 Pr. there to
traverse, so as to fire up a Ravine in front.

Q. Could an Embrazure have been Opened
on the left of this Work, to have moved the
same Gun to, from the front?

A. It appears to me a very great doubt,
whether there could, from the Narrowness of
the Work, which did not admit of room for
the Gun to recoil that way.

Q. Had this Work been en Barbette, could the
Gun have been made use of [203] to the left
flank?

A. It possibly might in a certain Degree, from

[203]Certainly, the 12 pounder at
fleche #1 would have been more
useful during the attack if it had
been mounted en Barbette.
However, as Lt. Horndon stated
previously, "I supposed the
Howitzer to have been the
principal piece" to guard the
south flank; besides, the
Howitzer could lob exploding
shells whereas a 12 pounder did
not have that capability.

taking the Advantage of the Angle of the
Work.

Q. Had the 17th Regt. their Battn. Guns?

A. No.

Q. Do you know Where Capt. Darby's post
was?

A. I do not. [204]

Q. Do you know of any rising Ground,
between the Work just mentioned in the
lower Abbatis, and the Strait Way to the
Upper Abbatis?

A. Yes. I do remember a rising ground
which was rugged.

Q. Was the Ground such, as to admit of a
Battery for light Artillery being Constructed,
so as to have fired down on the Ground,
between the two Abbatis & Haverstraw Bay?

A. Yes, I think that there might have been
such a Battery erected there.

Q. Had there been such a Battery, would it
not have considerably Annoyed the right
Column of the Enemy, on the Night of the
Attack?

A. Undoubtedly it could. [205]

Q. (by Lt. Colo. Johnson) Did you hear any
firing of Musquetry from the Howitzer
Battery, at the time you were going to it, or
before?

A. Yes, and it was that firing I alluded to in a
former Answer.

Q. How long did that firing continue?

A. It had not more than ceased, before I heard
the Man on the Howitzer Battery, call out,

[204] As Capt. Darby stated
previously, "at a rock between
the two abbatis."

[205] However, if the Howitzer had
fired, the proposed battery
discussed here would have been
unnecessary.

kill me, etc. which assured me that the
Enemy was in the Work, and the firing in the
Upper Works immediately began; I heard
several Persons round me then cry out don't
fire or you will kill our own People.

Q. Do you conceive that any of the Guns in
the inner Work could have been of Service,
had they been fired on the Night of the
Attack?

A. I do not.

Q. In answering the former Question, do you
look upon the Howitzer, as part of the
defence of the lower or upper line of Work?

A. I do not think that it was connected with
either Line. [206]

Q. (By the Court) Do you know why the
Signal was not fired on the Night of the
Attack?

A. The Men of the Guard at the Artillery
Encampment having carried away with them
the Match intended to light the Signal; I upon
discovering this, from the Information of the
Conductor, hailed the Vulture, told them the
Post was Attacked, and that they were not to
expect the Signal.

Q. Do you know Whether the Vulture heard
your hail?

A. I do not. [207]

Q. Do you know What Orders the
Commanding Officer of the Vulture, had for
his Conduct in case of an Attack on
Verplank's or Stoney Point?

A. I do not, but I heard Capt. Sutherland say,

[206] The Howitzer was part of the
inner abatis that ran below and
in front of the Upper Works.

[207] Because of high winds and
the sound of gunfire, it seems
very unlikely that Lt. Roberts
could have been heard.

when I got on Board afterwards, that it was very Unfortunate, that he did not know of the Attack, or he would have immediately sent off the Gun Boat. [208]

The Court adjourned till 11 o'Clock next Morning
Friday February 2d 1781
The Court being Met pursuant to Adjournment

<u>Lieut. John Roberts</u> of the Royal Artillery was again examined.

Q. What was the Signal intended to be made to the Vulture and Verplank's Point?

A. It was a Composition of Mealed Powder & other Materials, made up so as to serve for a light ball. [209]

Q. Do you know Where the Gun Boat lay on the Night of the Attack?

A. I do not know, nor did I inquire, as I was very ill & therefore went immediately to bed, after getting on Board the Vulture. [210]

Q. Can you describe Haverstraw Bay, both with respect to the Depth of Water, at high & low Water, & the Nature of its Bottom, whether Sandy, Muddy or otherwise?

A. At low Water & at half tide, I have gone off the rocks immediately in a line with the Magazine, [211] and have Waded in a Southerly direction for about a Mile, without the Water ever coming higher than my Chin, generally breast high, the Bottom was Soft, but not so

[208] Lt. Roberts' use of the word "immediately" suggests that the Gun Boat was close by, perhaps tied to the *Vulture* because of the high winds.

[209] It will be recalled that Ensign Hamilton and Capt. Darby were asked previously about beacons. Light balls are simply another illuminating device.

[210] The Gun Boat may have been close but not very visible. Lt. Roberts testified earlier that it was so dark that he could not see the *Vulture*, locating her only because she fired a gun.

[211] The magazine was located below the Upper Works, near the point of the peninsula.

much so, as to admit me sinking above my Ankle; my reason for going so far was with an intent to discover the Channel of Water that came out of Haverstraw Creek; I have also Waded Westward towards the Shore, [212] for about an hundred & an hundred and fifty Yards, and found very little difference as to the depth of Water; after that the Water began to grow Shoal by degrees, and by the time I reached between the two Abbatis, the Water was about three feet high at high Water, & the Bottom hard; at low Water the end of the Outward Abbatis was quite bare; at half tide I suppose about a foot and a half deep, and at high Water about three feet; the bottom was so hard that it admitted the Landing of all the Artillery (by the Assistance of the Devil Cart) that were at Stoney Point.

Q. Do you know whether it was high or low Water at the time of the Attack?

A. I conceive that it was very near high Water, [213] because when I made my escape, I went into the Water a very little below where I used to Bathe and could not find the Bottom, & therefore inclined towards the Shore.

Q. What was the Usual Station of the Gun Boat?

A. About an hundred and fifty Yards from the Shore, and much in line with the inward Abbatis.

Q. Supposing the Gun Boat at her Usual Station at the time of the Attack, and it being

[212]Lt. Roberts refers to the area through which the American Right Column launched its attack.

[213]Nonetheless, high water would still have been only about three feet deep between the two abatis, as Lt. Roberts has just testified.

221

very near high Water, as you have given reasons to suppose it was, could this Boat have perceived the Approach of a Column of the Enemy, and afterwards have taken such a position as to have Annoyed them?

A. I think that those in the Boat, must have heard the Enemy, and that the piece of Ordnance in that Boat must have been of much more Service than any in the Work, as it could have taken the Enemy in flank; and even at low Water the station of the Gun Boat was such, that Case Shot must have taken place; [214] the Usual Station of the Gun Boat was, as I have described, but I have sometimes known her moved further out, so as to be a float, in Order as I understood, to prevent the Enemy wading to, and surprizing her, but never so far as to be out of the reach of Case Shot.

Q. Do you conceive, merely as it relates to the Water, that a Body of the Enemy's troops could have crossed the Bay, between the two Abbatis at any time of the Tide?

A. I conceive that they could have crossed from the Bottom of the Bay, to between the two Abbatis, at any time of the Tide. [215]

Q. Does it come within your knowledge, or information, to know what the Object of the Vulture's Station was, and Whether she had Orders to move off the East Point of Stoney Point, to where the most seeming danger was, in case of Attack?

A. I do not.

[214] Roberts' answer to the predictable question about the effect of the Gun Boat adds much to the growing body of opinion that it was a crucial element of defense. Even if it were far from shore at low tide, its cannon, firing "Case Shot", could have "taken the enemy in flank," thereby countering the view of Lt. Armstrong of the 17th Regiment who had testified "the Gun Boat must have lain at so great a distance as its fire could not have been of any consequence." Roberts, an artillery officer, thought differently.

[215] Here, Lt. Roberts clarified what he stated earlier: the water on the south flank was not deep enough to prevent enemy troops from wading through it. That is why the Gun Boat and the Howitzer (or either one) were the only defense that might have halted the attack by decimating the 700 men of American Right Column. Further, that shallow part of Haverstraw Bay was only place in the battle area where there were no British troops mingling with the enemy, thereby eliminating "friendly fire" and reducing the confusion that was so apparent everywhere else.

222

Q. Were there any light balls prepared and ordered to be fired in case of an Attack, to gain a View of the Enemy's Movements?

A. I do not recollect that we had any such. [216]

Q. Was the Station of the Vulture such, as to be of any Service on the Night of the Attack?

A. I do not conceive that it could be of any Service.

Lieut. William Nairne of the 71st Regimt. of Foot being duly Sworn, deposed: that on the Night of the Attack of Stoney Point, I had the inlying Picquet [217] of the two Companies of the 71st Grenadiers; the other two Officers to the Company to which I belonged, were also on Duty that Night; that some time after Dusk, I received a Verbal Order, by a Serjeant of the Company, who told me that it was the Commanding Officer's Orders, that the Men should lay in their Cloaths and Accoutrements; that a little before 12 o'Clock the Picquets fired and as Lieut. Cumming, who was then in the Tent with me & Orderly Officer under Captain Darby, was going to Visit the Picquets, [218] I desired him to tell the Company to stand to their Arms and immediately followed him, & found the Men getting under Arms; that I detached a Serjeant and Sixteen Men of the inlying Picquet of the 71st Regimt. (Grenadiers) to a fleche of Rails [219] on my right near the Water side, on the road leading to the Ferry; Another Serjeant and 8 Men of that Picquet

[216] These devices would have improved visibility, but would have otherwise made little difference to the outcome, in part because of the rapid pace at which the Americans advanced.

[217] The inlying picket of the 71st Regiment was located near fleche #3.

[218] See No. 2 in the appendix for Ensign Hamilton's Detail of Picquets and Guards.

[219] This infantry "fleche of Rails" was one of three mentioned earlier by Ensign Hamilton and contained 1 corporal and 6 men.

joined the Company, whose Station was upon the left of the 12 Pr. in the right hand Work [220] of the outward Abbatis, Where I also took Post, being the only Officer then with the Company; that Captain Campbell who Commanded the two Companies of Grenadiers of the 71st Regt. called out to me to keep my Men low, upon which I ordered them to kneel; that in about 8 or ten Minutes afterwards, a firing began from the four Companies of the 17th Regt. which were on my left, and the two Companies of Grenadiers, [221] and this firing continued for some time, when I heard Lt. Colo. Johnson or Capt. Tew call out to stop firing, as some of our own people were coming in; at this time I believe the Picquets came in; I could not see them, but I heard people coming in, which I supposed to be the Picquets; that firing began again from these Six Companies, with some intervals, and I heard a Scattering fire from the inner Work, but not so heavy a One as that from the outer Abbatis; that I soon after heard several Voices in the inner Work, which I supposed to be Rebels, call out the Fort is our own; [222] at the same they still kept up a Scattering fire from the lower Abbatis, the Enemy not having gained any Ground there; that about this time the left hand and part of the right hand Grenadier Company, were taken into the Upper Work by Captain Tew, and very soon after a large Party of the Rebels came upon our left flank,

[220] Lt. Nairne is referring to fleche #3.

[221] These men were at their alarm posts, established by Col. Johnson on July 11, and were lining the outward abatis.

[222] "The Fort's Our Own" was the American watchword as given by General Wayne in his order of battle.

and charging our Bayonets called to us to surrender; that I had then about 9 or ten Men with me and I was made Prisoner with those Men, and those of the Artillery, who were with the Brass 12 Pr. in No. 3; [223] I cannot say whether the Party of Rebels, by which I was taken, came in by the left, or by the fleche upon the right; that I was kept there till about an hour before day break, when I was carried into Lt. Colo. Johnson's Marquise; that sometime after I was taken prisoner I heard scattering fire from the inner Work, which I supposed was upon the British Troops, who were endeavoring to drive the Rebels out of that Work. I further observed that the Road that led to the ferry would not admit of above One Man or two coming abreast & therefore I think it probable that the Enemy came around the Abbatis; [224] but I cannot say with any Certainty that any of them came this Way.

Q. Did the Serjeant and 16 Men whom you detached to the rail fleche retire by Order, or were they forced?

A. I neither heard of an Order for them to retire, nor do I know of their being forced; nor ever see or hear any thing of them till next Morning.

Q. To what Object was the fire of the Company you Commanded, directed; Whether towards the front or Obliquely to either of the flanks?

A. It was directed towards the hollow Way in

[223] There were also two Royal mortars at fleche #3, but none of the artillery at that location – including the brass 12 pounder mentioned here by Lt. Nairne – fired during the battle. Had they done so, the effect in the dark would have been minimal and might have injured or killed the returning pickets.

[224] Lt. Armstrong voiced the same opinion in earlier testimony after conversing with Major John Stewart, the American officer who led the vanguard of Col. Butler's column.

the front. [225]

Q. Did you see a Column of the Enemy Approaching that way?

A. I could not see any of them, except by the flash of the 3 Pr. which also fired at the time; but by this I perceived some Men coming on in my front, but whether they were a Column of the Enemy or only the advanced Party, I cannot say.

Q. What Men were posted between the fleche No. 3 where the 12 Pr. was and that made of rails, where the Serjeant and 16 Men were?

A. None at all; the ground I think, would not have admitted of it, it being quite a Precipice. [226]

Q. Did you see any Scattered Parties of Rebels, within the outward Abbatis, during the Attack?

A. I did; there were a few of them got possession of my Tent, and fired upon us from thence, & very shortly after, charged us with Bayonets, with a much larger Party than when they fired, having as I imagine, been reinforced, and made me Prisoner, as I have before described.

Q. Did you ever hear from the Rebels themselves, where the Party who took you Prisoner, got in?

A. I never did.

Q. Was there any Officer Commanding to your right?

A. There was not.

[225] The "hollow Way" mentioned here refers to a ravine in front of fleche #3.

[226] The precipice referred to here is the base of fleche #3 and should not be confused with the use of the same word in other testimony that refers to another location altogether - i.e. the steep area at the north end of the inner abatis, through which Lt. Armstrong testified earlier some of the Americans of the left column entered the Upper Works.

Corporal Simon Davies of the 17th Regimt. of Foot, being duly Sworn, deposed: that a Serjeant, corporal and 15 Men were a Picquet detached to the left; [227] that I with 9 Men were advanced an hundred Yards beyond the Creek upon the rising Ground, close to the Water side, and the Serjeant with the remaining 6 Men was left about as far on the other side of the Creek so that they were about two hundred Yards asunder, that Capt. Darby as Captain of the day, gave me my Orders soon after Gun firing, and amongst other Orders, directed me to keep my Men awake, and in case I could not maintain my Post, to retire to the Serjeant, who was left in the rear to cover me; that the two Advanced Sentries from the part of Picquet with which I was detached had small rail fleches to cover them; that the first Alarm I heard was, between 12 & 1 o'Clock as I imagine; we used to relieve our Sentries in general by the Ship Bells, but it blew so hard that Night, [228] that I could not hear them, the Alarm was from the advanced Sentry or Sentries of the Officer's Picquet [229] on my right firing; that I immediately ordered the Men of my Picquet to stand to their Arms, but hearing no more firing, then Ordered my Men to sit down on their Packs, but not to go to Sleep; but I had Scarcely sat down, when I heard another Sentry from the Officer's Picquet Challenge twice, then fire, upon which I ordered the Men again to stand to their Arms, and the

[227] Cpl. Davies was part of the picket located between the water on the south flank and fleche #1.

[228] Cpl. Davies is the third witness so far to comment on the high winds on the night of the battle. They did not abate until July 18, three days later.

[229] As previously indicated, the officer's picket was commanded that night by Lt. John Ross of the 71st Regiment.

Drum of the Officer's Picquet beat to Arms, and the two advanced Sentries of my Post both fired; that I took two Men with me, with an intention of going to my advanced Sentries, and enquiring the Cause of their firing, but about half way thither, I met them both retiring as fast as they could, and upon my asking them the reason of their retiring, they said that there was a large Body of the Enemy advancing; that I knelt down the better to hear and see them myself, and perceiving that there was a large body of them advancing, [230]I brought in my Sentries and returned with my whole Picquet to the Serjeant's Post, as I had been Order'd to do, but found the Serjeant gone; I at the same time heard a Noise in the Water on my left, which appeared to me to have been Occasioned by a large body of Men wading through it and from thence concluded that a Column of the Enemy were also coming that way; that upon finding the Serjeant gone, I retired into the Work, [231] where Lt. Horndon of the Artillery was, with a Short 12 Pr. that on passing the outward Abbatis in retiring, I found a Corporal and three Men left to close the Opening of it, [232] as soon as I with my Picquet should come in; & the Corporal and three Men after doing this, immediately joined me, and the Whole together formed in the Work and along the Abbatis, some to the right and some to the left of this Work, I being on the left myself, some directing their

[230]Despite the high winds, Cpl. Davies had heard the 700 men of the American right column.

[231]Cpl. Davies is referring to fleche #1.

[232]There were several openings – the exact number is not known - in the outer abatis for the passage of sentries, as stated earlier by Capt. William Darby. Cpl. Davies' testimony appears to clarify the issue of whether the openings in the abatis were closed or not. At least one was open, but there were "three Men left to close the Opening. . ."

fire towards the Bay, and some towards the Swamp [233] in front, Mr. Horndon at the same firing from the 12 Pr. towards the Swamp, as he could not turn the Gun towards the left flank, it being in an Embrazure; that as they were but a small No. of Men, [234] they could not extend above Six or Seven Yards along the Abbatis, to the left of the Work; that we ceased firing for some little time upon hearing some Voices from the Upper Work, crying out, the Fort is our Own, not knowing whether they were Rebels or our own People; but Lt. Horndon told us we might Continue firing if we choose it, as he should fire the Cannon, upon which we again directed our fire as before, and were fired upon from the Upper Works; that Lt. Horndon then sent a Serjeant of the 17th Regimt. to see whether or not, the Enemy were in the Upper Works, which Serjeant was killed [235] in his Way thither; that not finding the Serjeant return, we fired several Shots more, in the same direction as before; that Lt. Horndon, then conceiving the Post to be really taken, offered if we would stand by him, to turn the Gun about, and defend the Work, or he would put himself at our head and lead us towards the Shipping; but he previously ordered two Men to turn their Coats, in order to examine if there was passage out, but these Men found that the Enemy were also in front; Lt. Horndon upon this information, told us that he would go to the Rebel Commanding

[233] "Swamp" and "marsh" are used interchangeably in the court-martial.

[234] Lt. Horndon testified previously that because of sentries coming in, there were now twenty-seven men at fleche #1 in addition to his own four artillerymen.

[235] This is a slightly different account than the one given earlier by Lt. Horndon in which there is no mention of a sergeant who is killed.

Officer and desire that we might not be ill treated when we Surrendered, for rather than that should happen, he would stand by his Gun [236] till he and all the Men fell. And the Men agreed to the Lieut's Proposal; that he accordingly went to the Rebel Commanding Officer, & returned with a Company of Rebels headed by two Officers, to whom we Surrendered and were not ill treated.

[236] A later witness, Cpl. William West, gives a more detailed account of Lt. Horndon's determination to "stand by his Gun."

The Court Adjourned till next Morning at 11 o'Clock
Saturday, Febry 3d 1781
The Court being Met pursuant to Adjournment

Corporal Simon Davies of the 17th Regimt of Foot was again Examined
Q. Whether when you retired within the Abbatis did you make any report of what you had seen and heard, and to whom did you make the report?
A. I should have made the report to the Serjeant, could I have seen him, but upon not finding him I retired within the outward Abbatis, and the firing having Commenced before I got in, I formed my Men and fired away amongst the rest.
Q. Was the fire general from all the lower Works?
A. Yes.
Q. Was there any firing from the Enemy, either from those you first discovered in

front, or from the Column, which you supposed to be coming thro' the Water?

A. Not till after I got within the outward Abbatis; [237] whilst I was kneeling down in order to discover if the Enemy were Approaching in front, as I have already mentioned, I heard their Officers (as I supposed them to be) telling the Men not to fire and to keep Silence.

Q. After you got within the outward Abbatis, did you see or hear the Column of the Enemy, that you first discovered in front, or that which came thro' the Bay, still advancing?

A. I did not.

Q. During the Attack, did you observe any of the Enemy in your rear, between the two Abbatis'?

A. I heard a great Noise in the rear, but I did not know whether it proceeded from the Enemy or our own people.

Corporal John Ash of the 17th Regt. of Foot, being duly Sworn, deposed: that I belonged to a Serjeant's Picquet of 15 Men, from which I was detached with Six; [238] the Serjeants Picquet was on the right of the whole, without the outward Abbatis; and I, with the 6 Men, was posted close by the Water side, [239] at about a quarter of a Mile distance from the outer Abbatis; that I posted my Sentries, according to the Orders that I had received; that Capt. Darby went the

[237] Of course, in the dark it would have difficult to tell who was firing especially since the distinction between friend and foe had become increasingly blurred.

[238] The "Serjeant's Picquet" described by Cpl. Ash was located outside the outer abatis near fleche #3.

[239] This detachment was located near King's Ferry "close by the Water side."

rounds between 10 and 11 o'Clock, and told me that it was Lt. Colo. Johnson's Order not to let any of my Men sleep on any Account, but to keep them very Alert; that about 12 o'Clock, or between 12 and 1 o'Clock, there were two Shots fired (as I supposed) from the Officer's Picquet, [240] upon which I formed my Picquet, upon a Rock, according to the Orders I had received; that I afterwards heard four Shots more fired, but no body Approached towards me, but seeing the Works in general in Alarm, I tryed to retreat with my Picquet according to the Orders I received from Capt. Darby, in case of an Alarm; that I Attempted to make my retreat the shortest way I could, which was close along the Water side and through the right flank of the Abbatis; [241] but when I got into the Swamp just under the Abbatis, meaning to go through it, the Rebels were extended from the Wharf along the outside of the Abbatis, but between myself & it, so as to prevent me and my party getting to it, and the Shots from the 71st Grenadrs. came so thick amongst us, as to Wound one of my Men, [242] upon which I thought it proper to retire a little further back under Cover, and placed a Sentry between my party and the Rebels; that I remained there till day break in the Morning, when finding myself Surrounded, I gave myself up and was carried into the Upper Work.

Q. What were the particular Orders you

[240] This is the picket commanded by Lt. Ross and referred to by several previous witnesses.

[241] Cpl. Ash and his men were attempting to enter the outer abatis through an opening on the road leading to King's Ferry, the same route that some of the American Light Infantry in Col. Butler's column had taken.

[242] The Grenadiers had accidentally fired on friendly troops - not the first instance of mistaken identity during the darkness and confusion of battle.

received from Captain Darby, respecting your Picquet?

A. The place at which I was Posted was Supposed to be fordable, and where the Rebels could have crossed; that I had double Sentries planted there; one had Orders to keep a particular look out towards the ford, and the other to the River, in case of the Approach of Boats; that the Sentries were loaded and had particular Orders to fire on any boats that attempted to come down the North River [243] and within their Picquet.

Q. Do you, from your own knowledge or from information, know how that Body of Rebels got between you and the Abbatis?

A. According to the best of my knowledge and belief, they came in by the Officer's Picquet at the Bridge on my left, [244] for I am certain that none came in by my Picquet, or the Serjeant's, from which I was detached, that the distance between me and the Serjeant's Picquet which was in my rear, Obliquely to the left, was about two hundred Yards, and the ground between us was very craggy and full of Rocks.

Q. When you were taken Prisoner in the Morning and carried into the Upper Works, through what part of the lower Abbatis did the Rebels carry you?

A. Through the same part as I meant to have gone myself, close to the Shore.

Q. When you went thro' the Abbatis, did it appear to have been pulled up?

[243] As noted in a previous comment, the boats that could have "come down the North [Hudson] River" refers to American vessels that might sail from West Point down the Hudson, but there was no naval force involved in the American Light Infantry assault.

[244] Cpl. Ash agreed with the observation of other witnesses that the first contact with the enemy was made by Lt. Ross's picket.

A. It seemed to have been pulled and cut away, and the pieces thrown down the Rock into the Water. [245]

Q. How Wide was the Opening in the Abbatis, at the time you were carried thro' it in the Morning?

A. Wide enough to admit ten Men passing abreast; it was not exactly at the place I meant to have gone, but rather to the right of it, as I was coming in, opposite to the rail fleche, [246] which had been made by Order of Lt. Colo. Johnson.

Q. Had you any conversation with the Party that took you, and did you ask them what part of the Abbatis they had got through the Night before, or did they tell you that they had got through at that part?

A. When I was first taken, the Rebel Captain (as they called him) led me to the right of his Party and pointed to a Hill between where there was a long 12 Pr. and a 3 Pr. and told me that I was a Rascal, that we were all alike and that many a good Man had fallen on that Spot the Night before, [247] and asked me if I chose to stay or lay there likewise, or something to that purpose; that I asked him if they were his Men or British, and the Captain answered to his grief they were theirs, the chief of his Company being killed there; that he then asked me Whether I would go into the Works, or into the Country and enlist; that I answered that I myself chose to go into the Works & share the fate of my Comrades;

[245] Apparently, part of the American left column under Col. Butler entered the opening in the abatis referred to earlier by Cpl. Ash and then widened it to admit a larger force. Pulling up the abatis and removing barriers were the tasks of the Forlorn Hope.

[246] This rail fleche is located by the King's Ferry road inside the outer abatis.

[247] The reference is probably to casualties caused by the 3 pounder which, according to testimony previously given by Lt. Horndon, fired 69 rounds during the battle.

that as to the Party they were in his hands they however all did the same; that the captain afterwards brought a Serjeant and 12 Men to conduct me, and my Party into the Upper Works with our Firelocks Clubbed, [248] and gave the Serjeant Orders, that in case any of us carrying our Firelocks any other Way to put us to death, but I did not hear them say where or how they had got through the Abbatis.

[248] Clubbed firelocks are shouldered with their muzzles pointed to the ground.

Corporal William West of the 17th Regiment of Foot being duly Sworn, deposed that I [249] was on Picquet with Lieut. Ross, on the Night of the Attack of Stoney Point; that on relieving the sentries at 9 o'Clock that Night, those that came off informed me, that they had heard a Noise in the front, [250] like the Clashing of Arms; that I took all the pains I could to see if I could perceive any thing myself, but could hear Nothing; that immediately after relieving the Sentries I reported to Lt. Ross what I had heard from the Sentries, & Lt. Ross asked me if I had given particular Orders to the Sentries to be Alert, to which I answered that I had; that Lt. Ross said that he would walk about himself and try if he could perceive any thing, and accordingly Walked about, for about an hour, and every thing remained quiet, till 11 o'Clock, when Corporal Cummings relieved the Sentries, and on his return from relieving them he reported to Lt. Ross that the Sentries

[249] The testimony of Cpl. West is an anomaly: during the entire trial, he is the only witness who was not asked any questions.

[250] The "Noise in the front" reported by sentries at 9PM may have been caused by the nearby presence of some enemy troops, high winds, or the understandable anxiety resulting from having been put on alert. In any case, the American Light Infantry did not launch its attack until more than three hours later.

had informed him, that every thing was very quiet, but about an hour after the two advanced Sentries fired; I, pulling out my Watch, found it to be just 12 o'Clock; that I immediately ran towards the hill, from which the Sentries fired, but met one of them in the way, who told me that there was a large body of the Enemy [251] on the other side of the Swamp, and that they were coming round towards the Bridge as fast as they could; that I knelt down & perceived them myself, upon which I Ordered the Sentry to go back to his Post, whilst I went and reported it to my Officer; that upon coming up to Lt. Ross, I found, that he had already formed the Picquet, and I informed him what both the Sentry and I had seen, on which Lt. Ross ordered the Serjeant to retire the Picquet about twenty Yards, whilst he (Lt. Ross) went forward, to endeavor to see them himself; that Lt. Ross returned in about two Minutes running, as fast as he could, and Ordered the Drummer to beat to Arms, [252] and Ordered me to take four Men from the right and to form them about forty Yards in the front, which I accordingly did, and just as I had formed them, I received two Sentries, whom the Enemy had driven from their Posts, and I ordered them to join the Picquet, but I do not think they had reached it, before I heard a terrible Noise in the rear, between the lower Works and the Picquet, and looking back, I saw Lt. Ross and the Picquet retiring,

[251] The "large body of the Enemy" was probably Col. Butler's column rather than the diversionary force under Major Murfree.

[252] The account given here is substantially the same as provided in earlier testimony by Lt. Ross, only from a slightly different perspective.

and I thought it my duty to do the same; that I heard the Men of Lt. Ross's Picquet calling out to charge thro' them, as they had got into their rear, & Lt. Ross and his Picquet being so far before me, I could not come up with him, but when I did come up I saw a large Body of the Rebels on the outside of the outward Abbatis, pulling it up just under the right hand Work called No. 3, where a long 12 Pr. Was; [253] that I at first took this body of Rebels to be Lt. Ross's Picquet, but finding my Mistake endeavored to get through them and to go in at that Work but this I found impossible; that I then retired from amongst them, thinking that I should be able to get in some where or other, and did accordingly get in at the Work where Lt. Horndon of the Artillery with a short 12 Pr. was, having lost one of the Men of my Party by the way; [254] that the Moment I entered this Work Lt. Horndon asked me, where the Main body of the Rebels was, and I showed him as nearly as I could; that Lt. Horndon pointed the 12 Pr. to the Spot I had shewn him and desired the Infantry to fire Cross Ways, one Party towards this same Object and the other towards the Water on the left, and they obeyed his Orders and kept up as constant a fire as they could till we saw the Shipping drop down the River & the Guns in the Upper Works fire upon the Shipping; [255] that Lt. Horndon advised with the Non Commisd. Officers, What was best to be done & sent a

[253] Cpl. West's testimony reveals where the American left column breached the lower works – by dismantling the abatis under fleche #3. Some of the Light Infantry also entered by the right flank near King's Ferry, as stated earlier by Cpl. Ash.

[254] Enemy infiltration prevented Cpl. West from getting inside the Outer Works at fleche #3, so he gained entry instead at fleche #1 and joined Lt. Horndon and his men.

[255] It will be recalled that part of Gen. Washington's plan was to turn the captured artillery against British ships and the garrison at Verplanck's Point.

Serjeant to see whether the Enemy were in the Upper Works or not, but this Serjeant was killed in his Way thither; that after waiting a while and the Serjeant not returning, and perceiving that all the Works, except the one they were in, were taken, Lt. Horndon asked the Men, if they would stand by him, and that he would turn the Gun about & Maintain the Work; that the Non Commissioned Officers and Men in general said, they were ready to do any thing that he Ordered them, but some one Non Commisd. Officer said, that as the Enemy had carried all of the other Works, they must be very strong, and as they (the British) had but 26 Men in this Work, it would only be throwing our Lives away; that Lt. Horndon then asked what we thought about making our Escape, and we Answered that we were all ready to attempt it, Lt. Horndon at the same time declaring that he would Die with us or effect it; [256] that Lt. Horndon thought it prudent first to Order two Men to turn their Coats by way of Disguise, and examine whether it was possible to make their Way towards the shore of Haverstraw Bay, but these Men on their return reported to Lt. Horndon that the Rebels were as thick on the Water side as they could be, upon this Lt. Horndon said, My Lads I believe we are Prisoners; that after waiting in this Situation for half an hour, and no body coming near us, Lt. Horndon desired some one to go out in search of some Rebel Officer with whom he

[256]Lt. Horndon's age is not a matter of record, though in his testimony a year and a half after the battle he referred to himself as "being then a young officer." His youth may help explain his bravado in the face of overwhelming proof that all was lost. By contrast, the comments of the unidentified non-commissioned officer sound very much like the experienced voice of an older, and perhaps wiser man.

might make some sort of terms; that I accordingly went out, and in going towards the Upper Works just below the flagg Staff, [257] I was challenged by a party of the Rebel Army, to whom I answered, that I was a friend to King George, upon which a Party of the Enemy came up to me with fixed Bayonets, and one of them ran his Bayonet thro' my Coat, but a Rebel Officer coming up protected me, and asked me what I was come for; I answered that I had been sent by a British Officer who Commanded in a Work that had not yet been taken, to find out some Officer of the Enemy, with whom he wished to speak; that the Rebel Officer asked if we meant to fire upon him, as he went down, I Answered, not before he had spoke with him, upon which he went down with me, leaving his Men behind him, and when we had got near the Opening, he desired me to go in and call the Officer out, and Lt. Horndon came to him; & I accompanied him; that the Rebel Officer declared himself to be An Officer, commanding a party of the Rifle Men [258] and Lt. Horndon answered that he was also an Officer, and Commanded that Work, which had not yet been taken, and asked if he could tell him, in whose hands the Works were; Whether in the those of the King's Troops, or of the Congress; the Officer Answered that the Works had been in possession of the Continental Troops above an hour and a half, & Lt. Horndon replyed that he then supposed

[257] Cpl. West approached the main entrance to the Upper Works, located between the Flag Staff battery and the left flank battery.

[258] A discrepancy is apparent here since there were no "Rifle Men" involved on either side of the battle, except possibly part of Major Henry Lee's command which was held in reserve by the Americans. Further, Lt. Horndon in his previous testimony identifies the officer to whom he surrendered as Lt.Col. Fleury, who led the vanguard of the American right column. However, Lt. Horndon also states that he "went into the upper works" whereas Cpl. West claims that the enemy officer (presumably Fleury) went to fleche #1 where Lt. Horndon and his men were awaiting their fate.

239

that he was also to be a Prisoner of War, and desired to know Whether he and the Men in that Work, were to be treated as such, and added that if they were not to be treated as such or Plundered, he would return into the Work and defend it as long as he had a Man alive; the Officer Answered that they should be well treated, and a Sentry should be sent with every Man to see him get his things; to this Lt. Horndon replyed that if he would give this in Writing, [259]he and his Party would Surrender themselves Prisoners; the Officer said he could not do this, but if Lt. Horndon would go with him to General Wayne, he would do it; that Lt. Horndon went with the Rebel Officer, and returned soon after saying, that Gen'l Wayne had Consented to those Terms; that Lt. Horndon then desired the Serjeant to form the Men and March them out, leaving their Arms behind them, and when we got our Tents, the Rebel Officer sent off his Guard with the British Prisoners, Man for Man, as far as they would go, to our Tents to get our things, but the Prisoners exceeded the Guard in point of Numbers, and therefore several of them did not go, and indeed most of the things were taken away before they got to the Tents, and they then Marched us to the Upper Works and we Joined the other Prisoners.

The Court Adjourned till next Morning At 11 o'Clock

[259]Lt. Horndon's concern about surrender terms and written guarantees does not appear in his account, but plundering, unfortunately, is as old as warfare itself, and would have been especially difficult to control if it was directed against enemy soldiers during the initial stages of their surrender. Later, when Lt. Horndon was marched with the other prisoners to Pennsylvania, their passage was observed by Ensign Thomas Hughes, a British officer who had been taken earlier in the war. In his diary, Hughes noted that the officers "were all plundered."

Monday, February 5th 1781

The Court being Met pursuant to
Adjournment

Corporal Joseph Newton of the 17th Regimt.
of Foot being duly Sworn, deposed: that on
the Night of the Attack of Stoney Point, I was
posted with 12 Men [260] on the Howitzer
Battery and Order'd my Men to Lodge their
Arms in such a manner against the Parapet,
that they should easily get at them, in case of
an Attack; that about 10 o'Clock at Night the
Captain of the day (Capt. Darby) came round
& enquired who was the Corporal of that
Picquet, & I informed him that I was the
Man, that Captain Darby order'd me in case
any Alarm should take place before he
returned, I should give him Notice of it as
early as possible; that upon the first two
Shots being fired from the Officer's Picquet, I
ordered the Men of my Picquet to stand to
their Arms, whilst I myself went to acquaint
Capt. Darby of it; that Capt. Darby
immediately quitting his Tent, passed my
Picquet and went towards the outlying
Picquets; that I remained at my Post at the
Howitzer Battery, not thinking proper to fire,
till I saw some Object to fire at; [261] that soon
after Bombardier Swain, who is still a
prisoner in Philadelphia Gaol, with a party of
the Artillery (I cannot ascertain the Number)
came out; Whether from the darkness of the
Night, or from the implements being

[260] According to Ensign Henry
Hamilton, 12 men, a corporal
and a sergeant comprised the
Howitzer detachment.
Apparently, the sergeant that
night was missing.

[261] Of course, the darkness of the
night would have made it very
difficult to see "some Object to
fire at," but it was not necessary
to do so. Lt. Roberts stated
earlier that the Howitzer "could
not have missed its object," no
doubt because at such close
range, case shot or exploding
shell would have been equally
effective even when a target
could not be discerned.

241

Misplaced, I cannot tell, but they were sometime looking for them, but after a time a Man came with a lighted Portfire, which they endeavored to extinguish but could not; that by this time we heard a Noise in the Water to our left, and the Men called out, that the Enemy were coming that way; that I upon looking over the Work, saw Something, which I supposed to be the Enemy advancing by the outward Abbatis which run into the Water; Upon which I ordered my Men to direct their Fire as nearly as they could to that Object; that some of the Men of the Artillery spoke at this time, and said that they wished that the Officer of Artillery that commanded that Gun that Night would come and give them Orders to fire, that having a lighted Portfire, the Men of the Artillery saw the Enemy before we did and made their Retreat to the Flagg Staff Battery, [262] but I with my Party maintained my Post, till I was charged by the Enemy; that upon a Column of the enemy coming on the left flank, I turned about and charged them, just on the edge of the Platform; that the whole of my party, myself excepted, then retreated into the Upper Works, and I received two Slight Bayonet Wounds, and was knock'd with the Butt of a firelock, which render'd me insensible for a quarter of an hour, that when I came to myself again, the Enemy were all round me.

Q. What length of time intervened between

[262]Cpl. Newton and his detachment were infantry soldiers, defending their position with musketry and awaiting the appearance of the artillerymen, who, when they finally arrived, spent some time looking for necessary implements and then tried to extinguish the very portfire – a paper tube filled with a gunpowder composition and used instead of slow match - needed to fire the Howitzer, possibly because the glowing light helped pinpoint their location. The artillerymen chose not to take the initiative (and the responsibility) for firing at an unseen target without orders, and went to the Flag Staff battery on the opposite end of the Upper Works, and (it appears) may have taken the portfire with them.

your hearing the two first Shots fired from
the Officer's Picquet and your hearing &
seeing something coming thro' the Water on
your left which you supposed to be the
Enemy?

A. I suppose about ten Minutes.

Q. How long was it between this point of
time and the Enemy entering the Howitzer
Battery?

A. I apprehend, it might be about a quarter of
an hour.

Q. From whence did the Column of the
Enemy that took possession of the Howitzer
appear to have come, did they seem to have
gained the rear of the Battery, or to have
landed between the two Abbatis, and forced
their Way thro' the inward one?

A. They appeared to have gone round the left
flank of the inner Abbatis, and to have come
up by Capt. Darby's Tent, which stood in the
rear, upon the left of the Howitzer Battery[263.]

Q. How long did the Men of the Artillery
arrive at the Howitzer Battery, after the first
alarm?

A. About five Minutes. [264]

Q. How long before the Column of the
Enemy charged your Picquet, did the
Artillery retire into the Upper Work?

A. About a Minute.

Q. Did they give any reason for retiring?

A. They did not.

Q. Was the Portfire alight from the time of
the Men of the Artillery coming into the

[263]Cpl. Newton is describing the advance of the American right column.

[264]These men "lay the furthest off of any of the troops in the garrison," according to the previous testimony of Lt. John Roberts.

Howitzer Battery, to their Retiring from it?

A. It was.

Q. Do you know whether the Howitzer was loaded with a Shell or Case Shot?

A. I do not.

Q. Had you any Consultation with the Men of the Artillery about firing the Howitzer?

A. I had not.

Q. Had you a Slow Match under your care at the Howitzer Battery?

A. I had not.

Q. Was there any such thing burning there before the Arrival of the Men of the Artillery?

A. I did not see any. [265]

Q. What Number of the Enemy, do you suppose charged the Howitzer Battery?

A. About Fifty, with others following close; they were marching up, as thick as they could.

Q. Did you think it necessary to wait for Orders to fire on the Enemy, when you saw them Advancing in front?

A. I did not; I thought it my duty to fire upon them as soon as I saw them. [266]

Q. Did the Enemy charge you in front, Rear, or flank?

A. In my rear, and I Accordingly turned about to face them, in Order to charge through them, and all my Picquet got through, myself excepted, me being Wounded, as I Mentioned before.

Q. Whilst you were in the Howitzer Battery,

[265] Lack of preparations, as well as poor communication between the infantry soldiers and the artillerymen who shared the same post, practically eliminated any effect the Howitzer might have had even before the Americans captured it.

[266] As Cpl. Newton has previously stated, the artillerymen held a different view about firing without orders, and were apparently reluctant to assume the authority of command.

244

did you hear any of the Enemy, breaking through the inner Abbatis?

A. I did not.

The Court Adjourned till next Morning at 11 o'Clock

Tuesday, February 6th 1781

The Court being Met pursuant to Adjournment

Captain Alexander Mercer, Commanding Engineer being duly Sworn, deposed: that a few days previous to my quitting the Posts of Stoney and Verplank's Point, the Commander in Chief [267] Visited these Posts, and I attended him; And as the Works Appear'd to me to be in a state of defence, and it being near the expiration of a Quarter [268] & my presence necessary at New York, I begged his Permission to quit the Post, leaving Lieut. Stratten Engineer, and Lieut. Marshall, Assistant Engineer [269] to proceed with such Additional Defences as might appear Necessary, in their opinion and that of the Commanding Officers, but before I quitted these Posts, I thought it Necessary to leave a Letter of Instructions, with Lieut. Stratten, which Letter I read to Lt. Colo. Webster, the Commanding Officer of both Posts, and it was approved of by him, and Lieut. Stratten was Ordered to give him a Copy of it; that I had several Conversations with Colo. Webster with respect to the state

[267] Sir Henry Clinton.

[268] The "expiration of a Quarter" refers to a three-month tour of duty.

[269] Lt. Stratten was assigned to Verplanck's Point, and Lt. Marshall, detached from the 63rd Regiment, was posted to Stony Point.

of both Posts, and he did me the honor of desiring my Opinion & advice, with regard to the disposition of the Troops who were immediately under his Command at Verplanks Point; Upon my return to New York with the Permission of Lt. Colo. Webster, I left a Copy Officially of this Letter of Instructions with Lord Rawdon, then Adjutant General, and did not return again to Stoney or Verplanks point.

The Letter of Instructions from Captain Mercer to Lieut. Stratten was then laid before the Court. No. 4. [270]

Q. Is the Letter produced before the Court, the Original Letter given by Captain Mercer to Lieut. Stratten?

A. It is not the Original, but a true Copy of it, both written and Signed by myself.

Q. Can you describe the ground, Situation of the Works and Objects of the different pieces of Artillery, on the several Works, at your departure from Stoney Point? [271]

A. The front of the Table on top of the Hill was nearly an hundred Yards; and nearly in the Center of that Front was a very high Rock, which would have taken too much time to have blown, it was therefore thought Necessary to Crown it with a Line of musquetry; upon the left of that Rock and greatly raised likewise, a Battery was constructed for one Gun; [272] upon the left of that was a fleche for a Howitzer for the

[270] See No. 4 in the appendix.

[271] As Deputy Judge Advocate Adye well knew, Capt. Mercer, as commanding engineer, had designed the fortifications at Stony Point, and is therefore the only witness thus far to describe them in their entirety. The "Table on top of the Hill" is the most level ground in the Upper Works.

[272] Capt. Mercer refers here to the Flag Staff battery.

defence of the left flank; in the rear was a Strong line (with a Ditch) for a Battery of One 18 and One 24 Poundr. [273] and the rest a line of Musquetry, this run down to the beginning of the Declivity on the left flank; the right flank consisted of a Battery of one 18 and one 24 Poundr. and lines of Musquetry, [274] flanking each other, as well as the Nature of the ground would admit of; the declivity on the right side to the edge of the Precipice; That the Abbatis on the left ran down a Steep craggy Ridge, from the left of the line; the Ground in the rear of that ridge formed a Gulley or throat; this was Occupied and Commanded by a fleche or line of Musquetry, which fleche would hold nearly 20 Men; that I gave positive Orders, to Lt. Marshall to close that fleche to the left of the line; that the Ground, as nearly as I recollect, in the rear of that fleche formed on the Small Gulley, which was likewise Occupied by another fleche, or line of Musquetry; that I have to Observe, that neither of these Gullies entered the Water by a direct declivity, but were bounded by a Precipice; the Object of the 12 Pounder, [275] which was en Barbette, was entirely for a defence against the Opposite Points in front, in case the Enemy should attempt to establish themselves; the Medium Distance of these two Opposite points was about two hundred Yards; & these points were Crowned by fleches; [276] the intention of these Fleches were for

[273] Capt. Mercer is describing the left flank battery.

[274] The "lines of Musquetry" and the infantry fleches mentioned several times are obvious attempts to protect the flanks, and Capt. Mercer probably considered that these measures would be sufficient. In his letter to Lt. Stratten, dated June 26, 1779, about three weeks before the battle, he wrote "The works upon Stony and Verplanck's Point are now in such a state of defense as to be able, in my opinion, to resist the attacks and repel the insults of an enemy."

[275] Capt. Mercer refers again to the Flag Staff battery. The gun there, like most of the others, was not fired during the battle, and, according to the previous testimony of Lt. Roberts, an artillery officer, it could not have been brought to bear on the Americans.

[276] The points "Crowned by fleches" refer to the three fleches of the Outer Works.

Picquets by day, and a Chain of Sentries by Night; the 24 and 18 Pounders upon the body of the place [277] (if I may be allowed to call it so) were for the more distant ground, should any regular Attack be Attempted; and to plunge into the <u>fleches</u> in front, in case of a lodgment being attempted, and likewise for the defence of the body of the place itself; the reason for establishing the <u>fleches</u> in front for Picquets by day, or a chain of Sentries by Night, was because they obstructed the View from the body of the place, of the nearer Avenues of Approach, and give time, by an Alarm for the Garrison to get under Arms; in the intervals of these <u>fleches</u>, there was likewise an Abbatis carried down on the left flank into the Water, and on the right to the edge of the Path, near the Precipice, with loose Abbatis, ready to be drawn in; this Abbatis was also intended as an Additional Security against an Enemy, and to throw Obstructions in their Way, in case of their Approach; I take no Notice of the advanced fleches or the Guns placed in them, as they were never intended as points of defence, in Case of an Attack; these fleches were immediately begun on taking Possession of Stoney Point, and the Guns were placed there, merely to keep the Enemy at a distance, whilst we were at Work upon the body of the place, but the defence of the Works, as an established Post was intended to be confined to the Table of the Hill, and

[277] The "body of the place" is Capt. Mercer's term for the Upper Works.

Major Robertson of the Corps of Engineers can testify to a Conversation I had with him at Verplank's Point, relative to the Advanced fleches at Stoney Point. [278] Added to this the Vulture, Sloop of War was to Cover the right flank and the Gun Boat the left.

Q. Were not both Abbatis perfectly good and Strong, and do you think it is possible for the Enemy to have penetrated them in any part, except at the Barriers?

A. As far as I can judge, the Abbatis were strong and good.

Q. Were they pinn'd down?

A. By report made to me they were; there were some parts of the Abbatis that could not be pinn'd down, on Account of their being on Rocks, but they were chocked.

Q. Had you any report made you after you left Stoney Point, either from Lieut. Stratten or Lieut. Marshall, how far the Orders you had left for Compleating the Works at Stoney Point were Obeyed? [279]

A. I had not.

Q. Did you ever see the Journals of Lieut. Stratten or Marshall, relative to the Works that were carried on at Stoney Point?

A. Yes.

Q. Are those Papers, marked 5 and 6, as far as comes within your knowledge, Authentic?

A. They are; Lieut. Marshall gave me his Journal upon his return from Captivity, and Lt. Stratten upon going on the Expedition with Brigr. Genl. Arnold, left with me the

[278] The strategy Capt. Mercer outlines here – basically to abandon the Outer Works and concentrate defensive efforts in the Upper Works alone – is a sound one – at least in daylight when an enemy could be seen, but was not followed by Lt. Col. Johnson. Even if it had been, however, the Upper Works would still have been vulnerable since it was not enclosed.

[279] Capt. Mercer's order mentions several directives, of which "the principal one" is the construction of a new battery to help protect Verplanck's Point, followed by creating another magazine and preparing new fleches, but does not include instructions to enclose the Upper Works (See No. 4 in the appendix).

Extract from his Journal, now produced before the Court. [280]

Q. As you have said that you had several Conversations with Lt. Colo. Webster, relative to the defence of Verplank's and Stoney Point, do you recollect whether you gave your Opinion relative to the Number of Men, necessary for the defence of that of Stoney Point or the disposition of the Troops? [281]

A. I cannot recollect that I did.

Q. Had you any Conversation with Lieut. Colo. Johnson relative to the defence of Stoney Point?

A. I do not recollect that I had.

Q. Whether you Offered any lights or Instructions to the Commanding Officer for the defence of Stoney Point?

A. I do not recollect that I had.

Q. Did you Consult with any body, with regard to the disposition of those Works in the defence of Stoney Point?

A. I cannot recollect that I particularly Consulted with any Person on these Works, as they were carried on, in some measure under the immediate Eye of the Commander in Chief; I have talked to Lord Rawdon [282] and Major Robertson on the Subject, but I cannot say that I had any regular Consultation on the Occasion.

Q. Is it not usual and proper in the Service for a Commanding Engineer, being Ordered to fortify a Post, to give his Ideas of the

[280] Unfortunately, Lt. Marshall's journal (No 6 in the appendix) is missing from the court-martial records, but excerpts from Lt. Stratten's journal (no. 5 in the appendix) have survived.

[281] Capt. Mercer's answers to this question and the two that follow (to which his responses are almost identical) seem to suggest a lack of communication with those in charge of defending the fortifications he had designed - a failure which may well have reduced the ability to provide an adequate defense.

[282] Lord Francis Rawdon-Hastings was a British officer who had formed the Volunteers of Ireland, a provincial regiment.

Defence, to the Officer who is left to defend
it? [283]

A. Yes, and as Lieut. Colo. Webster was left
in the Command of both Posts, Viz.
Verplank's and Stoney Point, I did in general
Conversation, and as I think, on delivering
him a Copy of my Letter of Instructions to
Lieut. Stratten, give him my Ideas on this
Subject.

Q. Did you, at your departure, think the
Number of Men left for the defence of
Stoney Point, competent to that defence?

A. Upon the principal of defending the Table
of the Hill only, as I have before mentioned, I
thought 500 Men a Sufficient Number for the
defence of Stoney Point. [284]

Q. You having said, that in your Idea, the
defence should have been confined to the
Table of the Hill, were you ever consulted, or
did you ever give it as your Opinion
Officially to Lieut. Colo. Johnson, or Lieut.
Colo. Webster, that the pieces of Artillery in
the fleches, along the outward Abbatis,
should remain in their <u>fleches,</u> after the
Works were reported to be in a state of
Defence?

A. I do not recollect that I ever had any
Conversation with Lieut. Colo. Johnson,
relative to the defence of Stoney Point, but I
very well remember in general Conversation
with Lieut. Colo. Webster, on this Subject,
telling him that these fleches were never
intended as Objects of Defence; [285] and I

[283] After receiving negative or non-committal answers - expressed in almost identical language - to his previous questions about consulting with those who would have to defend Stony Point, Deputy Judge Advocate Adye's exasperation in the present query is almost palpable.

[284] According to Ensign Hamilton's list of the distribution of troops at Stony Point (no. 3 in the appendix), Col. Johnson had deployed only 177 soldiers, exclusive of artillerymen, to defend the Upper Works.

[285] Capt. Mercer tells Lt. Col. Webster of his recommendations for defense, but for the second time, states he had not spoken directly to Webster's subordinate, Lt. Col. Johnson.

251

further recollect, on returning to Verplank's Point, with the Commander in Chief, I used this Exclamation to Lieut. Colo. Webster, Good God! Colo. Webster, did I not always say that these Points ought not to be defended? [286]

Q. Were there any Roads by which the Cannon in these fleches might have been withdrawn occasionally?

A. There was a Path made by the Soldiers in going backwards and forwards, by which, as they were mounted on travelling Carriages they might have been withdrawn. [287]

Q. Were the Cohorns or Royal Mortars intended to be occasionally brought in?

A. They were.

Q. Were the Guns in the Advanced fleches en Barbette, or in Embrazures?

A. In the right fleche, there were two Embrazures, and in the left fleche One.

Q. Did the Embrazure in the left hand Work [288] command the Abbatis of that flank?

A. It did not; it was never intended for it.

Q. Could the Guns of the Upper Works, see all parts of the lower Works, between both flanks of the lower Abbatis?

A. According to the best of my recollection they could, Where one Gun could not take up a point, another could. [289]

Q. If the fleche No. 1 had been en Barbette, could not the Gun posted there have borne upon Haverstraw Bay?

A. It certainly would, but it was never

[286] Capt. Mercer's comments were made in the presence of Sir Henry Clinton, and therefore may be viewed as exculpatory.

[287] However, it would have been impossible to withdraw them during a nighttime attack that lasted less than half an hour, and would have served no purpose: the only captured artillery the Americans used were those in the Upper Works, and these heavy guns were turned against British ships and the British fort at Verplanck's Point.

[288] The "left hand Work" is fleche #1 in the Outer Works.

[289] "All parts of the lower Works" did not include the abatis which ran below them. Lt. Roberts, for instance, testified that the flank batteries and the flagstaff battery could not be depressed enough to strike the lower abatis.

intended for the defence of that flank; the Howitzer was the piece of Artillery meant for that purpose.

Q. Was there any other piece of Artillery on the Battery intended for the defence of the left flank towards Haverstraw Bay?

A. There was: [290] but the Howitzer, Musquetry, & the Gun Boat were intended for the defence of that flank.

Q. Were both the flanks at Stoney Point so secure, as to cause an Enemy to make an Attack in front with a greater prospect of success?

A. I should think that they were. [291]

Q. Were the Works on the Table of the Hill at Stoney Point so Constructed, as to have Mutual dependence and serve reciprocally as flanks to each other?

A. They were as far as the Nature of the ground would admit of, and wherever a flank could be gained it was; they consisted (if I may use the expression) of a Connected line of Defence. [292]

Q. The Works being detached Ones, did they Support themselves?

A. I can hardly call any of them detached Works, for even the Howitzer Battery, was immediately Commanded by the Works behind it. [293]

Q. Was there an enclosed Work of any kind, upon the Table of the Hill?

A. There was not; but, I refer to my Letter of Instructions to Lieut. Stratten, for the Orders,

[290] The transcription of Capt. Mercer's answer must have been incorrect: there was no other artillery piece "on the Battery [in fleche #1]", only the 12 pounder commanded by Lt. Horndon, and that gun was not intended for the defense of the left flank.

[291] The American Light Infantry attack which swept around the flanks as well as through both abatis apparently did not cause Capt. Mercer to revise the opinion expressed here.

[292] It must be pointed out that the "Connected line of Defence" was disconnected in many locations and was no substitute for an enclosed defense

[293] The Howitzer was in line with the inner abatis located below the Upper Works -- and too close to be "commanded" by them if one recalls that the guns were intended for distant targets and could not be depressed.

wherein 'tis directed that he was to strengthen the present defences and to persist in carrying on such Works, as may most effectually Cover and protect the Garrison; and where it is further said fleches, as lines of Musquetry, [294] must be gained on both sides, to prevent the possibility of Turning the flanks.

Q. Was Lieut. Marshall, the Acting Engineer at Stoney Point, implicitly to Obey any Orders he might receive from Lieut. Colo. Johnson, or was he to apply to Lieut. Stratten, or was the participation of Lieut. Colo. Webster, whom you call Commanding Officer of both Posts, necessary for making any Alterations for the defence of Stoney point?

A. I should imagine that he (Lieut. Marshall) was in the first instance immediately to Obey the Orders of the Commanding Officer on the Spot, tho' it might be necessary afterwards to report to the Commanding Engineer. [295]

Q. Did you often Visit Stoney Point, whilst Lt. Colo. Johnson Commanded there?

A. I lay in a Sloop between the two Posts of Verplank's and Stoney Point, and constantly Visited them both.

Q. Did you observe in the Visits you describe, the encampments of the Troops at Stoney Point?

A. I cannot recollect the particular Spots they were on. [296]

Q. Did you see any Encampment between the

[294] Capt. Mercer's letter to Lt. Stratten (see No. 4 in the appendix) says nothing about closing the works, emphasizing instead "lines of Musquetry" to prevent the flanks from being turned. These infantry fleches – not to be confused with the three fleches on the Outer Works – were, however, open in the rear and could themselves be turned.

[295] It seems unusual that Capt. Mercer is uncertain ("I should imagine") whether Lt. Marshall should obey Col. Johnson, the "Commanding Officer on the spot".

[296] Since Capt. Mercer has just stated that he "constantly Visited" Stony Point, it seems odd that he does not recall the "particular Spots" where the troops were encamped.

two Abbatis?

A. I think not.

Q. Having observed that you thought 500 Men sufficient for the Defence of Stoney Point, provided the defence was confined to the Table of the Hill, would there have been a sufficient Number of Men to have Manned the several Works, batteries and fleches, a Corps de Reserve been spared to support such points of Attack, as were most menaced and likely to be carried by the Attacks of an Enemy?

A. Upon the principal of 500 Men being sufficient for the defence, I would Appropriate 200 Men, two deep, for the front defence, 100 for that of each flank and a reserve of 100 Centrecally and to act occasionally. [297]

The Court Adjourned till next Morning at 11 o'Clock
Wednesday, Febry 7th 1781

Captain Mercer was again examined.

Q. During your residence at Stoney & Verplank's Points, was Haverstraw Bay sounded, so as to know how the exact fordable distances at all times of the tide, and was a description of those experiments made in a Report either to Lieut. Colo. Johnson, or to Lieut. Colo. Webster? [298]

A. No.

Q. To whom did you give your Ideas on the

[297] Capt. Mercer's deployment may have seemed a workable strategy if there had been sufficient advance notice of an impending attack, even in the dark, but in the battle that occurred, the flanks became entry points for an overwhelming enemy force, leaving the garrison in the hopeless position of attempting to defend a fortification open in the rear. Even the 500 men recommended by Capt. Mercer would have been outnumbered by more than two to one with little chance of reinforcements.

[298] Deputy Judge Advocate Adye's question may have been prompted by a feeling that if water was part of the British defense, then the depth and tides of that water should have been known.

255

proper disposition of the Vulture Sloop of War, and of the Gun Boat, in the defence of Stoney Point?

A. I cannot recollect giving my Ideas to any particular Person; [299] the Vulture and Gun Boat were left there by the Commander in Chief for that purpose.

Q. Do you know the several dispositions of the Gun Boat, at different times of Tide, for the defence of Stoney Point, during the Night?

A. As nearly as I can recollect, the Gun Boat might lay at her usual Station, which was about fifty Yards from the Shore, opposite the left flank of the inward Abbatis, at all times of the Tide.

Q. Do you not think the Gun Boat laying at her usual Station, would not only have heard a Column of the Enemy advancing on the left flank thro' the Water, but also have Annoyed them and impeded their March?

A. Positively Yes, and would have given great additional Security to that flank, particularly by firing case or grape shot. [300]

Q. Could the Gun Boat at her Station have flanked the inner Abbatis?

A. I think not; to have done that, she must have retired to too great a distance to have Answered the purpose that she was Stationed for.

Q. Do you mean, from the Idea you have formed and Mentioned, that the Table of the Hill only was to be defended; that this should

[299] It would seem that a cohesive plan of defense would have included direct communication with a "particular Person" – perhaps one in charge of both vessels.

[300] Once again, the importance of the Gun Boat in protecting the left flank is underscored. When high winds forced the Gun Boat (and the *Vulture* on the right flank) from their posts on the night of the battle, the only alternative defense to guard the shallow waters of Haverstraw Bay was the Howitzer – but that was overrun before it could be fired.

have been the Case in the Night only, or both by day & Night?

A. I will abide by the same disposition, by day and Night, only with this difference, that by Night I would have Beacons on the flanks to have lighted; And had I been informed of the Approach of an Enemy I would have the beacons constantly lighted. [301]

Q. Did you signify the forgoing Ideas to Lt. Colo. Johnson, or Lieut. Colo. Webster, or whom?

A. I do not remember to have mentioned the Idea to anybody; it appeared to me too Obvious to render this Necessary.

Q. Was there any Communication between, or disposition settled by the Commanding Engineer, who plann'd the Original System of Defence for Stoney Point, with the Senior Officer of Artillery at that Post, as it might relate to the best Use of the Artillery on the Batteries, in the defence of Stoney Point, considered in either in a general sense with a defence of all the parts, or in a more partial Manner, relative to particular points?

A. I cannot recollect any Official Communication with the Commanding Officer of Artillery, with respect to the Object of the several Guns, but it was frequently talked of, particularly the Object of the Howitzer.

Q. Whether as is Customary in most Services, the Commanding Officer of Artillery, had a previous knowledge given to

[301] Capt. Mercer holds to his view that only the Upper Works ("the Table of the Hill") should have been defended, night or day, adding that beacons should have lighted on the flanks. Questions about beacons and light balls had been asked of several previous witnesses, including Ensign Henry Hamilton who stated that he "did not know of any beacons " that had been prepared. Capt. Mercer did not think to mention this suggestion, thereby failing to consider that what may be "too Obvious" to one person may not be to another. Beacons would certainly have aided the British defense, but, as already noted, it seems unlikely that they alone would have altered the outcome of the battle.

him of any parts of the Plan of Defence, adopted for Stoney Point, particularly such as related to the Object of the Batteries?

A. In answer to this Question, there has been a want of form, as the Commanding Officer of Artillery had nothing on Paper, but as he was upon the Spot, whilst the Works were carrying on, they were Mutually talked of between them. Captain Traille was the Commanding Officer of Artillery at the time, and had he made any Objection to the disposition of the Guns, I would certainly have given him my reasons for disposing of them as I did. [302]

Q. Did you leave your Ideas of the defence of Stoney Point, as described in the course of your evidence, with the two Engineers, who were to carry on the Works, after your departure?

A. As Disposition & Defence rested with the Commanding Officers, I did not, I left nothing but my Letter of Instructions.

Q. Do you think it derogatory to the respect due to the Commanding Officer of any Post, let his Rank be what it may, to Submit your Ideas of that Post, fortified by you, to such Commanding Officer?

A. Very far from it. I did give my Opinion to Lt. Colo. Webster, with respect to the disposition of the Troops on Verplank's Point particularly, I am not so certain with regard to the Conversation, as far as it related to Stoney Point, and I had no Conversation on

[302] While there may well have been " a want of form," as Capt. Mercer testified, it does not seem as if the planning of the fortifications including artillery positions was a collaborative effort. Instead, Captain Traille could have "made an Objection to the disposition of the Guns," but it appears that such dispositions had already been determined by Capt. Mercer.

the Subject with Lieut. Colo. Johnson. [303]

Q. Do you know under whose Orders the Gun Boat was?

A. I do not, but I supposed under that of the Captain of the Vulture, as she was Manned by Seamen; that upon first taking Possession of Verplank's & Stoney Point, there were two Gun Boats which I supposed were both intended for the defence of the left flank of Stoney Point, as the Water was Shallow, but I do not know what became of the Second Gun Boat. The reason for the Vulture being stationed for the defence of the right flank was, that the inclination of the Ground was too Abrupt to have been Commanded by the fire of a Gun Boat.

Q. (by desire of Lt. Col. Johnson) What time & what Number of Men would it have taken, to have removed the Guns from the lower Works to the Table of the Hill?

A. I cannot pretend to say; during the Attack in the Night, I do not think that they could have been removed. [304]

Q. During your Stay at and near Stoney Point, and Occasionally Visiting it, did not Lt. Colo. Johnson supply the Number of Men required, and shew every inclination to perfecting the Works?

A. Lieut. Colo. Johnson, upon every Occasion, shewed the greatest Attention to every requisition made by me, both as an Officer and as a Gentleman.

Q. Whether even before Majr Genl Pattison

[303] Judging from this response and several earlier ones, it would appear that Capt. Mercer never had any direct communication with Lt. Col. Johnson. Perhaps Capt. Mercer thought it might have been improper to do so since Lt. Col. Webster was the commanding officer of both posts. The question – forever unanswered because of Lt. Col. Webster's absence and his death in battle a little more than a month after the trial ended - is: How much, if any, of Capt. Mercer's opinions and ideas for defense did Lt. Col. Webster convey to Lt. Col. Johnson?

[304] The guns could also have remained where they were and been spiked - by jamming the vent with a large nail or a bayonet tip - thereby disabling them, at least temporarily.

[305] left Stoney Point and the Command devolved upon Lt. Colo. Johnson, did not Lt. Colo. Johnson show every Inclination to forward the Service?

A. Yes, upon every Occasion.

The Court Adjourned till next Morning at 11 o'Clock

Thursday, February 8th 1781

The Court being Met pursuant to Adjournment

Major Archibald Robinson, of the Corps of Engineers being duly Sworn, deposed: that (as far as my recollection will carry me at such a distance of time) in a Conversation I had with Captain Mercer, [306] soon after going up with the Commander in Chief, to Stoney & Verplank's Point, and before the Works were begun, & after having been on the Spot with Captain Mercer, who did me the Honor to desire me to go to Verplank's Point with him, Captain Mercer told me that he had Order'd small fleches to be thrown up, which might protect the place and keep the Enemy at a distance from Stoney Point, whilst the principal defences or body of the Work were erected, [307] and that these fleches might afterwards serve for Small Picquets or Guards to place some Pieces of Cannon therein, as a defence during the day time.

Q. Did you ever see the fleches that were made in front?

[305] Major General James Pattison (1724-1805) commanded the British artillery during the capture of Stony Point from the Americans on May 31, 1779.

[306] Major Robinson had been to Stony Point with Sir Henry Clinton, and had conversed with Capt. Mercer about the defenses, but was not present during the battle.

[307] Major Robinson is describing fleches #1, 2, and 3 in the Outer Works, defensive positions which have been mentioned by many other witnesses. These simple fortifications may have received their designation from the number of artillery each contained: #1 had one 12-pounder gun; #2 had two Coehorn mortars; and #3 had two Royal mortars and a 12 pounder.

A. Yes.

Q. Can you describe the Construction of them?

A. They were three Small Simple fleches, advanced above two hundred Yards from the Summit of the Hill, and Open in the Rear, and occupying three particular points, from which you could see a good way round.

Q. Would not these Advanced fleches, had they been Abandoned, have afforded a Cover for the enemy?

A. I did not particularly attend to them, but they appeared to me to have been erected, nearly to Occupy particular points, as the Nature of the Ground directed.

Q. Had you, as Deputy Quarter Master Genl, [308] any Orders to give your Opinion of the Nature of the Ground at Stoney Point?

A. No, I had not.

Q. Had you have any directions as Quarter Mastr General to converse with the Captain of the Vulture, relating to it's Station and that of the Gun Boat?

A. I had not, but I understood that they were intended for the protection of the flanks at Stoney Point.

Q. In whose Department generally, are the Gun Boats?

A. They are generally in the Quarter Master General's Department. [309]

Lieutenant William Marshall of the 63rd Regimt. & Acting Engineer, being duly

[308] Apparently, Major Robinson was an engineer serving as a Deputy Quartermaster General.

[309] Major Robinson states that Gun Boats are "generally" in the Quarter Master General's Department, but Deputy Judge Advocate Adye does not follow up this answer by asking whether the Gun Boat at Stony Point was specifically under the QMG's command, and, if so, why it was missing during the battle.

261

Sworn, deposed: that I was appointed Acting Engineer at Stoney Point on the 26th of June, 1779, [310] and went thither by Order of Captain Mercer the Commanding Engineer, who was then at Verplank's Point., and on my Arrival there, I waited on Lieut. Colo. Johnson, who I understood, had the Command on that side; that I acquainted him of the Orders I had received from Captain Mercer, to Act on the side of Stoney Point and (I think) the next day, I went round the Works with Colo. Johnson and pointed out some things that I thought Necessary to be done for the better Security of the Post; the first thing, I think, that I recommended Lt. Colo. Johnson was to Coat the North side of the Powder Magazine with Sods, it being before Covered with dry, brushy fascines; that the next Work was thickening the Outward Abbatis, which in many places was not staked down, and very thin; that I next proposed thickening the inward Abbatis, just in the front of the line, upon the top of the Hill; [311] that Lt. Col. Johnson himself proposed to have an Embrazure cut on the right flank of the Upper Work, in order to bring a Gun to bear Obliquely on the River; [312] and the next Work proposed was the repair of the Embrazures in the advanced Works, particularly in No. 3, which was very much choaked, and a Working Party was immediately employed to effect this last piece of Business; that after I had compleated

[310] If length of time is any guide, then William Marshall is the principal witness in the court-martial of Lt. Col. Johnson. Lt. Marshall testified for four days-the longest of anyone - and, among other subjects, was queried about the design, strength and location of the British defenses.

[311] The improvements described here, including the use of fascines (bundles of branches tied together) must have been Lt. Marshall's personal recommendations since they are not mentioned in Capt. Mercer's letter (No. 4 in the appendix).

[312] Capt. Mercer had suggested a new battery for this purpose; Lt. Col. Johnson simply wanted another embrasure added to the present battery.

these Embrazures, Lieut. Stratten came to me with some written Instructions left with him by Captain Mercer, the Commanding Engineer on the 3rd of July as appears by my Journal; [313] I recollect perfectly well to have waited several days before he came, and upon Lieut. Stratten showing me Instructions, I recommended to him to shew them to Lieut. Colo. Johnson, who commanded at the Post; that Lt. Stratten desired me to take a Copy of these Instructions, as far as they related to the Works to be carried on on the Stoney Point Side, and that my shewing them to Lieut. Colo. Johnson would Answer the same purpose; that not above an hour after Lieut. Stratten had left Stoney Point, I recollect seeing Colo. Johnson in front of his Tent, and telling him of these Instructions, and I also recollect Lieut. Colo. Johnson at the time asking me what the Instructions tended to; that I pointed out to him some Works opposite his Tent which, by the Instructions were to be done; Lieut. Colo. Johnson did not then inspect them, but said that he would take another Opportunity of seeing them, and Ordered a Working Party to be employed on other Work than the Instructions tended to; [314] that July the 5th, Lieut. Colo. Johnson called upon me and inspected Captain Mercer's Instructions; the Conversation that passed at the time was, that Lieut. Colo. Johnson asked me for that Paper of Capt. Mercer's, which I gave him; that Lieut. Colo.

[313] Capt. Mercer's letter, however, is dated June 26, the same day that Lt. Marshall was appointed Acting Engineer. Marshall apparently did not see the letter until July 3, as he states. As previously noted, Lt. Marshall's journal has not survived.

[314] Lt. Marshall seems to imply here that Lt. Col. Johnson's work projects – at least at first - took precedence over those listed in Capt. Mercer's letter.

263

Johnson then asked me what Number of Men I should require, I recollect Answering that I could employ as many as he (Lieut. Colo. Johnson) could give me; Colo. Johnson asked if forty would do, and I Answered that that was very few; Colo. Johnson reply'd he could give me fifty which was all that he could spare, and as far as I can recollect this was all the Conversation that then passed; [315]that on July the 6th Lt. Colo. Johnson granted me a Working Party, and so on from day to day, which Working Parties were employed, as registered in my Journal produced before the Court, which I know to be just and exact, except the last paragraph that relates to the Attack of the Post and Which in haste I drew up from information of Others; that independent of the Working Parties, there were strong covering Parties sent out, [316] as they were frequently Obliged to go a Mile and a half from the Works, and often saw the Enemy in front.

Q. You have already pointed out the Additional Works you advised Colo. Johnson to have carried on, and have also said that one piece of Service in particular was executed, [317]were any of the other Objects you recommended attended to?

A. As nearly as I can recollect every thing I myself recommended to Lieut. Colo. Johnson, was put in Execution, as soon as possible.

Q. Were the Instructions of Capt. Mercer

[315]Lt. Col. Johnson agreed to assign men to the working parties needed to carry out Capt. Mercer's instructions, perhaps reluctantly, since the number he supplies is not as many as Lt. Marshall would have liked. For more details about the relationship between Lt. Col. Johnson and Lt. Marshall, see extracts from Lt. Stratten's journal, No. 5 in the appendix.

[316]The "strong covering Parties" may have been the reason why fewer troops were available for Lt. Marshall's work details.

[317]The "one piece of Service" probably refers to the embrasure Lt. Col. Johnson added to the right flank battery.

fulfilled ?

A. The Working Parties were not immediately employed in fulfilling these Instructions, upon Lt. Colo. Johnson's reading them, but were employed, as I have already said, on other Works ordered by Lt. Colo. Johnson himself; those proposed by me being previously finished; these Instructions of Capt. Mercer were afterwards fulfilled in part.

Q. On what day did you begin to fulfill Captain Mercer's Instructions, & how far were they carried into execution, previous to the Attack?

A. On the 7th of July, [318] we began to put into Execution the Commanding Engineer's Instructions; and the Battery on the right flank [319] proposed by Capt. Mercer to act in favor of Verplank's point, supposing it Attacked by the Enemy, was nearly finished on the Night of the Attack; and I recollect to have made a Return upon the Battery, which enabled me to Open three Embrazures instead of two.

Q. Did you look upon yourself, previous to seeing Capt. Mercer's Instructions, as under the immediate Orders of Lt. Colo. Johnson, with respect to any Works to be carried on at Stoney Point, or did you suppose that you were to Apply for Instructions to Lieut. Stratten, who resided at Verplank's Point, under the immediate Command of Lieut. Colo. Webster?

[318] Lt. Marshall has stated that he did not receive Capt. Mercer's letter of June 26 until July 3, though Lt. Stratten (see No. 5 in the appendix) claimed he delivered it on June 29. In any case, work parties to carry out the letter's instruction were not established until July 7, less than ten days before the American attack.

[319] The "Battery on the right flank" is the "principal one" of the improvements listed by Capt. Mercer. The priority assigned to it suggests that the most dangerous threat to the security of the British defenses, in his view, was not from the land or to Stony Point, since the new battery was intended to fire toward the river and help protect Verplanck's Point on the opposite shore.

A. I looked upon it that I was to apply to Lt. Colo. Johnson with respect to any Works that it might be necessary to carry on at Stoney Point, but I also thought it proper to make report of them to Lieut. Stratten, which I did.

Q. Did receiving Instructions from the Commanding Engineer, alter your Sentiments upon this Subject?

A. It did not.

Q. Did you not conceive that the Object of Captn. Mercer's Instructions left with Lieut. Stratten was to proceed with every Work, which might give Additional Strength to the body of the place, and to prevent in the literal Sense of the Letter, the flanks from being turned?

A. Yes. I certainly conceived that they meant that. [320]

Q. Can you describe the Ground of the Table of the Hill?

A. As nearly as I can recollect, the space of the Table of the Hill, upon which the Works were, was sufficient to contain 500 Men in Single Rank and Parapet sufficient for 300 Men drawn up in the same Manner.

Q. Did you understand that it was intended in case of a Night Attack to defend the outward line of Works with the Cannon posted in them, or that they were intended merely as a line of Musquetry, to keep the Enemy at a distance during the day time; the Cannon drawn into the Upper Works at Night, and what is called the body of the place or Table

[320] The phrasing of Deputy Judge Advocate Adye's question and Lt. Marshall's response are interesting. Certainly, the purpose of at least some of Capt. Mercer's instructions is to prevent the flanks from being turned, but the best way to have accomplished that would have been to enclose them. Military hierarchy and protocol were very important, so even if Lt. Marshall disagreed about the effectiveness of Capt. Mercer's defenses, as a temporary ("Acting") engineer, he could hardly have expressed it since to do would be to criticize the judgment of his superior. Perhaps that is why Adye does not ask Lt. Marshall's opinion of the effectiveness of the measures proposed by the commanding engineer.

of the Hill only to be defended?

A. On my first coming to the Post and inspecting the line in front, I did suppose that it had been Constructed to cover the troops in case of an Attack, previous to the upper Works being finished, but the Guns having never been withdrawn from those Out Works, during the time of my Stay at the Post, I did suppose that it was meant to defend them; [321] Lieut. Stratten never mentioned to me any thing contrary to this latter idea, nor did Capt. Mercer's instructions mention these Guns being withdrawn, and therefore I naturally imagined these Works were intended to be defended.

Q. Had you ever any Conversation upon this Subject with Lieut. Colo. Johnson, or upon the defence of the Place?

A. I never had; I supposed that Lieut. Stratten as Commanding Engineer, had conversed with Colonel Johnson upon this Subject. [322]

Q. Whether from your Observation of the Encampment of the Troops in the Upper Work, and between the two Abbatis, you supposed they were so encamped as to defend the interior line of Work and also the outward Abbatis? [323]

A. I looked upon it, upon seeing the Troops thus drawn up, that in case of an Attack, a sufficient Number would be sent to defend the Works along the outward Abbatis, and that the rest, the Picquets excepted, would be stationed for the defence of the inner Works;

[321] This is a crucial point and goes to the heart of a divided defense and the lack of a clear line of communication from the engineers to the officers in command. Lt. Col. Johnson may have made the same assumption that Lt. Marshall did: the Outer Works should be defended.

[322] It could be argued that this vital part of Stony Point's defensive plan was too important for Lt. Marshall to have only "supposed" that Lt. Col. Johnson knew of it from Lt. Stratten.

[323] In previous testimony, Ensign Hamilton stated that four companies of the 17th Regiment were placed between both abatis. As already noted, in daylight, they could have been withdrawn to the Upper Works in the event of an attack, but in the darkness and turmoil of an unexpected nighttime assault, that would have been virtually impossible.

it was impossible to line the Outward Abbatis, with the Troops that were there.

Q. In case it had been found Necessary to draw the Cannon from the Outer to the inner Works, as also to retire with the Troops, what sort of Ground had they to go over?

A. Very uneven, broken ground, and it would have been very difficult, if not impossible, in a Night Assault, to have drawn in the Guns, as besides the badness of the Ground, the distance from the 3 Pounder to the Flagg Staff was near 300 Yards. [324]

Q. Was there any Platforms or Batteries in the Upper Works, for the Reception of the Guns in the lower Works, in case of their being withdrawn?

A. There were not any; I supposed that had they been withdrawn, they would have been sent away, as they could be of no use there.

Q. Had the advanced Works, having each of them three faces, been abandoned without being levelled, would they not have served as Cover to an Enemy, in case of an Attack?

A. I do not think they could have been of any Cover, as they were open in the Gorge and Commanded by the Guns in the Upper Works; besides, they were constructed according to the Shape of the Hill on which each of them was erected, and Men could not have stood on the Outside of them, so as to have been Covered, on Account of the declivities in front. [325]

Q. What was the thickness of the Parapets of

[324] Lt. Marshall is certainly correct about the difficulty of withdrawing the artillery from the Outer Works during a night attack, and the reasons he gives are compelling ones – not to mention that the artillery (with the sole exception of the Howitzer) would have been of little use in the kind of battle that the British were compelled to fight.

[325] As the engineer assigned to Stony Point and having, among other projects, repaired the embrasures in the fleches of the advanced works, Lt. Marshall would certainly have been familiar with their design and construction.

those Advanced Works, and of what Materials made?

A. I think their profiles were twelve feet at the Base, and declined to eight feet at the Top, and made of earth, coated with Fascines. [326]

Q. Were both Abbatis perfectly good and strong at the time of the Attack, and do you think it possible for the Enemy to have penetrated them in any part, except at the Barriers?

A. I do not think that they could have penetrated at any part, even the barriers, without some difficulty, with Troops in the lower Works, as some parts of the Outward Abbatis, tho not all, were covered by the Guns in the Upper Works. [327]

The Court Adjourned till next Morning at 11 o'Clock
Friday, February 9th 1781
The Court being Met pursuant to Adjournment

Lieut. William Marshall of the 63rd Regimt and Acting Engineer was again examined.

Q. Did the Creek make Stoney Point an Island, at all or any time of the Tide?

A. I do not recollect that it did; there was a Swamp ran all round our front, and I think a small inlet which came from the River on the right of the Works, and went about half way round. [328]

[326] The fascines provided support for the earthen walls, but these "Advanced Works" or fleches were still open at the rear.

[327] Nonetheless, the abatis were penetrated in several places by the forlorn hopes of each column. Small hatchets, a weapon that Light Infantry troops normally carried, were probably used to cut through these barriers. Also, Lt. Marshall disagrees with the view, expressed earlier by Lt. John Roberts of the Royal Artillery, that the guns in the Upper Works were unable to fire on the outward abatis.

[328] This familiar question is part of Deputy Judge Advocate Adye's continuing attempt to determine the defensive situation in front of the Outer Works.

Q. Was the Creek practicable at all times of the Tide for Infantry?

A. At Flood tide I do not think that it was.

Q. What was the State of the Tide at the time of the Attack?

A. I think from the Report of the Rebel Officers, who got into the Upper Works, that it was about one third Ebb; [329] I asked General Wayne the Question, and received this information from him, and made a remark upon this matter in Writing after I got to Lancaster.

Q. Did the two Abbatis run into the Water on each flank?

A. They did not, I think, only upon the left flank.

Q. Were there any beacons or other Signals established to be made, in case of a Night Assault?

A. I know there were no beacons, but I understood there were fire balls [330] to be made use of, in case of a night Attack; I got this information from Capt. Traille.

Q. Were any fire balls made use of on the Night of the Attack?

A. Not to my knowledge.

Q. Do you remember Chevaux de Frize being sent from Verplank's to Stoney Point?

A. I do, in consequence of Lt. Colo. Johnson's Application.

Q. How were those Chevaux de Frize disposed of, or to what use put?

A. They were placed from the left of the

[329] As Lt. Roberts had previously testified, the water at the south end of the outer abatis was "about a foot and a half deep" at half tide, and "at high water about three feet." One third ebb would be about two feet deep – shallow enough for enemy troops to wade through. Lt. Marshall's comment about making "a remark upon this matter in Writing" probably refers to a notation in his journal.

[330] "Fireballs" are composed of mealed gunpowder, sulphur, saltpeter, and pitch; the term is used interchangeably with "rocket" and "light ball," by witnesses in these proceedings. All are illuminating devices rather than weapons.

Battery on the right flank, nearly filling up the Interval to the right of the line. [331]

Q. Were you ever present at any discourse or Consultation between Lt. Colo. Webster, Lieut. Colo. Johnson, Capt. Ferguson, & Lieut. Stratten, relative to closing the rear of the Works on the Table of the Hill, if you were, what Resolutions were taken on that occasion, and what Orders given to you, as the executive Engineer at Stoney Point?

A. I never was at any such Conversation with all these Gentleman. [332]

Q. Had you ever any Conversation or did you receive any Orders from Lieut. Stratten upon this Subject?

A. I remember going with Lieut. Stratten to Lt. Colo. Johnson, in the forenoon of the 14th July, as appears by my Journal, and Lieut. Stratten proposing to Lieut. Colo. Johnson, to have the Upper Works so closed as to connect the left of the Line with the left of the larger of the two fleches, & I recollect Lieut. Colo. Johnson, from not understanding rightly what part of the Works Lieut. Stratten meant, asking if he had a plan of the Works; he Answered that he had not, but endeavored to explain himself as well as he could; Lt. Colo. Johnson observed, What Works were then carrying on, but did not, as far as I recollect, determine at that time, Whether the works proposed by Lt. Stratten should be carried on or not. [333]

[331] Lt. Marshall is describing the area between the right flank battery and the Flag Staff battery.

[332] A later witness, Capt. Robert Douglass of the Royal Artillery, will provide more details about this important conversation.

[333] Lt. Stratten may have been attempting to comply with Capt. Mercer's directive as expressed in his letter –"fleches, as lines of Musquetry, must be gained on both sides to prevent the possibility of turning the flanks." It seems strange that Lt. Col. Johnson does not appear to comprehend this plan, especially since all three officers – Stratten, Marshall and Johnson – were at Stony Point and could have examined the ground first-hand. Lt. Stratten's attempt, however, occurs on July 14 – nearly three weeks after the date of Capt. Mercer's letter – and there was simply not enough time or materials to complete the project before the attack during the early hours of the 16th.

Q. As this Conversation did not happen till the forenoon of the 14th of July and the Post was carried by the Enemy on the Evening of the 15th or Morning of the 16th do you think it was possible from the greatest exertion that could be made by such Men who could be spared from the Garrison, as a Working Party, that the Works proposed by Lieut. Stratten could have been compleated, or even in any sort of forwardness, at the time of the Attack?

A. It was not possible, we had not Materials to have prosecuted this Work; we had just a Sufficiency of Fascines to have finished the Work they were upon on the Night of the Attack, which I believe would have been compleated the next day, had not the Attack taken place.

Q. You having observed in your Journal that the Commanding Engineer's Instructions to Lieut. Stratten dated the 26th June, were not Communicated to you till the 3d of July, do you suppose that had (in consequence of these Instructions) the closing of the Works been begun on the 27th of June, that they would have been compleated or in any forwardness on the 15th of July, the Night of the Attack?

A. I think that it would have been nearly compleated, but on my producing Capt. Mercer's Instructions to Lt. Colo. Johnson on the 3d of July he (Lieut. Colo. Johnson) did not seem inclined[334] to put them into

[334]One can only guess why Lt. Col. Johnson did not accord Capt. Mercer's instructions priority. There was no direct communication between the two men, as Capt. Mercer has testified, and Lt. Col. Johnson may have resented not being consulted about the fortifications he was expected to defend.

Execution.

Q. Was not a part of the Commanding Engineer's Instructions relative to the Upper Works, namely a Battery on the right flank, began to be put into Execution in consequence thereof & on what day?

A. Yes, on the 7th of July this Work was begun.

Q. Did you represent to Lt. Colo. Johnson, that it might be better for the Service of the Post, to begin immediately upon these particular additional Strengthenings in the Upper Works, mentioned in the Commanding Engineer's Instructions, and in consequence propose to Lt. Colo. Johnson to leave off such Works as he (Lt. Colo. Johnson) had proposed, pre ious to his knowledge of those Instructions?

A. I did not, but I recollect perfectly well writing to Lieut. Stratten on this Subject. [335]

Q. Did Lt. Stratten, according to your knowledge, ever make any representation to Lt. Colo. Johnson relative to the Strengthening of the upper Works previous to the 14th July?

A. Not to my knowledge.

Q. Did the Works ordered by Lt. Colo. Johnson, appear to you to be Serviceable [336] towards the defence of Stoney Point, either against a regular Attack, or an Assault by Night, and what were those Works?

A. I think that they were serviceable and that the Works ordered by Lt. Colo. Johnson

[335] Since Lt. Marshall was a low-ranking commissioned officer and only an acting engineer, his decision not to speak directly Col. Johnson about his non-compliance is understandable. Instead, he very properly referred the matter to Lt. Stratten, who, in the absence of Capt. Mercer, had been appointed as commanding engineer for both Stony Point and Verplanck's Point, as Lt. Marshall later testified.

[336] Deputy Judge Advocate Adye by his use of the word "Serviceable" avoids the direct question of whether Lt. Col. Johnson's works were effective. Lt. Marshall includes "serviceable" in his response.

273

were, a Rail Defence for Musquetry, placed at the entrance of the right Flank of the outward Abbatis; the next Work was making a Causeway over the Swamp in front of No.1 (an Advanced Work) for the Picquet to retire over, in case of Necessity. [337]

Q. Whether upon going to take upon you the charge of Assistant Engineer at Stoney Point, you had any previous communication with the Commanding Engineer & received from him such lights & knowledge of the System of Defence of that Post, as might enable you to form an immediate Idea of it, or were you left to the instruction of your own information & Observation?

A. I received no other Orders from Capt. Mercer than that I was to repair to Stoney Point, on the next day, & Act as An Assistant Engineer, under Lt. Colo. Johnson, and that Lt. Stratten was to be left as Commanding Engineer on the two Posts of Verplank's & Stoney Point; Capt. Mercer also gave me to understand that Lt. Stratten was soon to go down to New York & that I was then to Act as Commanding Engineer at both Posts, at that Lt. Stratten was to give me written Instructions upon leaving the Post. [338]

Q. Did Lt. Stratten give you any Instructions or lights for your Conduct, as Assistant Engineer at Stoney Point, in the manner described by Capt. Mercer as mentioned in Answer to the former question?

A. I never received any Instructions whatever

[337.] The causeway had been completed by the time of the battle, and is referred to by Lt. Horndon in previous testimony.

[338] As Lt. Marshall states, the only instructions or "lights" he has received for the defenses at Stony Point were those listed in Capt. Mercer's letter. Apparently, the three engineers never conferred.

274

from Lt. Stratten, till he came over with those of Capt. Mercer.

Q. From your own Observation and professional knowledge, as an Assistant Engineer, were the Works in general upon the Table of the Hill upon Stoney Point so constructed, as to have a Mutual dependence upon, and to be able to support each other?

A. The line round the front of the Hill was reciprocally flanked, as well as the Nature of the Ground would admit of, but was open at the extremity of the Flanks, and in danger of being carried by an Assault, if Attacked at Night. [339]

Q. Was not the Table of the Hill open towards the Rear, and what do you imagine the distance of that Rear was from the right and left flank?

A. The Table of the Hill was Open in the rear and I think the distance of the Flanks might be about One hundred Yards, taking it in a right line.

Q. The Commanding Engineer's Instructions to Lt. Stratten directing that, fleches, as lines of Musquetry, must be on both Sides to prevent the possibility of turning the flanks, do you not suppose that it was imagined, that the flanks might be turned by Surprize, or a very Superior force?

A. It is impossible to say that they might not have been carried by a very superior force, but I think that had the Works proposed by Capt. Mercer been finished and they had

[339]In the nearly six weeks since the British occupied Stony Point on May 31, very little action had been taken to address the concerns expressed here by Lt. Marshall whose response has the benefit of hindsight.

been sufficiently manned, the Enemy could not easily have gained their flanks, as the Ground was very Strong. [340]

Q. Which flank did you conceive to be the Weakest?

A. I always looked upon the right flank to be Weakest, and for this reason, we had no Work that sufficiently covered the right flank and the Enemy would not have been so much expected in coming upon that flank in the Night as on the left, particularly as the Shipping did not always lay so as to cover that flank, in the day time they must have been exposed to the Shipping. [341]

Q. What was the Depth of Water on the right flank, and breadth of the beach, so as to permit Troops marching?

A. I think that at no part of the Tide, it admitted of a dry beach, but at low Water Troops might come round; there being at low Water, only about four feet in depth.

Q. What was the nature of the Precipice in the Extent between the two Abbatis on the right?

A. Steep, cragged Rocks, very difficult of Access, Men must crawl up with great care and caution in order to gain the Summit. [342]

Q. Did the Vulture in her common Station, prove a defence for the right flank, and could her Guns bear upon the beach before described?

A. In the Station I have usually seen her, I think not; she might be brought to bear.

[340] Notwithstanding Lt. Marshall's opinion, expressed nearly a year and a half after facts to the contrary, the American Light Infantry had not been deterred by the "Strong" ground and, despite Captain Mercer's proposed defenses, would probably still have gained the flanks so long as the Upper Works was open in the rear.

[341] Lt. Marshall's opinion that the British right flank – especially from the right flank battery in the Upper Works and fleche #3 in the Outer Works down to the water – was vulnerable is supported by the fact that the American right column broke through the outer abatis below fleche #3 as well as skirting the end of the outer abatis since "at low Water Troops might come round", as Lt. Marshall states and as Lt. Armstrong in previous testimony confirmed.

[342] Nonetheless, the precipice, just like the strong ground referred to earlier by Lt. Marshall, did not prevent the Light Infantry's advance.

Q. Had she begun to bear properly, [343] would it have been possible for an Enemy to have forced a passage, thro' the Water, and, by climbing up the Steep and craggy Rocks before described, gained the right flank?

A. I do not think it possible.

Q. Were there any Guns in the Upper Works appropriated for the defence of the right flank of the inner Abbatis?

A. There never was any Gun that bore upon that point.

Q. What were the particular defences of the ground upon the right flank between the two Abbatis, either of Artillery or Musquetry?

A. Between the two Abbatis and in the front of the right there was a Small fleche for Musquetry; at the extremity of the right flank of the Upper Works, there was an 18 and 24 Poundr Iron Guns on truck Carriages, [344] which were meant to defend the ground in front, with Grape and bag Shot, both which were left upon the Battery for this purpose, but these Guns did not bear above half way down the hill, on Account of its being broken ground; the whole line of Parapet, [345] part of which acted as a flank to the inner Abbatis, from that Battery to the flag staff was intended for Musquetry.

Q. Had you any Orders from Lieut. Stratten to, or did you yourself, sound Haverstraw Bay, upon the left flank of Stoney Point, so as to know the exact fordable distances at all times of the Tide?

[343] In the *Vulture*'s "common Station," the steepness of the shoreline combined with the lack of elevation of her shipguns would have severely reduced any effect she might have had – and, as previously noted, in the darkness, she might well have accidentally fired on British troops.

[344] All the artillery at Stony Point had been offloaded from ships when the British captured the peninsula on May 31, 1779, and with the exception of the 3 pounder, the Howitzer, and the four mortars, were mounted on small-wheeled truck carriages. Grape shot and bag shot are two variations of scatter projectiles. As Lt. Roberts of the Royal Artillery testified previously, the guns in Upper Works – including the 18 and 24 pounder on the right flank - were unloaded at night.

[345] The "whole line of Parapet" was located between the Flag Staff battery and the right flank battery.

A. I never had any Instructions from Lieut. Stratten upon that head, but for my own satisfaction, I sounded the depth of Haverstraw Bay, particularly at the extremity of the Abbatis which ran into it.

Q. Did both Abbatis run into Haverstraw Bay?

A. Only the outer one; it was very deep Water at the extremity of the inner Abbatis. [346]

Q. Did you from Observations of Officers and Men bathing in Haverstraw Bay, know the fordable distances?

A. I did; I often observed them bathing near half a Mile from the Shore. [347]

Q. Do you Conceive that a Column of Troops with an extended front could ford thro' this Bay, without any Obstruction from the Water itself, so as to prevent their advancing towards the left flank of Stoney Point?

A. I think they might have passed without Obstruction from the Water, as they would not have been Wet above their Waists at ebb tide; I saw several of the Rebels, who said that they came in upon the left Flank thro' Haverstraw Bay, and who were not Wet above their Waists. [348]

Q. A Column of the Enemy having gained the Shore on the left flank, how was the Access to the Upper Works, defended by Cannon and Lines of Musquetry?

A. By an 8 Inch Howitzer en Barbette which

[346] The inner abatis (which included the Howitzer battery) is the one that the American right column broke through rather than attempting to wade around.

[347] It will be recalled that previous witnesses have made similar observations about the shallow water of the Bay.

[348] Lt. Marshall is referring to the American right column which carried the main thrust of the assault.

had a prodigious Command of Ground; I think I never saw a piece of Artillery have a greater Command; there was hardly a Stone upon the face of the Hill, that Case Shot would not have reached; above this, there were an 18 and 24 Poundr. in the body of the Place, which bore down upon the parts of the Hill, to the right of the Howitzer Battery, [349] and I remember to have seen both bag Shot and Case Shot laying upon this Battery; upon the left of these two Guns, there was a Parapet for a line of Musquetry, which covered the face of the Hill; on the Return of the left flank there was a small fleche, which flanked the Opening, and on the left of that, was another fleche larger than the former, which Covered its front towards the Bay, and Acted as a flank to the smaller fleche.

Q. Did the 18 & 24 Pounder you have described, bear upon the left point of the outward Abbatis?

A. I think not.

Q. Could that Battery with Embrazures opening to the front, be considered in any respect as a direct defence of the left flank?

A. It certainly could not. [350]

Q. Were there any pieces of Artillery, besides the 8 Inch Howitzer, bore upon the left flank for its defence or into Haverstraw Bay?

A. There were not.

Q. Did you ever receive any Orders to close up the Interval between the Return of the Line upon the left flank of the Upper Work,

[349] Lt. Marshall's description of the Howitzer and its "prodigious Command of Ground" emphasizes once again how indispensable the weapon was for defense of the watery south flank. His opinion, however, of 18 and 24 pounder in the left flank battery was not shared by Lt. Roberts, commander of the artillery in the Upper Works on the night of the battle, who felt that these guns were intended only for long-range daytime defense. The opening referred to is the main entry of the Upper Works. As stated in a prior comment, it was located between the overlapping segments of the inner abatis.

[350] Here, Lt. Marshall's opinion of the guns on the left flank battery coincides with the view expressed by previous witnesses.

and the smaller fleche upon the left, either with an Earthen or fascine parapet, or by Chevaux de frize?

A. It was recommended to be done, and I recollect that Lieut. Stratten proposed it to Lt. Colo. Johnson on the 14th July, but I never received any Orders for doing it. [351]

Q. Supposing the Quantity of line that was necessary for the Battery on the right flank, which was to serve in the defence of Verplank's Point; (supposing it Attacked) had it been carried to the defence of the left & rear, would it not have been a considerable Strengthening to that left, and a great Obstruction to the Enemy's forcing the Upper Work on the Night of the Attack?

A. I believe that it might. [352]

Q. Was the Rocky Shore from the left of the Outward Abbatis, to what is termed the point of Stoney Point, so inaccessible to Enemy, as to render additional Strength upon the left flank unnecessary? [353]

A. I do not think that it was, as there were many Parts where an enemy might get up.

Q. Had there been a common Redoubt on the Summit of the Hill, capable of containing 150 Men, would it not have served as a point of retreat from the Works already described, supposing them forced, and possibly have prevented the Enemy from becoming Masters of the Posts of Stoney Point, on the Night of the Attack?

A. I think that it very possibly would.

[351] In previous testimony, Lt. Marshall described Lt. Col. Johnson's meeting with Lt. Statten on July 14.

[352] Deputy Judge Advocate Adye is describing the new battery that Capt. Mercer wanted on the right flank of the Upper Works. It was unfinished on the night of the battle, and in any case was intended for the defense of Verplanck's Point on the opposite side of the river. Had it been completed and expanded as Adye proposes here, it is remotely possible that it might have slowed temporarily the advance of the American left column, but that column – 300 strong – was the smaller of the two. The 700 men of the right column would have been unaffected.

[353] The form of this question is a bit convoluted, but apparently Marshall understood it since he answered it. (PL)

Q. How many days do you think it would have taken to have Constructed such a Work, with the powers, namely 50 or 60 Men per day, which was the Usual, and greatest Number Lt. Colo. Johnson could spare from the other duties of the Post?

A. I think that I could not have constructed such a Work in less than Six days, from the great distance I had to go for materials. [354]

Q. Supposing the Idea of defending the advanced fleches dropt, and supposing two hundred Men two deep, posted for the defence of the front of the Table of the Hill, 100 Men for the defence of each flank, a reserve of 100 Men, the Vulture Sloop of War at her intended Station upon the right flank, and the Gun Boat at her Station on the left flank, could the Post of Stoney Point, in the State it was at the time of the Attack, have been defended against a very superior force of the Enemy? [355]

A. I think that it might.

Q. Do you know with what force the Enemy made the Attack on the Night of the 15th or Morning of the 16th of July, 1779?

A. I do from a particular inquiry; whilst I was at Lancaster, I met with a Colo. Gibson of the Rebel Army, who had been at the Attack of Stoney Point as I understood from him, that the Enemy consisted of 2300 Men; he gave me a detail of every Corps & Regiment that were there; that about 1500 Men approached the Works, and the remainder were Posted to

[354] For only the third time during the trial (Capt. Darby and Capt. Mercer were also asked), Deputy Judge Advocate Adye inquires about this missing yet crucial element of defense – an enclosed work or redoubt – expanding his question to inquire how long it would have taken to construct.

[355] This deployment of troops in the Upper Works was first proposed by Capt. Mercer during his testimony. Adye might also have added "and if the Howitzer had fired, the water on the flanks been sounded, and the possibility of a night attack been taken into account."

281

cover the Retreat, in case that had been repulsed, and I think that General Wayne told me after the Attack, that there were 1300 Men, who entered the Works, besides those left without to cover the retreat; there was a large body lay under a hill, in the front of the Picquet and Colo. Gibson told me that he himself was posted there, and had Command of that Party. [356]

The Court adjourned till next Morning at 11 o'Clock
Saturday, February 10th 1781.
The Court being Met pursuant to Adjournment

Lieut. Marshall, Assistant Engineer, was again Examined.
Q. Was there not a Gun Boat usually stationed in Haverstraw Bay, as one of the defences of the left flank?
A. There was; and there was also a 10 Inch Mortar which was used to stand in the body of the place, and which I did not mention Yesterday. [357]
Q. Was the Gun Boat at her usual Station on the Night of the Attack?
A. I think she was not.
Q. Do you not think, that had the Gun Boat been at her usual Station on the Night of the Attack that she would have been of essential Service, not only to have given a timely alarm to the Garrison of a Column of the

[356] Modern readers may wonder about the apparent lack of hostility between captured British officers and their American counterparts. An 18th century officer who had fallen into enemy hands was considered a gentleman in distress, and was treated with courtesy rather than ill will. The British did not always abide by this unspoken agreement because many American officers were not gentlemen in the aristocratic European sense. General Wayne, for example, like many of his American counterparts who were also tradesmen, was a tanner and surveyor in civilian life.

[357] This mortar had been mentioned previously by Capt. Tiffen and Lt. Roberts, but played no role in the attack.

Enemy advancing thro' Haverstraw Bay, but to have harrass'd and probably impeded the March of that Column?

A. I do, as the Gun in this Boat must have acted as a flank to the Howitzer Battery. [358]

Q. Were all or any of the several Defences both of Cannon and Musquetry of the left flank made use of on the Night of the Attack?

A. Musquetry I know there was, but as to Cannon I think there was not any fired.

Q. Do you know from your own Observation or any information afterwards received, at which point of the left flank the Enemy Landed, after wading thro' Haverstraw?

A. I do not; I recollect a Scattering fire from the extremity of the left flank of the Upper Works.

Q. Do you know what Signals were intended to be made in case of an Attack, and what were they?

A. I think that three Rockets [359] were to be fired; I remember some few days before the Attack, seeing some Officers of the Enemy reconnoitering upon an adjacent height; and I mentioning to Captain Traille how useful the 10 Inch Mortar would be in case of the Enemy breaking Ground upon that height, which was about 700 Yards distant; that Capt. Traille at that time shewed me an Order for sending that Mortar away, and also a Memorandum for firing these Rockets in case of Alarm, and upon Capt. Tiffen taking the Command of the Artillery in Stoney Point, he

[358] Lt. Marshall concurs with what virtually every witness has testified to so far: The Gun Boat was not at its post on the night of the battle, and could have "impeded" the enemy if it had been present.

[359] As stated in a previous comment, rockets are types of warning or signaling devices rather than weapons. Other witnesses have been asked similar questions on the same subject, and all the answers without exception express uncertainty or lack of knowledge.

283

applied to me to point out to him a proper place for firing these Rockets, and Nails were Accordingly drove into the frame of a Hut, to the left of the Magazine, [360] for fixing them on; I also recollect that having conversed with Capt. Traille, of the advantage there would be of firing light Balls from the Cohorn Mortars, in case of a Night Attack, and Capt. Traille answered that he had a Composition for them ready, and he himself expressed that he thought they would be useful. [361]

Q. Were any light Balls fired on the Night of the Attack, or do you know of any Signal to the Vulture being framed & prepared?
A. I think that no light Balls were made use of on the Night of the Attack, nor do I know of any Signals being prepared in Order to be made to the Vulture.

Q. Did you not write on the 4th of July in these words to Lt. Stratten, "Lt. Col. Johnson does not seem inclined to grant Parties any longer to the fulfilling the Instructions given by Capt. Mercer, I shall have more Conversation with him on this Business, & finally settle this Matter one way or other"?[362]

A. I do not remember the particular Words I made use of, but I recollect writing to Lieut. Stratton the next day after I had been to Lt. Colo. Johnson with Capt. Mercer's Instructions, that Lt. Colo. Johnson did not then seem inclined to grant Men to put them

[360] As previously indicated, the magazine was located below the Upper Works near the point of the peninsula.

[361] Captain Traille left Stony Point the night before the battle because of illness, and his departure may have created an unfortunate disruption in the flow of important information to his subordinates and his replacement, Captain Tiffen, who testified earlier that he had received "no written orders" from him. Captain Traille did not testify at the court-martial, perhaps because of his health, though no reason is stated in the record.

[362] Lt. Marshall did indeed write those words which are found in Lt. Stratten's journal, No. 5 in the appendix.

284

in execution & I recollect also that the next
working party that was granted, Lt. Colo.
Johnson gave me Orders how to employ &
they were employed in increasing the two
Abbatis by carrying them round the front of
the Out Works, particularly the Howitzer
Battery. [363]

[363]Capt. Mercer does not
mention "increasing the two
Abbatis" in his letter (no. 4 in
the appendix). The project
appears to be one of Lt. Col.
Johnson's own devising.

Q. Did you not consider the carrying the
Abbatis round the front of the advanced
Works, particularly the Howitzer Battery, as
fulfilling a part of the Commanding
Engineer's Instructions, which say that Lt.
Marshall, is to strengthen the present
defences, so as may most effectually cover &
protect the garrison?

A. This did in some measure tend to
Strengthening the Works, but was not the
principal point of the Commanding
engineer's instructions, & it is to that I allude,
when I say that Lt. Colo. Johnson, did not
seem inclined at that time to grant Men for
carrying on those Works. [364]

[364]For reasons that can be only
be surmised, Lt. Col. Johnson
continued to advance his own
defensive measures over those
mandated by Capt. Mercer.

Q. Did not Lt. Stratton Visit the Post of
Stoney Point on the 5th July?

A. I do not recollect that he did, I think that if
he had come over that day, I should have
remarked it in my Journal. [365]

[365]Excerpts from Lt. Stratten's
journal (No 5. in the appendix)
confirms that he went to Stony
Point on July 5 to confer with Lt.
Marshall.

Q. Do you recollect at any time that you saw
and conversed with Lt. Stratton at Stoney
Point, your telling Lt. Stratton that Colo.
Johnson did not intend to continue the
Working Parties longer than that day?

A. I do not.

Q. Had you ever any Conversation with Captain Traille relative to the Objects of defence of the Guns in the out works, & what was that Conversation?

A. I had often Conversed with him & I think that Captn. Traille expressed his dislike of the situation of these Guns & I have expressed to Captain Traille my Ideas of the intention for which that Line was constructed, which were that I thought that that line was erected to cover the troops, whilst the inner Works were building, and that was as soon as they were completed, the Guns in the outer Works should have been withdrawn; [366] but as I never received any Orders or Instructions on this head from the Commanding Engineer or Lt. Stratton, who had Visited the post of Stoney Point, I was led to suppose that the Guns were to remain there.

Q. Did you ever any Conversation Officially, with Lieut. Colo. Johnson, on the foregoing Subject?

A. I do not recollect that I ever had, as I thought it would have been interfering with Lt. Stratton's Command, as Commanding Engineer. [367]

Q. Do you know of Lt. Colo. Johnson's having received any information of the Motions of the Enemy on the Evening of the Attack?

A. I had not the smallest knowledge of it.

Q. Did you not see the Enemy often reconnoitering [368] in the front previous to the

[366] The subject of withdrawing the artillery from the Outer Works once the Upper Works was completed is another of Deputy Judge Advocate Adye's repeated inquiries. The question had been asked of Capt. Mercer, for instance, and Lt. Marshall was himself asked previously, on the first day of his testimony. The point remains that regardless of whether or not the artillery was removed and the Outer Works abandoned, the main fortification – the Upper Works – would have remained open on the sides and back and therefore have been impossible to defend for any prolonged period of time.

[367] It may be that Lt. Marshall could have been perceived as "interfering", but the question still arises: Could not Lt. Marshall have communicated his concern to Lt. Stratten?

[368] Stony Point was reconnoitered a number of times by American officers, including Major Henry Lee, General Rufus Putnam, and General Wayne.

Attack?

A. Sometimes I have.

Q. Did you not once see a Rebel Officer approach so near, that you had reason to think by looking at him with a Spy Glass, that it was General Washington himself, or some other Rebel General?

A. I have known them approach so near, that had any one whom I had known before been amongst them, I think that with a Telescope I had, I could have distinguished him; I once saw one with a Star and a Ribbon; I cannot speak as to the Colour of the Ribbon, [369] but I could distinctly distinguish the Nature of his Boots.

Q. Did not the Person you describe, approach so near that you could distinguish his pointing to the left flank of Stoney Point?

A. I recollect his pointing to our left; & I remarking it to several Officers who were standing by at the time.

Q. Did you ever mention to Lt. Colo. Johnson these Circumstances?

A. I do not recollect my mentioning them to Lieut. Colo. Johnson, but I remember Lt. Colo. Johnson looking at those Officers who were reconnoitering & my recommending it to him to fire at them, as I suspected they were reconnoitering with intention to gain a knowledge of the ground in front.

Q. (By desire of Lt. Colo. Johnson) Could not the Enemy with almost perfect Security from a Hill in the front of Stoney Point, have

[369] A single star on an epaulette denoted a Brigadier General. Ribbons or sashes worn diagonally from shoulder to waist were also badges of rank, with different colors for different grades.

Acquired a knowledge of the Works at that Post?

A. There was a Hill in front about Sixteen or eighteen hundred Yards Off, from which with good Glasses, they might have gained a knowledge of the Upper Works with tolerable Security, But when I saw them and recommended the firing at them, they were not above a thousand Yards Off & Consequently within reach of a 24 Pounder & I Apprehended the firing upon them might prevent their Approaching nearer. [370]

The Court Adjourned till Monday Morning at 11 o'Clock
Monday, February 12th 1781
The Court being Met pursuant to Adjournment

Lieut. William Marshall was again examined.
Q. By Lt. Col. Johnson Do you recollect on what day the Chevaux de Frize was sent from Verplank's to Stoney Point?
A. I do not recollect the day it was sent, but I think it was about the time that I broke Ground for erecting the Battery in the rear of the Works. [371]
Q. On the Chevaux de frize being sent from Verplank's to Stoney Point, did you understand that Lieut. Colo. Johnson had made Application for any other Materials, & for what purpose?
A. I can recollect that Lt. Colo. Johnson

[370]Lt. Marshall may have seen Generals Wayne and Washington observing the British defenses from the top of Buckberg Mountain on July 6, though no date is specified in his testimony.

[371]Capt. William Darby, the second witness to testify in the trial, was also asked about Chevaux de Frize, though not by Lt. Col. Johnson. One possible motive for raising the question of Chevaux de Frize and other materials now by Lt. Col. Johnson was to emphasize his concern for the open nature of the defenses and his attempt to correct that situation. The battery referred is the new battery which, as noted earlier, Capt. Mercer thought the "principal one" of his proposed measures.

applied to for Fascines to be made on the side of Verplank's Point, as we were Obliged to go a great way for them on that of Stoney Point, and I think, I also recollect, an Application from Lt. Colo. Johnson for Tools.

Q. Were those Fascines & Tools sent over to Stoney Point, if not, what was the reason Assigned for not sending them?

A. There were neither Tools nor Fascines sent Over; I do not recollect the reason for not sending them, but I had a sufficiency of Fascines to finish that Battery I was then carrying on, as also a sufficient Number of Tools to employ the Working Party that was usually granted.

Q. For what other Works, do you suppose the fascines & Tools Lt. Colo. Johnson applied for from Verplank's Point, were intended?

A. As I had never received any Orders for closing the line in the rear, I supposed that these Fascines and Tools were intended for the further carrying into Execution Captain Mercer's instructions, [372] & it was also necessary to have a Store of Fascines, in case of the Enemy breaking Ground.

Q. Did you look upon the erecting of the Battery above alluded to, so essentially Necessary for the Strengthening of the Post of Stoney Point, as to have inclined you to direct your Attention more particularly to that, than to the Works, proposed by Lt. Colo. Johnson?

[372]Lt. Marshall refers to Capt. Mercer's directive to construct infantry fleches on the flanks. Progress, however, was slow on all of Capt. Mercer's projects. On July 2, for example, Lt. Stratten wrote in his journal that the new battery was only "traced out". Three days later, on July 5, the battery was still "only traced out", and Lt. Marshall had told Lt. Stratten that "Col. Johnson did not intend to continue the working parties longer than today." Thus, work proceeded but at an unhurried pace.

A. I conceived that the Works order'd by Lieut. Colo. Johnson, were more essential at that time for the defence of Stoney Point than the immediate Construction of that Battery[373]

Q. Do you conceive from your own Observation, or the information or sentiments of other Officers of the Garrison, that Lt. Colo. Johnson could Consistently have spared you more Men for carrying on the Works, than he did?

A. I have often Conversed with Lt. Colo. Johnson on the Subject of Working Parties, and had in Consequence thereof been sent by him to the Adjutant of the 17th Regimt to give me as many Men as he could grant. [374]

Q. Do you think that the Creek could have been a considerable Impediment to the Enemy's Approach, the Attack being made at Night?

A. It was an Impediment but could not be looked upon as a very considerable one, as some parts of it were fordable.

Q. (By the Court) What was the first Alarm you received on the Night of the Attack?

A. The first Alarm I received was an Artificer belonging to the Engineer Department, coming into my Tent, and informing me there was some firing in front.

Q. Where were you taken Prisoner?

A. I was first taken Prisoner on the Table of the Hill, near where an Old Rebel Block house had stood. [375]

Q. What length of time elapsed between your

[373] As described in previous testimony, the battery was intended to cover an approach to Verplanck's Point.

[374] Lt. Marshall does not directly answer the question, thereby avoiding the issue implied by Deputy Judge Advocate Adye: Did Lt. Col. Johnson withhold the men needed to carry out the work assigned by Capt. Mercer?

[375] The Engineer's Tent is shown clearly on Lt. Marshall's own *Sketch of the Works at Stoney Point,* and is located below the new battery. The "Rebel Block House" was at the open back of the Upper Works and is also depicted by Lt. Marshall.

hearing the first Alarm, & your being taken Prisoner?

A. Fifteen or twenty Minutes, as nearly as I can recollect; the Troops had taken their Ground, before I got up to the Table of the Hill.

Q. (By Lt. Colo Johnson) How long do you suppose the firing continued, between your being made Prisoner & the Rebels being in full Possession of Stoney Point?

A. It had nearly ceased when I was taken, a few scattering Shot were fired afterwards, & I believe a round or two was fired from the Gun in front where Lt. Horndon was, [376]but when I was taken, the Rebels in the Upper Works were calling out, the Fort's our own.

The Deputy Judge Advocate then laid before the Court, the Instructions of Major General Vaughan to Lt. Colo. Webster [377]and then closed the Prosecution on the part of the Crown. The Court in Order to give time to Lt. Colo. Johnson to prepare his Defence Adjourned till Monday Morning at 11 o'Clock.

Monday, February 19th 1781
The Court being Met pursuant to Adjournment

Lieut. Colo. Johnson Address'd the Court as follows, Vizt.
Gentlemen:

[376]The shots Lt. Marshall heard from Lt. Horndon's gun – the 12 pounder in fleche #1 – must certainly have been at the start of the battle since Lt. Horndon had testified that he fired approximately 27 rounds until ammunition had run out.

[377]See No. 7 in the appendix.

291

His Excellency The Commander in Chief having been pleas'd to grant my Request for a General Court Martial to inquire into my Conduct, I stand here Accused of having suffered the Post of Stoney Point, with the Troops in Garrison, the Artillery & Stores to fall into the Hands of the Enemy on the Night of the 15th, or Morning of the 16th July, 1779, when I was Commanding Officer of said Post. [378] A Charge indeed of such Weight as nothing but a Consciousness of having us'd every Exertion in my Power for the Honor of His Majesty's Arms and the Maintaining of the Post could alleviate. The Judge Advocate, in Opening the Court, reserved to himself a power of Answering any New Matter, that might arise in the course of my defence; but my wishes have been so far Anticipated thro' the course the Prosecution as to render it unnecessary for me to take much more of your time. I shall therefore confine myself to certain Particulars, in what I have now to Offer, referring to the Evidences already examined & some few others I shall call upon in further Confirmation of the same.

Major General Vaughan's Instructions to Lt. Colo. Webster clearly prove, [379] that he (Lt. Colo. Webster) was Commanding Officer of both the Posts of Verplank's and Stoney Point, and, as such, on visiting my Post, I communicated to him the Disposition I had made of the Troops, which met with his

[378] Seven days after the Prosecution's final witness, Lt. Col. Johnson began his defense. His reason for requesting the court-martial is not a matter of record, but it seems probable that the unexpected loss of such an important military post should require some explanation, and Lt. Col. Johnson probably thought that, if all the facts were known, a trial would result in approval for his efforts to stem defeat. Lt. Col. Johnson had also just returned from nearly a year and half of captivity, during which time questions about his competence and reputation may well have been raised without his being able to respond.

From a legal standpoint, Johnson's opening statement is excellent. He may have been coached by Deputy Judge Advocate Adye, since he makes a good summary of the evidence and responds to it point by point. He also either made excellent notes of his own or had access to Adye's record, in order to be able to make such detailed comments. (PL)

[379] While Major General Vaughan's instructions (No. 7 in the appendix) do not "clearly prove" that Lt. Col. Webster is the commanding officer of Stony Point and Verplanck's Points, that is certainly the implication, since orders regarding both posts are addressed only to him. Lt. Col. Johnson is not mentioned.

entire Approbation, nor did he ever afterwards alter it. In Consequence of this Idea, I always conceived the Works carried on at Stoney Point, as directed by Lt. Colo. Webster or agreeable to Instructions left by the Commandg Engineer. The only point of this Nature in which I ever interfered was the constructing of some fleches of Rails and repairing the Abbatis, with the Assent of the Acting Engineer. Also, the demanding Fascines, Chevaux de Frize, & Tools to compleat a Work proposed by Lt. Colonel Webster. It appears by the Evidence of the Commanding Engineer (Capt. Mercer) that the Vulture Sloop of War and the Gun boat were Comprehended in the Original System of Defence of the Post of Stoney Point, the former being destined to cover the right, the latter the left Flank. Why they were not in a proper Situation to Act on the Night of the Attack, neither becomes me to Answer, nor can I suppose this Court will consider me as Amenable for the Consequences. [380]

The Intelligence I received between Eight and Nine on the Night of the 15th from the Scouts I had sent out the preceding Evening, tho' it gave me reason to expect an Attack, yet from the Enemy's Moving with heavy Cannon (as by then represented), I did not apprehend it would have been so sudden. [381] Notwithstanding which I gave out the Orders, dated 9 at Night 15th July & took every other precaution which I could have thought

[380] Lt. Col. Johnson was, of course, present during the trial; it therefore could not have escaped his notice that almost every witness was asked about the location and the possible effectiveness of the Gun Boat on the night of the battle.

[381] Lt. Col. Johnson's statement regarding "Intelligence" on the night of the battle is confirmed by Ensign Henry Hamilton, among others. Washington's instructions to General Wayne, dated July 10, 1779, included providing a "couple of light field-pieces" which then could be left behind when the Light Infantry marched. The purpose of this ruse was to create the impression that an artillery attack was part of the American plan, thereby leading to the false information supplied by Johnson's scouts.

Necessary, had I been Absolutely apprised of their immediate Intention. This Appears by the Evidence at large.

It may perhaps be expected that I should take some Notice of the Plan of Defence pointed out in the Evidence of the Chief Engineer wherein the advanced Fleches are said to have been thrown up merely to cover the Troops, whilst the Works on the Table of the Hill were Constructing. The Artillery was then to have been withdrawn, and the fleches have served for Infantry, who were to have retired to the Upper Works when the Nature of an Attack rendered it necessary; but it is probable this Idea was not thought Necessary to be communicated to me, till the Works on the Table of the Hill were compleated. It therefore never came to my knowledge. [382]

It appears by various evidences that previous to the Attack, the Advanced Centinels gave such timely notice of the Approach of the Enemy, that the whole Garrison were at their several destinations & fully prepared to receive them. [383] It also Appears that the Corporal of the Advanced Picquet on the left Flank, at the time of his and his Picquet being driven in by a Party of the Enemy, heard a considerable body of Men wading through Haverstraw Bay, which Body there is great reason to suppose turned the left Flank, by pursuing that Track in which the Gun Boat might probably have Acted to great Advantage.

[382] It will be recalled from previous testimony that Capt. Mercer never communicated directly with Lt. Col. Johnson about withdrawing the artillery from the Outer Works and abandoning those defenses, or about other important concerns on which perhaps the chief engineer and the commanding officer "on the spot" might have conferred. Other witnesses, Lt. Marshall being the most recent, thought that, in the absence of explicit orders, that the guns should remain where they were and, by implication, the work defended.

[383] While Lt. Col. Johnson's statements about the "timely notice" given by the sentries are confirmed by other witnesses – Lt. John Ross and Cpl. Simon Davies, for example – it is also true, as noted earlier, that the intended time of the enemy attack was not clear to some officers. Capt. Campbell of the 71st Regiment thought the attack would occur at night, while Lt. Armstrong of the 17th Regiment "did not understand" that a night attack was expected. Mixed opinions like these may have undermined Lt. Col. Johnson's claim that his men were "fully prepared."

I shall here beg leave to call on Capt. Douglass of the Royal Artillery, and likewise Lieut. Simpson.

Capt. Robert Douglass of the Royal Artillery, being duly Sworn, was examined.

Q. By desire of Lt. Colo. Johnson Do you recollect having Accompanied Lt. Colo. Webster & Captain Ferguson to Stoney Point, some few days before that Post was Attacked? [384]

A. I do.

Q. Do you know their Intention, in Visiting that Post?

A. It was to Consult upon the propriety of enclosing the inner line of Intrenchment.

Q. Did you accompany Lt. Colo. Webster & Captain Ferguson to the Table of the Hill?

A. I did.

Q. Do you recollect the Conversation that took passed between Lt. Colo. Webster, Capt. Ferguson &Lt. Col. Johnson, on the Table of the Hill?

A. Having the Misfortune to be deaf, [385] I did not hear the Conversation in general, tho' I now & then catched a Word, which Circumstances united with others which happened before and after, led me to a Certainty that it was relative to closing the Works on that Post.

Q. Do you know of Lt. Colo. Johnson having made application to Lt. Colo. Webster for Materials, such as Tools, Chevaux de frize, &

[384] Captain Patrick Ferguson was part of the garrison at Verplanck's Point, and exerted an influence far beyond his rank. He had a reputation as a military strategist and innovator, and had invented a highly effective, breech-loading rifle which might have affected the course of the war had it been widely adopted. Capt. (later Major) Ferguson accompanied Sir Henry Clinton on his expedition to Charleston in early 1780. At the age of 36, Ferguson was killed at the battle of King's Mountain, South Carolina on October 7, 1780, several months before Lt. Col. Johnson's trial began.

[385] As an artillery officer, Capt. Douglass's disability was common to his profession. It does tend however, to weaken the defense's credibility when testimony to a conversation is offered by a witness who admits he is deaf (PL).

Fascines for closing this Work? [386]

A. I believe Lt. Colo. Johnson did; I know that Chevaux de frize were sent in Consequence of Lt. Colo. Johnson's Application, & that Fascines were made for the Post of Stoney Point, but am not certain whether they were sent over; it was a very few days before the Attack of the Post, that they went over, but I cannot say how many.

Q. Prior to the night of the 15th of July 1779, had you any reason to imagine that that was the particular Night fixed upon by the Enemy for the Attack?

A. By no means, for a fortnight before (as far as comes within my knowledge) we had equally a right to expect an Attack, as on the Night it happened; [387] I recollect making an Application to Capt. Traille several days previous to the Attack, for a Reinforcement of Artillery Men for Verplank's Point, & Capt. Traille's Answer was, that he could not then Comply with my request, as Mr. Wayne had threatened them with an Attack at Stoney Point.

Q. (By the Court) Do you recollect, or can you ascertain by any Means, how long time intervened between the hearing of the first firing at Stoney Point and the first Huzza from thence?

A. I cannot take upon myself to say the length of time, but think that I heard Lt. Colo. Webster say that it was about 18 Minutes, none of the officers I heard speak of it, said

[386]Lt. Col. Johnson's request for these defensive materials had been discussed previously by Lt. Marshall.

[387]While there may not have been specific information about an impending attack prior to July 11 when scouts reported to Lt. Col. Johnson, there were probably rumors, and the British certainly knew that American forces were in the area.

that it exceeded twenty; at the same time I think it probable that those on Verplank's Point did not hear the first firing, I think that it was hardly possible for any one to have ascertained the exact time without looking at a Watch, as our Attention was drawn off by a firing which also took place at the time, on the side of Verplank's Point. [388]

Q. Do you recollect hearing a Huzza, on the Night of the Attack of Stoney Point?

A. I did not, on Account of my being deaf, hear the Huzza myself, but I recollect other Officers on the side of Verplank's Point, saying that they heard two Huzza's.

Q. Do you know why Capt. Ferguson became a Party in the Conversation with Lt. Colo. Webster & Lt. Col. Johnson, with respect to fortifying the Post of Stoney Point? [389]

A. Captain Ferguson from the first Moment disapproved of the Mode, in which Stoney Point was fortified; it was his almost constant Conversation in my hearing, and I have every reason to believe he held up the same Idea to Lt. Colo. Webster, that if ever Stoney Point was Attacked during the Night, that it would be carried, & that he himself with Six or 7 hundred Men would undertake to effect it.

Q. Whether from Capt. Ferguson's discourse of Stoney Point, you had reason to suppose that it was to be carried generally or at any weak part of the Post?

A. I believe that Capt. Ferguson meant the Post in General, as his common Objection

[388]Capt. Douglass is referring to the feint being conducted by Col. Rufus Putnam less than a mile away across the Hudson to divert attention from the attack on Stony Point, and deprive the embattled defenders there of possible assistance.

[389]Despite being a fairly low-ranking commissioned officer, Captain Ferguson was not shy about expressing his opinions, and also had the ear of Sir Henry Clinton, the Commander-in-Chief. Ferguson was adamant on the subject of closing the works at Stony Point, and in addition to the conversation recounted here, wrote to Sir Henry on July 6, 1779 – eleven days before the battle – stating that the enemy "could enter any Part of the abatti, the flanks of which may be turn'd almost unseen from the works. . [and] the Post and Garrison might be lost in a few minutes as the works are all open behind." In his memoirs, Sir Henry stated "I had. . . on the 14th [of July] suggested . . .the necessity of *at least one close work* to obviate the conse-quences of a possible surprise." [italics in original] The Commander-in-chief's suggestion is not mentioned in the court-martial. In any case, by July 14 – little more than 24 hours before the American attack – there was simply not enough time left to carry out his proposal or that of Capt. Ferguson.

was that there was no enclosed Work.

Q. Did you not Conceive from your common Observation, that Lt. Colo. Webster was as constant in his Attention to the Post of Stoney Point, as to that of Verplank's?

A. I believe that he was.

Lieut. William Simpson of the 17th Regt, already Sworn was again examined:

Q. Had you at any time any Conversation with Capt. Ferguson relative to the Works of Stoney Point?

A. From an intimacy with Capt. Ferguson I frequently spoke to him upon the subject of the Works at Stoney Point, and he always said that he looked upon our situation there, to be rather dangerous; he one day in particular, in Company with Lt. Colo. Webster, came over from Verplank's to Stoney Point, and I Accompanied them to Lt. Colo. Johnson; Captain Ferguson then mentioned to Lt. Colo. Johnson that he thought his Situation at Stoney Point rather disagreeable, [390] and said that with 800 Men, as good Troops as those Lt. Colo. Johnson had at Stoney Point, he would be Answerable to Attack & carry that Post at twilight, from the flanks being exposed & from the Number of Men it must take to line the outward Abbatis & defend the Artillery in those Works, but that he (Capt. Ferguson) was of Opinion that he could in 48 hours enclose the Upper Work, & then withdrawing the

[390] Capt. Ferguson apparently did not hesitate to approach where others might fear to tread, speaking directly to his superior officers about the dangers of Lt. Col. Johnson's situation not only to Johnson himself, but also to Lt. Col. Webster, commander of both posts.

Artillery & Troops from the Outer Works, defend the post against Washington & his Whole Army; [391] I believe that Col. Johnson said that he did not know how far he could be Answerable for making such Alterations, but that if Lt. Colo. Webster was of the same Opinion, he would do all in his Power to enclose the inner Works, but at the same time remarked that his Garrison was already greatly fatigued by Working Parties, & that there was besides a difficulty of cutting Fascines in his front; that Lt. Colo. Webster then said, that any little Assistance, he could give him on his Side of the Water, he would do most chearfully, which Offer Lt. Colo. Johnson accepted, but the Enemy Attacked us v ry soon after & before any thing could be effected.

Q. Can you recollect the day the above recited Conversation took place?

A. I cannot recollect the day; I suppose it to have been about three days before the place was Attacked. [392]

Q. Did not you Act as Assistant Engineer at Stoney Point?

A. I assisted Capt. Mercer, & Surveyed the Posts of Stoney Point & Verplanks Point for him.

Q. Do you know Whether any Measures were taken towards enclosing the Upper Work, which was proposed by Capt. Ferguson, apparently approved of by Lt. Colo. Johnson, & by inference complyed with by Lt. Colo.

[391] Apparently for the first time, Lt. Col. Johnson learns of a different strategy - that enclosing the Upper Works and removing the artillery and troops from the Outer Works would greatly improve his defensive capabilities, and might even turn defeat into victory. The advice, however, went largely unheeded. As Lt. Col. Johnson stated, at least according to the present witness, Lt. Simpson, he "did not know far he could be Answerable for making such Alterations", and that his "Garrison was already greatly fatigued." Lt. Col. Johnson did accept Lt. Col. Webster's offer of help – but too late to translate it into action.

[392] The date would have been approximately July 12. There is no indication that any of the engineers aside from Lt. Simpson was present during the conversation recounted here. Capt. Mercer was in New York, having gone there on or near the date of his June 26 letter to Lt. Stratten.

Webster?

A. Some Chevaux de Frize, which had been round the Rebel Fort called <u>LaFayette</u>, on Verplank's Point, were sent over to Stoney Point by Lt. Colo. Webster, I believe, at the request of Lt. Colo. Johnson, as being the most Speedy Method of making some kind of Enclosure; there was likewise began a Trench from the right flank of the inner Work to the left Flank of the New Battery. [393]

Q. During the Conversation between Lt. Colo. Webster, Lt. Colo. Johnson & Capt. Ferguson, relative to the Necessity of enclosing the inner Work, Did Lt. Col. Webster give Lt. Col. Johnson any orders respecting the withdrawing the Guns from the lower fleches & confining the Mode of Defence to the Table of the Hill?

A. He seemed to agree in Sentiment with Capt. Ferguson, but as to giving it as an Order, he certainly did not. [394]

Q. How far can you Authenticate the two Plans of Stoney & Verplanks Point, laid before the Court, with respect to the Nature of Ground and Distances?

A. With respect to the Plan of Stoney Point which is drawn by Lt. Fyers, as I Surveyed the Ground at that Post, & gave the Survey to Capt. Mercer; if Lt. Fyers has Copied from that Survey I can Answer for the Accuracy of it. The Plan of Verplank's & Stoney Point I drew & can speak to the exactness of the distances & Nature of the ground, as far as

[393]These measures certainly helped the defenses in the Upper Works by "making some kind of Enclosure" but no concerted effort was made to address the concern that Capt. Ferguson had repeatedly expressed: the Upper Works were open in the rear and therefore extremely vulnerable.

[394]As previously indicated, Lt. Col. Webster was away from New York on duty at the time of the trial, and therefore could not comment on whether or not he ordered Lt. Col. Johnson to withdraw the guns from the Outer Works.

possible on such Occasions. [395]

Lt. Col. Johnson having laid before the court a plan of the works erected for the defence of Stoney Point after its being retaken by British troops. [396]

Major (late Captain) William John Darby, already Sworn was again Examined.

Q. What reason had you to suppose the Plan produced of the Works constructed of the Post of Stoney Point, upon the retaking of it by the British troops, is an exact one?

A. I can only say that I copied from one, which I was informed was a just Survey. [397]

Major Charles Graham of the 42nd Regt of Foot, being duly Sworn, was Examined.

Q. By Lt. Col. Johnson As you Commanded at Stoney Point after that Post was repossessed by the British Troops, can you from your knowledge of the Ground & Works say, Whether the Plan now produced before the Court is a just One?

A. I can't possibly say that it is a just Plan, but it appears as exact a representation of the Works thrown up as I can recollect; there were some trous de Loups under the Block House at the barrier on the left of the Works, which I do not Observe to be inserted in the Plan. [398]

Q. Can you describe the State of the Works, as laid down in the Plan from the Retaking Possession of Stoney point to the time of

[395] The plans referred to here – of Stony Point and Verplanck's Point – are not contained in the court-martial records.

[396] The plan produced by Lt. Col. Johnson (also missing from the original record of the court-martial) was that of the second British fort, built after the Americans abandoned Stony Point.

[397] Lt. Col. Johnson has apparently called Major Darby as a witness to authenticate the Plan – but in fact he cannot do so since he can only testify that he copied it from another plan which he "was informed" was a just survey. The following witness, Major Graham, provides the necessary testimony to authenticate the Plan. One assumes that Adye took Johnson aside and explained to him what testimony was required (personal knowledge of the "Ground and Works") in order to get the Plan admitted in evidence. Assisting Johnson in this way was part of the duty of a Judge Advocate General. (PL)

[398] Trous de Loups ("wolf's holes") are a series of circular pits, each with a sharpened stake set in the bottom.

your quitting it?

A. Brigr. Genl. Sterling's Brigrade Retook Possession of Stoney Point about the 21st or 22d of July & found the Works dismantled & the Abbatis torn up, & the Platforms destroyed; [399] that we immediately began upon the defence of the Post, first by carrying an Abbatis round the Table of the Hill, & then erecting the enclosed Work, with Six Block Houses, as delineated in the Plan; that the Work upon the Table of the Hill being enclosed, a Block house was built in front, upon a Knoll where there had latterly been a fleche. [400]

Q. What time did it take to enclose the Work before the Block House in front was began?
A. I cannot exactly recollect; but I know that it was enclosed before Brigr Genl. Sterling left the Post, which was in about Six or Seven Weeks afterwards, when I was left to Command there.

Q. What Number of Men were left at Stoney Point under your Command, upon Genl. Sterling & his Brigade leaving it?
A. Including Pioneers & Batteaux Men (to whom we gave Arms from the Sick of the Garrison, as also Assigned Alarm Posts) about 1200 Men, between the Posts of Stoney & Verplank's Point; the Number at the former was sometimes varied, but generally consisted of 5 or 600 Men.

[399] After their plan to capture Verplanck's Point miscarried, the Americans abandoned Stony Point on the night of July 18, destroying the fortifications and removing military stores and equipment.

[400] In a previously cited July 6 letter to Sir Henry Clinton, Capt. Patrick Ferguson suggested that Stony Point could be "put in Condition to stand a Siege with a Garrison of 300 men for which purpose it is only necessary to occupy the Table of the hill with one good capacious closed work, surrounded by a thorough abbati." The British incorporated some of these changes – particularly building an enclosed work - in their new fortifications, with Capt. Ferguson playing a key role in the design and construction. At the time of the trial, Crown forces had abandoned Stony Point, after destroying their own second fort.

Lt. Colo. Johnson continued thus, "Having so far produced such Evidence as I have thought Necessary, towards Signifying the Sentiments of Lt. Colo. Webster, Capt. Ferguson & Myself, respecting the Necessity of having an enclosed Work on the Table of the Hill, and also having laid before the Court a Plan of the Works afterwards constructed for the defence of that Post, I am fully persuaded that had that Plan been originally adopted, the Enemy never could have taken it by Assault & from the Opinions given one by several of the Rebel Officers, have reason to think that they never would have attempted it. [401]

The indisposition of Lt. Carey of the 17th Infantry (who Commanded in the fleche No. 2, lower line of defence, & to whom I gave my Orders in Consequence of my having received Information of a body of the Enemy being in Possession of the Upper Works,) not admitting of his Attendance on the Court, I shall next call upon the Serjeant of his Detachment, who in all probability may recollect the Orders given by me to Lt. Cary.

Serjeant Henry Gillott of the 17th Regt of Foot being duly Sworn, was Examined.
Q. By Lt. Col. Johnson. Under whose immediate Command & Where were you Posted on the Night of the Attack of Stoney Point?
A. I was posted at the fleche No. 2, in the

[401] Lt. Col. Johnson makes a valid point, though without stating that he himself might have made more exertions to adopt and carry out Capt. Ferguson's ideas. Of course, Sir Henry Clinton knew of Capt. Ferguson's suggestions by letter before the battle, but there appears to have been no great urgency on anyone's part to make these vital defensive improvements. One plausible explanation for this dilatory behavior may have been the common conception– at least until the battle of Stony Point – that "rebel" forces under the command of "Mr. Washington" were simply not the equal of trained, professional European troops whose skill and experience would have necessitated the measures that the British failed to put into place against the Americans.

lower Abbatis, under the Command of Lt. Carey.

Q. Did you at any time during the Attack, hear Lt. Colo. Johnson give Orders to Lt. Carey, & what were those Orders?

A. The Orders I heard Lt. Colo. Johnson give to Lieut. Carey were, first that the Men would be very sparing of their Ammunition, & Secondly not fire unless there was an Object in Sight, by the Enemy approaching near the Works, as from the darkness of the Night we could not see them unless we did so; that after the Attack had continued for some time, Lt. Colo. Johnson gave an Order to Lt. Carey to withdraw the Men from that Work, & to March them very Slowly, and very Silently towards the Upper Works and that he (Lt. Colo. Johnson) would go along the lower Abbatis himself and collect such Men as he could find, [402] in Order to join Lt. Cary, and go with him into the Upper Works.

Q. Do you understand that it was in Consequence of any information Lt. Colo. Johnson received of the Enemy being in the Upper Works, that he gave those Orders to Lt. Cary, or what reason did he give them?

A. Lt. Colo. Johnson had Information that the Enemy were in the Upper Works, & I believe that Serjeant Major Webb, who is now to the Southward, was the Person who brought this information, & it was in Consequence thereof, that Lt. Colo. Johnson gave those Orders.

[402]Many witnesses have commented on Lt. Col. Johnson's part in the battle, leaving no doubt that he was actively engaged in mounting the best defense he could under the circumstances. However, Ensign Henry Hamilton, adjutant of the 17th Regiment, had already indicated (see No. 3 in the appendix) that -- excluding artillery -- there were more men (220) on the Outer Works than on the Upper Works, which had only 177 defenders –even though that main fortification would have been the objective of any attack. If the Outer Works had been abandoned, then the garrison could have been concentrated instead in the Upper Works.

304

The Court Adjourned till Next Morning at 11
o'Clock
Tuesday, February 20th 1781
The Court being Met pursuant to
Adjournment

Serjeant Henry Gillott was again examined.
Q. Whilst you were at the fleche No. 2, do
you recollect being fired upon by the Enemy?
A. Yes; I had One Man killed and two
Wounded by a fire from the Upper Works.
Q. Can you ascertain from any Circumstance,
or even Conjecture, whether this fire from the
Upper Works, was given by the Enemy, or by
the British Troops?
A. We at first supposed it to Come from the
British Troops, posted in the Upper Works,
but from the fire becoming very heavy, we
suspected it must be from the Enemy.[403]
Serjeant McAlister was therefore sent to the
Upper Works to gain Information, but he was
taken Prisoner in his Way thither, and
consequently did not return.

Lt. Colo. Johnson then Concluded his
Defence with the following Address to the
Court.
The Unfortunate Death of Captain Tew
deprives me of very essential Evidence on
this Occasion. [404]
I purposely avoid entering into a more minute
Detail of Particulars, but most Ardently

[403] Since the American element
of surprise was in part predicated
on not firing their weapons, the
volleys from the Upper Works
were undoubtedly those of
British defenders. Sgt. Gillott's
mistake was understandable in
the darkness and turmoil of the
battle.

[404] The death of Captain Tew,
referred to here by Lt. Col.
Johnson, was described by an
earlier witness, Lt. John Ross,
and may have been brought
about by the very shots that Sgt.
Gillott has just mentioned.

embrace this Opportunity of paying the just Tribute of Applause to the Officers and Men I had the Honor to Command.

The Justification of my Conduct, I most readily leave in your hands, not without feeling the highest satisfaction, at the Candor & Attention you have been pleased to shew me through the whole of these Proceedings, which will ever make the most lasting and grateful Impression on my Memory.

The Court having Considered the Evidence for and against Lieut. Colonel Johnson, together with what he had to Offer in his Defence, is of Opinion that he is, in suffering the Post of Stoney Point to fall into the hands of the Enemy, Culpable in the following Instances, viz. 1st. In a mistaken Disposition of the Troops, which for the Defence of the Post, ought to have been confined to the Table of the Hill. 2dly. In not remonstrating against the frequent Absence of the Gun Boat, notwithstanding he knew of it, which the Court is of Opinion, are Errors of Judgement, and consequently think his Conduct reprehensible; the Court therefore adjudge that he (Lt. Colo. Johnson) be informed thereof,[405] by such Officer, as His Excellency the Commander in Chief shall be pleased to appoint for that Purpose. At the same time, the Court is of Opinion that on the Night of, and during the Attack, Lieut. Colonel Johnson, in common with the

[405] Although not stated in the transcript, it is apparent that the court martial deliberated in private, since Col Johnson had to be informed of the decision. It is also interesting to note, that in his Treatise on Courts-Martial, Deputy Judge Advocate Adye recommended that the most junior officer of the court martial give his opinion first, so that considerations of rank did not bias the final determination. (PL)

Officers and Soldiers at his Post, behaved
with an Alertness, Activity and Bravery that
do them Honor.

W. Phillips, Major General

Step. Payne Adye
D. Judge Advocate

Confirmed, H. Clinton.

APPENDIX

New York, April 25th, 1781

Sir,

I have the Honor of transmitting to you, some Papers referr'd to in the Proceedings of Lt. Colo. Johnson's tryal which were unfortunately mislaid at the time the Proceedings were sent home.

> I am, Sir,
> With great Respect & Esteem
> Your most Obedient
> And most humble Servant,
> Step. P. Adye

Sir Charles Gould
Major Genl.

Schedule of Papers, referr'd to, in the Proceedings of the General Court Martial, held for the Tryal of Lieut. Colonel of the 17th Regt of Foot, Major General Phillips, President.

No. 1 & 2 - Detail of Picquets and Guards posted at Stoney Point, 15 July 1779, together with Lt. Colo. Johnson's Orders, given out at 9 o'Clock that Night.

3. Distribution of the Troops at Stoney Point, 15th July 1779.

4. Captain Mercer's Instructions to Lt. Stratten.

5. Extract from Lieut. Stratten's Journal for June and July 1779.

6. Lieut. Marshall's Journal, kept at Stoney Point.

7. Major General Vaughan's Instructions to Lieut. Colo. Webster, dated 27th June, 1779.

No. 1
Copy of an Order Issued by Lt. Col. Johnson
Garrison Orders 9 at Night 15th July, 1779

The troops 'till further Orders is to Lay with all their Cloaths on at Night (Except Coats which with their Arms, Ammunition, & Accoutermts is to be Carefully put up in such a manner as they can get them upon the Shortest Notice. This Order the Adjt wrote in the presence of Captn. Robinson, L. A. Regt. & sent it to Captn. Campbell in a Note by Lt. Col. Johnson's Orders, and Given out by the Serjt Major in the Adjt. presence to a Non Commissd Offr of a Company.

The above Order was given in Consequence of two Men havg Come in the Lines with Intelligence.

Henry Hamilton, Adjt. 17th Regt. Foot

No. 2 - Detail of Picquets and Guards

Courtesy Public Records Office, London

Nᵒ 3.

Distribution of the Troops under the Command of Lieut Col Johnson Stoney Point 13ᵗʰ July 1779.

Places to Defend	Captains	Lt. Marines	Sergeants	Drummers	Rank & File	Captains	Lt. Marines	Sergeants	Drummers	Rank & File
For the defence of the lower Works of Abbatis	..	..	..	..	..	3	11	8	11	187
For the defence of the Upper Works upon the Table of the Hill	2	4	7	10	105					
Howitz: Battery & Fleche upon its Right	..	1	2	..	30	2	5	11	10	149
Gun Boat Guard in Wait of Inner Abbatis	..	..	1	..	7					
Ferry Guard	..	..	1	..	7					
	2	5	11	10	149					
Out Piquets who were to Retire within the Lower Abbatis upon the Approach of our Enemy	..	..	..	..	..	1	5	1	81	
Total Strength doing duty	..	..	..	..		5	7	24	22	417

N.B. The Lieut Col. Adjutant & Surgᵉⁿ of 17ᵗʰ Infᵗ not Included — besides the Royal Artillery & Artificers.

Henry Hamilton
Adjutant 17ᵗʰ Foot

No. 3 - Distribution of the Troops
Courtesy Public Records Office, London

Copy of a Letter of Instructions left with Lt. Stratten, Engr.
Verplanks Point, 26th June, 1779

Sir,

The Works upon Stoney & Verplanks Point are now in such a State of Defence, as to be able, in my Opinion, to resist the Attacks & Repel the Insults of an Enemy. In short, they are not to be taken by Surprize, nor by a Rash, or Violent Effort. This being understood, I have the Commander in Chief's Orders to Join Him, at Head Quarters, & to leave You & Lt. Marshall, to Strengthen the present Defences, & to persist in carrying on such Works as may, most Effectually, Cover & Protect the Garrison.

Upon Stoney Point - Some additions are still wanted. The Principal One will be a Battery for the Two 24 Prs to Act as a Flank to Verplanks Point, in case of an Attack upon that Quarter, in the mean time, the Guns may be Reversed upon their present Platforms. Fleches, as Lines of Musquetry, must be gained on both Sides, to prevent the possibility of turning the Flanks. Another Magazine is wanted, which may be made by Squared Trees, Covered with Boards & Earth, & a Road must be made from the Magazines down to the Point.

Upon Verplank's Point – The New Redoubt, upon the left, must be strengthened, immediately, by the proposed Stockade, by thickening the Abbatis, & by the Felling of the Trees. in the Front, which will render the Approaches very difficult. A Platform may be raised in the Point of the Work, for a 6 or 4 Pr in case of Necessity. The Half Bastion, upon the Right Flank, must be Closed in the Gorge, by a thin Parapet, & a Ditch, the Abbatis carried round it, & down the Side of the Hill, into the Water. The Redans, or Fleches, upon the Curtain, may be closed in the same manner; they will, then, form Two Small Squares, and, in case of our being obliged to withdraw Our Men from the Upper Block house & Stone House, will contain & Cover those Parties.

The Curtain ought to be continued, both as a Line of Defence, & a safe Communication to the Works, in case the Enemy should get Possession of the Hill in Front. This You will mention to the Commanding Officer upon the Spot. If the Enemy should bring Cannon to the Bluff Point, on the other side of the Bay, You will find it necessary to raise a few Traverses, or Counter Parapets, to prevent an Enfilade, or the being taken in Reverse. A small Magazine is wanted in each Work. You will be pleased to make Your demands for Working Parties, in Writing & keep an Account of the Numbers granted, from Day to Day, & upon what Service employed.

I am Sir, Etc.

A. Mercer
To: Lt. Straton, Engineer

Extracts of My Journal for June & July 1779.

June 29th Went over this day to Stony Point & gave Mr. Marshall a Copy of Captn. Mercer's Instructions concerning that place, He complained that Colo. Johnston would let him have but few Men, on Account of their hard Duty.

July 2d This Morning went over to Stony Point. Mr. Marshall had traced out the Battery that is to Act as a Flank to Verplanks Point.

July 4th - Mr. Marshall in his Note to me of this day -- says -- "Col. Johnston does not seem inclined to grant Parties any longer to the fulfilling the Instructions given by Capt. Mercer. I shall soon have more Conversation with him on this Business & finally settle this Matter one way or other." N.B. this I shewed to Colo. Webster.

July 5th - This Morning went over to Stony Point. Mr. Marshall told me that Colo. Johnston did not intend to Continue the Working Parties longer than today. Mr. Marshall did not begin the Works proposed by Capt. Mercer, for want of Men -- All that He has hitherto done, is to open an Embrazure in the Battery on the Right to Act as a flank to Verplanks Point, 'till the other Battery is finished -- it is at present only traced out -- & about 300 fascines. I desired him to make a Journal, of what Men he had & how Employed, & let me know when Colo. Johnston desisted from giving Working Parties.

July 14th - Went over to Stony Point & desired Mr. Marshall to Close the Two flanks with a thick parapet, to go on with the Battery, & to close the Rear from the New Battery to the Line of Musquetry on the left Flank, with Rails Musquette Proof & Breasthigh. He has kept a Regular Journal of the Number of Men given him by Colo. Johnson & how employ'd therefore in case of Necessity, it can be referred to.

J. Straton, Lt. Engineers

No. 6
Extract from Lt. Marshall's Journal kept at Stoney Point
[Missing from record of court martial]

Major General Vaughan's Instructions to Lt. Col. Webster relative to the Posts of Verplank's Point and Stoney Point, 27th June, 1779.

One Captain & 50 Privates of the 33rd Regt. will take possession of the Block House upon the right of the Grenadier Encampment.

Provisions & Water Colo. Webster will take care to provide for that and all the other Posts.

One Hundred Men in the Block House near Fort La Fayette.

Fifty Men in the Stone House.

Fort La Fayette and the other Works hold the rest of the Garrison, which Colo. Webster will dispose of as circumstances may require.

Respecting Stoney Point

It will be absolutely necessary to draw your Picquets in much nearer than they formerly were, the Garrison being much reduced. This Col. Webster will inspect and order accordingly. Eight Batteaux will be left under Colo. Webster's care which he will dispose of, as he thinks Proper. Signals of Alarm to be communicated to the Commander in Chief, he will get from Capt. Sutherland. Signals of Alarm to be Communicated to the Commander in Chief, he will get from Captn. Sutherland.

In case of a Serious Attack he will be so good as to inform me at Phillipsburg, that I may send him such Assistance as may be proper in the absence of the Commander in Chief.

An Agent and Transports will be sent to this Place as soon as the Troops are Disembarked. I would wish to recommend a Rowe Boat for Dispatch to Phillipsburg, should the Wind not answer. Ammunition will be delivered to your Order by Captn. Traille Commanding Royal Artillery. One Months Provision is left for your Garrison under the Charge of Mr. Taylor.

The Engineer having left some directions relative to the Works, which in course is with the Commander in Chief's Approbation; you will forward the same as circumstances may require. The engineer, having left some directions relative to the Works, which in course is with the Commander in Chief's Approbation, you will forward the same as circumstances may require. Lieut. Stratton, Engineer, remain at Verplanks Point & Lieut. Marshall, Assist. Engineer, at Stoney Point, agreeable to the Plan left with Colo. Webster by the Chief Engineer.

Colo. Webster will be so good as not to Detach any part of the Troops out of his Post, or Lines, unless he has a most pressing necessity, or by order from the Commander in Chief.

All the Hutts left standing by the British & Hessian Troops as far as the Advanced Posts of the Yagers to be destroyed.

Signed, J. Vaughan, Major General.

AFTERWORD

The court-martial of Lt. Col. Henry Johnson was convened in New York City on January 2, 1781, during the sixth year of the American Revolution. The first day was taken up with the address of Deputy Judge Advocate Stephen Adye to the court of which the president was Major General William Phillips, a veteran artillery officer who would die a few months later of typhoid fever in Petersburg, Virginia, where he had joined the newly defected Benedict Arnold on campaign. The court may also have discussed procedural matters; in any case, it then adjourned until 11 A.M. the following day, Wednesday, January 3rd.

On that day the first of nineteen witnesses was called, and on February 12, the Crown rested its case. During the final days of the trial, February 19-20, five witnesses (two of whom had previously testified) were called by Lt. Col. Johnson. The court-martial had heard testimony for a total of 21 days, but there were also two lengthy adjournments: one for 20 days (from January 4 – 24) possibly because a member of the court, Lt. Col. John Gunning of the 82nd Regiment, had become ill and had to be replaced by Major Charles Stewart of the 63rd Regiment, necessitating a reconstitution; and a second adjournment for 7 days (from February 12 – 19) to allow Lt. Col. Johnson time to prepare his defense. Though he addressed the members of the court and called witnesses, he did not take the stand himself.

As stated in the annotations to the court-martial record, Lieutenant William Marshall, Acting Engineer, testified the longest, being questioned for all or part of four days. Lt. John Roberts of the Royal Artillery testified for the better part of two days, as did Capt. Alexander Mercer, Commanding Engineer. Except for occasional recalls, other witnesses testified for shorter periods of time, usually a day, though the length of the daily sessions

314

appears somewhat abbreviated, possibly because of the other duties that the members of the court had to perform in wartime.

The focus of Adye's interest was on the twin defensive components of fortifications and artillery, which accounts for time spent on those witnesses who were experienced in those military specialties and had first-hand knowledge of Stony Point's defenses. These were also areas that were not under Lt. Col. Johnson's control, and for which he could not directly be found responsible.

The court may have tacitly recognized that fact when, rather than issuing a general verdict to the charge against Lt. Col. Johnson – that he "suffered the post of Stony Point, with the troops in garrison, the artillery and stores to fall into the hands of the enemy . ." - they narrowed their findings to two specific instances; the first, where a decision that was his to make proved to be incorrect, and the second, where he could have expressed disapproval about defensive measures that were unreliable. Thus, the 33-year-old officer was found "culpable" for " a mistaken disposition of the troops, which for the defense of the post, ought to have been confined to the table of the hill," and for "not remonstrating against the frequent absence of the Gun Boat, notwithstanding that he knew of it." The court concluded that these were "errors of judgment," and that the Lt. Colonel's conduct was "reprehensible." The court seemed to be saying, in its finding, that if the garrison had defended only the Upper Works and the Gun Boat had been at its post, then the American attack might have been repulsed.

At the same time, however, the court made no comment about Stony Point's other defensive failures or omissions: artillery that didn't fire, fired ineffectively, or could not be brought to bear; fortifications that were open on the sides and back; the total lack of preparations against a nighttime assault. The inference that Lt. Col. Johnson may have drawn – and it must

315

have been a comforting one – was that the court recognized by implication that there were other contributing factors which led to the British defeat, factors that were normally outside the control of an officer serving in a subordinate capacity to the commander of both forts.

Nonetheless, the language of the court – "culpable," errors of judgment," "reprehensible" – must have stung the relatively young man who had recently returned from more than a year and a half in captivity, and who must have thought that requesting a trial would have cleared his name and reputation. The harsh words may have been tempered by a tangible form of partial vindication in the design of the second British fort – encircled by an unflankable abatis and containing several closed fortifications – thereby confirming the views not only of Capt. Patrick Ferguson, but also of Lt. Col. Johnson himself, who, somewhat belatedly, stated during the trial that "had that Plan [of the second fort] been originally adopted, the Enemy never could have taken it by Assault, & from the Opinions given me by several of the Rebel Officers, have reason to think that they never would have attempted it." The court's words of disapproval were also mitigated by their final statement – "At the same time, the Court is of opinion that on the night of, and during the attack, Lt. Col. Johnson, in common with the officers and soldiers at his post, behaved with an alertness, activity, and bravery that do them honour."

With this mixed decision, the beleaguered officer did his best to resume his military career. He served again with the 17th Regiment as it engaged in further operations during the war, and was captured once more with his troops at Yorktown, Virginia in 1781 when Lord Cornwallis surrendered. Later, according to Mark Mayo Boatner in his Encyclopedia of the American Revolution, he served in Nova Scotia and Newfoundland, and for several years was Inspector General in Ireland, and commanded troops during the defense of New Ross, in June, 1798. His service to his country after the American Revolution was recognized and honored: he was awarded the Order of the Bath, was promoted to full General in 1809, and became a baronet in 1818. He died in his 88th year in 1835.

Henry Johnson's thoughts about the court-martial and its verdict are unknown, but as he grew older, he probably revisited in his mind the scene of the trial and the battle for which, despite later achievements, he would be remembered most. As we age, the past can become an all-consuming place – perhaps because there is so much of it – and the old man may have refought the battle of Stony Point a thousand times, engaging in the all-too-human pastime of reliving the defining moment of defeat that might instead have turned to victory, thinking not only about the decisions that others could have made to thwart the enemy, but also about the determinations which had fallen to him. If all his troops had been concentrated in the Upper Works, could the Americans have been repulsed? Should he have protested about the missing Gun Boat and provided an alternate defense during its absence? Would the outcome of the attack - now so many years ago - have been different with better intelligence about the enemy's plans and movements? He would never know.

North

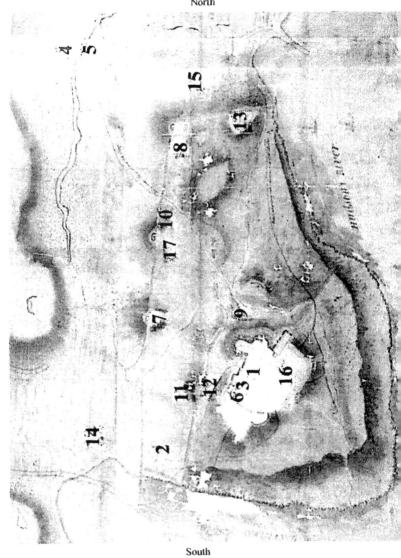

South

Approximate Location of British Officers and Men During the Battle of Stony Point

Based on their testimony at the court-martial of Lieutenant. Colonel Henry Johnson

1. **Ensign Henry Hamilton. 17th Regiment** - "At the first alarm, I was in the Upper Works with Lt. Col. Johnson who gave orders to the men to stand to their arms and I think to repair to their posts. . ."

2. **Capt. William John Darby, 17th Regiment** - " ...my Post was there [on the left flank between the two abbatis], and I did not see the enemy push up that way."

3. **Capt. Robert Clayton, 17th Regiment** - "[I took Post] Upon the Battery on the left hand near Haverstraw Bay, where there was one 24 Pdr. and one 18 Pdr."

4. **Lt. John Ross, 71st Regiment** - "I was posted with a Picquet of 30 Men at a place commonly called the Jaeger Post on the 15th of July, 1779.."

5. **Cpl. William West, 17th Regiment** - " I was on Picquet with Lt. Ross on the night of the Attack of Stony Point."

6. **Capt. William Tiffin, Royal Artillery** - "...I went immediately to the 18 Pdr on the left of the Upper Works...in about eight or ten minutes I was taken prisoner by the Enemy."

7. **Lt. William Horndon, Royal Artillery** - "...I immediately repaired to the work [fleche No. 1] on the left of the outward line of defense, where there was a brass light 12 Pdr."

8. **Capt. Lawrence Robert Campbell, 71st Regiment** - "The two companies of Grenadiers, which I had the command of immediately repaired to the Post [lining the Outer Abbatis near fleche No. 3] which had been previously pointed out by Lt. Col. Johnson."

9. **Lt. William Armstrong. 17th Regiment** - "I took upon myself the liberty of moving the company to cover the entry through the Inner Abbatis, ...and took Post between the flag staff and the battery on the right."

10. **Lt. William Simpson, 17th Regiment** -   "...I immediately repaired to my alarm post at the Outward Abbatis [near fleche No. 2] I belonging to Capt. Tew's company..."

11. **Lt. John Roberts, Royal Artillery** -   "...I went towards the Howitzer battery, knowing that the Howitzer could be of considerable service....When I got within ten or twenty yards of the Howitzer battery, I found the Enemy were in possession of it...."

12. **Cpl. Joseph Newton, 17th Regiment** -   "On the Night of the Attack of Stony Point, I was posted with 12 Men on the Howitzer battery...We heard a noise in the Water to our left, and the Men called out that the Enemy were coming that way..."

13. **Lt. William Nairne, 71st Regiment** -   "On the Night of the Attack on Stony Point, I had the inlying Picquet of the two companies of the 71st Grenadiers...."

14. **Cpl. Simon Davies, 17th Regiment** -   "I with nine Men were advanced an hundred Yards beyond the creek close to the Water side [to the left and below fleche No. 1]....I heard a noise in the water on my left, which appeared to me to have been occasioned by a large body of men wading through it...."

15. **Cpl. John Ash, 17th Regiment** -   "I belonged to a Serjeant's Picquet of 15 Men from which I was detached with 6. The Serjeant's Picquet was on the right of the whole without the outward Abbatis. and I with the 6 Men was posted close by the Water side at a about a quarter of a mile distance from the Outer Abbatis..."

16. **Lt. William Marshall, Acting Engineer** -   "It [the firing] had nearly ceased when I was taken [15 or 20 minutes later]... the rebels in the Upper Works were calling out 'the fort's our own' ..I was...taken prisoner on the Table of the Hill near where an old rebel Block house had stood."

17. **Sgt. Henry Gillott, 17th Regiment** -   "I was posted at fleche No. 2 in the Lower Abbatis under the command of Lt. Carey....I had one Man killed and two wounded by a fire from the Upper Works."

A former teacher of English, Don Loprieno has maintained a life-long interest in education and history, and for nearly twenty years, developed and implemented interpretive programs for two Revolutionary War state historic sites administered by the Palisades Interstate Park Commission in the lower Hudson Valley of New York: New Windsor Cantonment and Stony Point Battlefield, where he was also site manager. Since January 2001, Don has lived in Bristol, Maine with his wife Page and their cat Cato, where he is active in community affairs and writes a column for the local newspaper. *The Enterprise in Contemplation* is his first book.